Marry Me!

Relationships, Falling in Love & Marrying the Right One

by Denise Flynn

Marry Me!
by Denise Flynn

Editing / Page Design: Written Images, Detroit, Michigan

Cover Design: Christian Wetzel

Published by Arc Press

For more information, to order additional copies, or to book
Denise as a speaker, contact:
    Activate Life and Love Coaching
    P.O. Box 80246
    Rochester, MI 48308
    248-877-7078
    Denise@TheMarryMeBook.com

    www.TheMarryMeBook.com

DEDICATION

To my parents, Larry and Stella, who were lovingly
married 60 years.
How I love you and am highly blessed God placed me
in *this* family.
To my mother who always told her children and
grandchildren, "You should write a book." Thank you for
those seeds Mom. *Really* miss you.

Table of Contents

ACKNOWLEDGMENTS
<u>My utmost thanks to:</u>

My heavenly Father, my *sweet* Savior...this life would be hopeless and desolate without you. You are the most tender, caring, beautiful and giving lover of me. May my life *sing* to you. I owe you nothing less, but so much more. You are my joy! My joy! My heart delights in you!

My son, Cameron, who has seen and listened to my life as it goes—blessings, drama, tears, prayer, writing and all. Gosh I hope you'll learn from being with me through all this Babe! I pray for you and your future mate. Remember, girls like pressed clothes. ☺ You are my joy and delight! You're awesome! You were one of my heart's desires. Bless you fine, powerful man of God!

My parents and family: My father, brothers and families. Blessed I am! He could have placed me with any other, but he chose these parents and this family. For that and you, I am so thankful. I don't take what we have for granted! All my love to you!

My girlfriends in Christ: Penelope, Joanne, Linda, Karen, Brenda. You stood by me, were my greatest encouragers and the healing team. You were truly with me in the valley. You never forget times like those and the ones who helped bring you through with prayer and love. I love and thank you so. And oh, the laughter we've shared!

Cleo Spates, you encouraged me to step out and write! How much I owe to you!

Ron and Sue: You amaze me! We are family and I love you. Thank you, my prayer warriors.

Penelope: You brought me out! You make me feel great! I would not be who I am today without you Dear. Special, special God hook-up.

Ray Cooke: For your consistent belief in me and my calling to this book. For your faithful friendship, prayers, care and encouragement. Oh…and the fancy, red licorice too!

My rough draft readers: Cleo, Ellen, John, Tiffany. Thank you for your valuable time and input into this assignment! Thank you for your deep friendship, support, prayers and laughter!

Ptolemy and Tosha Pruden, my Strategic Planner of Arc Research and Arc Press: Isn't He amazing! To link us together has been so God, so helpful, so fun, so Destiny. There is no telling how this project would have come about if not for you. You brought me understanding, mentorship, wisdom, challenge, love and joy! Bless you! When I marry I want my guy to read your book and I want to be like the radiant family you are.

My utmost of thanks and honor to editor Diane Reeder. You are an amazing woman! Thank you for your energy in God's project!

Christian Wetzel: An anointed brother and designer you are! I LOVE what you've done with my covers! I am smiling!

Thank you David Perez and Dianna Sullivan Wizner of Dive Productions Photography for the Author vanity photo.

Zion Christian Church and Rochester First Assembly of God: You teach and encourage me. You provide a thriving place to worship in spirit and in truth experiencing His presence. You bless me with the love of Christ.

To all my friends, family and everyone God has given me the privilege of encountering: "I thank my God every time I remember you" (Phil. 1:3).

Psalm 40:1-5

I waited patiently for the LORD;
  he turned to me and heard my cry.
He lifted me out of the slimy pit,
  out of the mud and mire;
he set my feet on a rock
  and gave me a firm place to stand.
He put a new song in my mouth,
  a hymn of praise to our God.
Many will see and fear the LORD
  and put their trust in him.

Blessed is the one
  who trusts in the LORD,
who does not look to the proud,
  to those who turn aside to false gods.

Many, LORD my God,
  are the wonders you have done,
  the things you planned for us.
None can compare with you;
  were I to speak and tell of your deeds,
  they would be too many to declare.

God has created me to do some definite service; he has committed some work to me which he has not committed to another. I have my mission.

                             ~John Henry Newman

What causes you grief is a clue to that which you are called to heal.

~Dr. Lance Wallnau

Through everything in my life, good and difficult, by every way God made me, through everything I did right and did wrong, and through everything that has been done wrong and done right to me, I got a calling and a book out of it with the finger prints of God all over it. It has felt like I have been living out my own Hebrews 11 chapter. By faith, Denise walked into the plans God had for her before the beginning of time. Thank you Jesus. You do all things well.

"I have in writing from the hand of the Lord upon me, and he gave me understanding in all the details of the plan."

~1 Chronicles 28:19

Kids say the darndest things.

So I'm writing this book on *Relationships, Falling in Love and Marrying the Right One*. As time continues, I have more experiences and observations; so, I keep adding to the book. One day my son says to me, "Mom, what are you going to do when you meet a husband?" I said to my son, "I guess the book will be over then." He said, "If you get to page 1,000, that's not good."

1
Marry Me!

"Marry me!" What searching man doesn't want to say this to a woman? What waiting woman doesn't want to hear this from a man? This is a book that teaches dating *nots* to help forge marriage *knots* and relationship dating *to-do's* to get you to the *"I Do!"* It's about those beautiful thrilling words, "Marry Me!" It's about the marriage commitment of a lifetime.

Some things are *"basic."* Definition: the important foundations for which to build on; the ground rules. Don't mess up the "basic" rules or deviate from them, or undesirable outcomes could occur. *"Basic, in-depth"*— Definition: the basics are deep. There's much to them.

The breaking or keeping of basic principles can cause joy or pain to run deeply within our souls. There are basics to many things—algebra, cooking, automobile upkeep, dating and relationships. Go out of the bounds on the "basics" and you may flunk the test, eat the worst meal, ruin an engine or wind up heartbroken. Let's open up the last topic—dating. Handled properly with worthy "basic, in-depth" dating principles, you can take your algebra test happy and focused, actually have an appetite to eat with and drive your car lookin' good with a smile!

To prepare for marriage with wisdom, we have to know how to date or court as well. Check out Proverbs 3:13-23:

Blessed are those who find wisdom,
  those who gain understanding,
For she is more profitable than silver
  and yields better returns than gold.
She is more precious than rubies;
  nothing you desire can compare with her.
Long life is in her right hand;
  in her left hand are riches and honor.
Her ways are pleasant ways,
  and all her paths are peace.
She is a tree of life to those who take hold of her;
  those who hold her fast will be blessed.
By wisdom the LORD laid the earth's foundations,
  by understanding he set the heavens in place;
By his knowledge the watery depths were divided,
  and the clouds let drop the dew.
My son, do not let wisdom and understanding out of
  your sight,
Preserve sound judgment and discretion;
  they will be life for you,
  an ornament to grace your neck.
Then you will go on your way in safety,
  and your foot will not stumble.

What qualifies me to share some of that wisdom with you? Let me introduce you to your author. I am 46 and pushing to get this book out before the next birth year and the second digit of my age flips! I have been single for nine years now, something I never expected to be once I got married. God has blessed me with a wonderful 15-year-old son from that marriage, and since my divorce (one I did not initiate) I have been involved with many singles of all ages from various area churches. My son attends some functions with me as well. Some of us as singles have become like family.

I am an extrovert and reach out to others for connection and to provide connection for others. I host singles' gatherings in my home and round people up for other fun as well. I welcome anyone. As others report, they are truly blessed by meeting and connecting.

During and after my unwanted divorce from a 12-year marriage, I read books and attended relationship classes in search of healing, growth and a better future. I began writing dating/courting interview questions during my newfound singleness. I realize now that I was afraid of making a critical relationship mistake, but at the same time I believe it really made me think about what this next phase of my life should look like.

After my divorce, I dated a Christian man for five years on and off and we talked about marriage together. In my heart I felt he was the love of my life. The break up was heart-wrenching. There were times I wanted Jesus to take me home, nights I was doubled over in agony, nights I slept with my Bible held tightly against my chest. I was in the emotional Intensive Care Unit, with my spiritual heart open on the gurney. You will read more throughout and my full testimony later in this book.

So this book is written by a "real life" dater at one time who has learned much during these nine years. I dated others and was treated extremely well by quality Godly men, but we were not the ones for each other. I made mistakes. I learned. I repented. I grew. I have changed "from glory to glory" and am a different woman than I was nine years ago. God has used my misery to build my ministry.

I have come to the place where I will not complain about not being married. I am really content and pleased, though it was not always this way. I want to end up with '*my*' blessing. I've prayed for the Lord to open and close the doors in order to receive His will for my life. So that is exactly what is happening and I'll wait for it.

Writing about contentment as a single woman is something I never dreamed I would do. I always believed that marriage was the only way, and that singleness should only, for me, be a very short, temporary condition on my way to meeting the love of my life.

I have witnessed other unmarried Christian couples go in and out of dating and excruciating break-ups. It is horridly painful both to experience and to watch. So against the backdrop and experience of mine and others' tears, I share these observations and principles with you. I pray you will discover that you are not alone in how you may feel. You may not be unique in your situation. I pray that you will be able to relate to some things, release those feelings and then move on in healing. I pray this book will allow you to take control of your singleness and help avoid or minimize future heart ache. I pray that this may be part of your preparation and healing. It looks as though God is using my former misery and making it my ministry. I only wish I realized these things earlier. Imagine how much heartache could have been saved, but I also pray that I never lose the vividness of remembering that intensity so that I may be used to help another.

"The Lord gets his best soldiers out of the highlands of affliction."

~*Charles H. Spurgeon*

Praise be to the God and Father of our Lord Jesus Christ, the Father of compassion and the God of all comfort, who comforts us in all our troubles, so that we can comfort those in any trouble with the comfort we ourselves have received from God. For just as the

sufferings of Christ flow over into our lives, so also
through Christ our comfort overflows.

~2 Cor. 1:3-5

Relationships can be discouraging. "There are many
potential relationship opportunities; they come and go,"
several singles share. We wish the experience could be
cleaner, simpler, and the answers more obvious. I wrote
this book to make that a little more so—for myself as well
as for you.

May we keep our eyes fixed on Christ, and off some of
the craziness of male/female relationships, which is only
one of the largest areas and dynamics of your life. May we
live by His ways, with less drama and trauma. Fewer
distractions. Less gawking time. Less confusion and
mystery. Less gawking at the wreck or the bed mattress in
the middle of the road. Focus on Christ, focus on Christ. He
will give you that direction and peace that passes all
understanding.

I don't claim to have all the answers to the dilemmas of
singleness or relationships. There are a hundred shades of
gray... or grey in it. One answer may not work for all
people. I encourage you though, if you apply God's
principles in *Marry Me!* to your life, your $15 will more
than pay off! That's less than the price of a cup of fancy
coffee per month! Everything's compared to coffee
spending now days. Some of these strategies will take a
mature person to walk out. You may be challenged, but
challenge makes us better.

"Marry Me!" That beautiful invitation to intimacy and
closeness. God says "Marry Me!" to *us*. He says "Marry me
again every day. Fall deeper in love with me. Come into
that full, hold-nothing-back relationship with me. I'll make

you whole and joyous." He wants to be in an intimate, committed love relationship with us that only comes when we say "Yes" to Jesus's proposal of "Marry Me!" And then He allows us to marry another...human being.

I pray that you become more involved with and fall head over heels in love with Jesus, your bridegroom, in this reading.

> I will betroth you to Me forever; Yes, I will betroth you to Me. In righteousness and justice, in lovingkindness and mercy.
>
> *~Hos. 2:19 NKJV*

> ...as the bridegroom rejoiceth over the bride, so shall thy God rejoice over thee.
>
> *~Is. 62:5*

2
First Things First

First Things First. These relationship principals here are basic—the little bitty, BIG things people don't think about as often as they should. They consider these basics lightly or not at all, but they are hugely important!

God FIRST

All things in proper order…make sure you have the Lord positioned first in your life. God must be your first love and passion. You must not desire a mate more than you desire Him.

> But seek first His kingdom and his righteousness,
> and all these things will be given to you as well.
> ~Matthew 6:33

Adam had a walk with God alone before he ever had a relationship with Eve.

The Ties That Bind

If you are not legally divorced, you should not be dating anyone. That is infidelity. If you are divorced, *make sure* you are biblically free to remarry before you date or go into a relationship with anyone. If you do not know, meet with your pastor and get wisdom first.

Are you over your last love? You would be surprised how many look for the new when they still want the old. I know! I did this myself!

Why Are You Dating?

What is your purpose for dating? Are you seeking a companion, fun and activities, or do you hope for marriage? You should let your date know your purpose verbally within your first few get togethers.

Get these large dynamics all determined before involving anyone else. Know and communicate your availability and intent.

What Marriage Is...
Regarding marriage, the late Gina Cerminara (n.d.) writes:

> Marriage is not for a moment; it is for a lifetime. It requires long and serious preparation. It is not to be leaped into, but entered with solemn steps of deliberation. For one of the most intimate and difficult of human relationships is that of marriage. Infinitely rewarding at its best, unspeakably oppressive at its worst, marriage offers the uttermost extremes of human happiness and human bondage-with all the lesser degrees of felicity and restraint in between.

What Marriage Is NOT...
Marriage is not a car purchase. There are no trade-ins when it gets old! You wouldn't buy a car because you loved the exterior looks and feel of it if the engine was bad or it showed rust. Neither should you pick a marriage partner out of only comfort. Comfort or intrigue to you could be physical attraction, their personality or having common interests. Don't go into marriage or a relationship based on these things alone. There is no trade in! Don't end up stranded on the roadside.

On Your Mark...Get Set...
Are you ready? On your mark...Get set...WAIT!! There are a few more things to consider before starting to

pursue relationships either for your first time or after coming back into the single world again.

If you have experienced any kind of abuse or abandonment, especially from family either in childhood or later, I encourage you to look deeply into those places now. Malnourishment, hurt, emptiness, inability to trust others or be accepted by others should be healed before stepping into dating or relationships. Get rooted in the Father's strong love for you first. If you become involved with another before God fills you up, you will expect too much or accept too little from a relationship. You will accept the wrong kinds of love or less-than love to try to fill up the void or overcome the wrong done to you. You will not be able to give out whole love to another when you yourself have not fully experienced it or have it to give.

Know who you are. Take stock of your character, personality and how many Ho Hos or mangos you eat in a year. Take a spiritual gifts survey. Take a personality test. Study what your personal love language is.

Taken straight from Dr. David Hawkins' surmise of John Trent, author of *The Blessing*, "Almost without exception, our greatest weakness is our greatest strength taken to an extreme." (Dr. David Hawkins, *Are You Really Ready for Love?* p. 48.) That's pretty deep and I can see this within myself. A great strength of mine is sweetness, but when my son was younger and my sweetness could not discipline easily, it became a weakness. So I must apply the trait in a balanced and strategic way.

What is your greatest strength? There's your weakest. Balance. Once you understand yourself, you can better understand who God will—or will NOT—place you with.

When you have an idea of who you may be cut out for, it's easier to say no to the rest.

Equally Yoked?

One thing you can be sure of as a believer in Jesus Christ is that God will never put you in a relationship or bless you with a relationship with an unbeliever. This is basic. 2 Corinthians 6:14 says "Do not be yoked together with unbelievers. For what do righteousness and wickedness have in common? Or what fellowship can light have with darkness?"

Very seldom does the saved dating the unsaved work out. Don't even get involved in an unequal relationship. Let someone else evangelize them; it's not worth taking the risk of your attachment. Do not be deceived thinking you will get them saved.

I heard a woman who felt there were no Christian men around to date, so she dated an unbeliever. They shared many common interests and enjoyed each other's companionship. A year or so later, she was stumped in the relationship, not knowing whether to continue or end it. She felt trapped in the unequal relationship. If she kept on with the relationship, there would be pain; if she ended it there would be pain. She was caught. Catch 22. Catch zero man.

Even if your date were to receive Christ, there is no guarantee that they would fully mature. You would have no idea if you both even wanted to attend the same type of church. There would be just too many unknowns and possibilities for incompatibility.

Singleness is called "a gift," so treat it like a gift— carefully and cautiously.

How Much and How Long Do I Believe for Marriage?

Break off pacts and vows you have knowingly and unknowingly made or said to yourself. Statements such as "I'll never fall in love again" or "I'll never meet anyone" are statements put out into the atmosphere of principalities that may be holding up your blessing. Set yourself free to receive a blessing! Say "I am really hurting right now and find it hard to trust, but when God places the right person before me, 'perfect love will cast out all fear.' If he or she is from God, there will be that peace in the relationship."

Years ago, I was hurt and responded by declaring, "I will never do that (let a man know with words or actions that I had an interest in him, that is) again." I can't tell you how much that statement hindered me for years; it disabled my ability to show any degree of interest to a gentleman for fear of rejection. There are such things as good and bad pledges. Break off the bad ones in the name of Jesus. Break off negative things someone else has spoken over you as well.

Pray for God to pull up the roots of past rejections and disappointments regarding romantic relationships or hopes. Pray that the man or woman God sends for marriage would come in perfect love that would cast out any fear.

Nothing Wrong With Marriage!

Do not feel guilty or less spiritual for desiring marriage. Women are often told that "Jesus is your husband." That is definitely true; if you draw close to Him, he will fill the voids in your heart and life.

But again, there is the balance. A Christian radio announcer once said to listeners, "Please do not call me in the studio now; I am alone and it gets pretty busy." A caller responded to her with "You're not alone; you have

Jesus." The radio announcer, who overflows with the love and contentment of the Lord, replied, "Yes, I know, but Jesus doesn't press the buttons!" Jesus does not physically or practically do all the things a spouse could do for us or with us. The desire for marriage is legitimate and understandable.

However, Jesus can bring supplements and back-up to help you with the practical things of life. In a strong community of healthy believers men and women have come alongside to help me with certain tasks. There are several I can all on for help on my vehicle and home. One lent me his vehicle. One will take my son to church. One helps me with favors and party clean up. And a few I go to for a fatherly aspect of parenting advice. I bless back mutually in the ways that I can. The help is not to the same degree as a husband and of course there are no romantic affections in these friendships, but God can bring helps to us even in our singleness.

We should be *aspiring* to all He desires for us, not *perspiring* over finding someone to marry. But as long as you keep the desire for a mate in balance, do not feel less spiritual or guilty for desiring marriage. God may very well have put the desire there.

> For God is working in you, giving you the desire to obey Him and the power to do what pleases him.

> *~Phil. 2:13 NLT*

Ask Him to make your will line up with His.

Joel Osteen of Lakewood Church projects that it is important to know the difference between a God-given dream and just a wish. Wishful thinking you will grow out of. He encourages:

There are dreams put in us by the creator of the universe. The Latin word for desire means "from the Father." There are desires that God puts in our heart. The way you can tell if a dream is really from God, is if that desire won't go away. You'll know it's a real dream if you let go of it, but it won't let go of you. You push it down. You ignore it. You try to get rid of it. It keeps coming back again and again. That's a God-given dream.

~Joel Osteen Sermon

I think wanting a relationship is like wanting chocolate cake. Chocolate cake is good just as God made marriage to be. And there are times when we just want chocolate cake more than other times. SOMETIMES YOU CRAVE IT, sometimes you don't. And it's okay to eat it conservatively, but don't let the desire for it get the best of you. Different things and times can trigger the desire of marriage or chocolate cake. The perfect thing to me…is to eat chocolate cake ON your wedding day! Ha ha. Do not feel guilty or doubt your own love for the Lord because the desire for marriage may come up. So long as you keep that desire in balance and put all our adoration on the Lord, it is normal. Stay in faith, because without it He is not moved. It is good to be able to voice our desires to others who can support us when the desire becomes a little trying sometimes.

If the desire for marriage is not a good thing, the scriptures would not have been written.

Delight yourself in the Lord and he will give you the desires of your heart.

~Ps. 37:4

He who finds a wife finds what is good and receives favor from the Lord.

~Prov. 18:22

Marriage is an approved desire from God. The Lord knows that we will have longings sometimes and that the good ones are okay to be fulfilled.

> Desire realized is sweet to the soul.
>
> ~*Prov. 13:19*

And while you are waiting for your mate:

> My grace is sufficient for you, for my power is made perfect in weakness.
>
> ~*2 Cor. 12:9*

God will get you from point A to B to C. It's happened for me and at times I never dreamed how it could be so. Grace is the divine influence upon the heart. Grace is the helper, the comfort you receive in the midst of the tough situation. Grace is the sweet manipulator that enables you to do what needs to be done--what seems like the impossible; Grace is the invisible, beyond-understanding empowerment in your time of need.

Are You Supposed to be Single?

There are some who are called to be single or choose happily to remain single to serve God (Matt. 19:10-12). No matter what each of our callings will turn out to be, we each have to first surrender all to Jesus (maybe even repetitive times). After having surrendered and you just can't shake the desire for marriage, then perhaps you do not have that gift of singleness. Whatever God's plan is, our value is not in our marital status—it's just a setting. Our value is in the fact that God truly loves you and me in an amazing and never ending way! And it is a wonderful life He has planned for us if we will seek Him out fully.

In the story of God telling Abraham to sacrifice his son Isaac, God was after Abraham…not Isaac. God wanted

Abraham's full love first of all, it wasn't about Isaac. God needs to know that sincere love in your heart for Him first. God wants to know you are at least willing to go it as a single and you feel that He is enough for you. He wants your whole heart and He will know when He has your whole heart; you can't fake anything with God. Then, just the fact that you were willing to sacrifice something else you really wanted shows him your sincerity of heart and means so much to Him.

My personal statement is this: While singleness is not what I prefer, I am content and joyous with it and the Lord's presence. The experiences I have with Him fill me.

3
Getting Together

◊ Never make someone your priority that makes you
only their option.
◊ Never make someone your priority that makes you
only their option.
◊ Never make someone your priority that makes you
only their option.
(Watch your pearls)

What is Dating?

Dating has a casualness about it. It is fraught with the risk that you may connect, fall in love and *then* understand that you are incompatible, or had no green light from the Lord to go into marriage.

But should a Christian even date at all? Though I am not fond of the idea of casual dating, I would not feel comfortable with a complete dating ban. It is not our purpose to across the board say to each person, "Awwww! You're dating???" There are gray areas and variables on how or where people meet. Cautious dating seems to need to be reserved for people who don't believe they will run into each other again due to logistics. And in defense of cautious dating, I have heard stories from mature believers who received confirmation from God while on a few initial dates that they were with their intended mate. "Whatever you do, do it all for the glory of God" (1 Corinthians 10:31).

Start With Prayer. End With Prayer.

If someone asks you out on a date, immediately respond with "Let's wait a week and each of us pray and see if going on *any* date is the right thing to do." Don't just say yes to a date right off the bat. What's the rush? Usually, there is time in life. Like doctors and insurance companies tell us, we've got to be our own medical doctor. They tell us that the best patient is one who is involved in looking after their own care. They study their prognosis, communicate and play an active part in discussions and decisions with their doctor about their own well-being. As singles, we should study what is or may be about to happen between us and a possible partner, pray and discuss it all. YOU have to be an active participant in determining your path. This is *your* journey, with God as the mapmaker.

> A man's heart plans his way, but the Lord directs his steps.
> ~*Prov. 16:9*

Some people say that dating various potential partners lets you develop good relationship skills. While yes, it can do that, the risk for injury, I believe, is too high. You don't need to date to get good at relationships. You can practice, learn and develop your relationship skills with anyone, not just potential marriage partners. You can sharpen your relating skills with community, family, coworkers, or anywhere. Honor and respect can be practiced on anyone. Submission and deference can be practiced on anyone. Love can and should be practiced everywhere!

Limit Your Carbs
"Anthony! Anthony!" Wednesday is church service night, but also since the 70's, it was known as "Wednesday is Prince Spaghetti Day!" And that is where spaghetti should stay—on your dinner plate. There is a sales and marketing technique known as Spaghetti selling, (and let's face it, we are all trying to sell ourselves), but this

Spaghetti technique seems to resemble the dating lives of some. The theory is that a salesperson needs their prospecting numbers to be increased in order to hit good sales quotas. So they invest in as many sales calls and marketing contacts (or dates) as they can in hopes that any one of them will work out. It is not a focused plan, but a canvassing. They lack defined strategy.

It's like throwing spaghetti noodles on the wall and seeing which noodles stick—then those are the ones pursued. That's not God's plan. God's plan is much more than a numbers game. In fact, His plan is not a "game" at all. The relationships that He develops are strategically designed, not haphazard. God's sons or daughters must be thought of and treated with more respect than an abundance of carbohydrates. Better to look at the strands of spaghetti noodles and ask God which is the one. You know he'd say *wheat* noodles.

Spaghetti dating wastes precious time, effort, emotion and energy without prayer or a clearly defined plan. **If you or a friend is engaged in spaghetti dating, STOP!** It is time to rethink what is happening.

Spaghetti dating pegs you as a "player." Do you really want that tag? Why mess with the rest, when we can have the best?

Courting: Seeking God's Answer
Webster defines courting as "Flattering; attempting to gain by address; wooing; soliciting in marriage." Courting looks like this: The man would have studied the woman, prayed about it and if moved, asks the woman for a courtship. Whether one uses the term "dating seriously" "dating exclusively" or "courting," here are the goals that a Christian couple should have in mind:

1) A couple already has heard and understands from God that they are His match. I like to call this a "Mark 2:8 revelation": "Jesus immediately knew in his spirit that this was what they were thinking in their hearts." In other words, the two of you know in your spirits TOGETHER that God wants you together. Now, you go back to fill in the blanks and learn the details and fine intricacies of each other. Actually, that will take a lifetime; you should never stop courting and wooing each other! But for this period, courting is a time when the relationship is being set to function in marriage by learning each other and coming into agreement on how your lives will function. It would be followed by engagement, a time of actual wedding planning and setting up for the combining into one household after the wedding day.

2) With a strong mutual interest already in place, courting is an agreed time when a man and woman intensely set out to discern if they are for each other in marriage. It is a time of serious exploration. It's purposeful, not merely just going on fun dates. You are considering each other for lifelong blessings! Providing a courtship goes well, it would be followed by engagement. It's a time where you should see the man lead as he directs the courtship, its pace, discussions and the relationship.

Courting is deliberately setting outright to seek God's will if the relationship should move into marriage. It is talking about the big ticket items—the possible deal breakers. It's kind of like "cutting to the chase" without having to run around not knowing what's going on or what you're going after. (See Chapter 20, "Flip It;" pay special attention to "500 Questions Anyone?")

So how do you get to know someone at all or to see if you potentially want to court them if you don't go on a date with them? In groups! Try to have some conversation and interaction with people at church events or group gatherings of some sort. Or arrange a group gathering of your own. Meeting people in groups is supposed to reduce the danger of premature, close attachments. Of course, the danger cannot be completely eliminated; if you don't keep your eyes and heart fixed on the Lord, strong emotions and attachments can still develop.

If you find yourself attracted to someone in the group, the natural progression is to want to get together with them in closer situations, to have a time when you can focus more on them alone and directly. So when that happens, what do you do? Do you ask someone out automatically once you find them attractive in that group setting? NO! Follow the other guidelines here in *Marry Me!*

A mature single should wait for a word from the Lord to know who their mate is before courting them or be in prayer for some time and step out in cautious faith.

Matches Made in Heaven
Read and see how these couples were brought together:

Rev. Billy and Ruth Graham
Most all of us know and love Billy and Ruth Graham. I poured over their personal "Getting Together" chapter. I didn't want the chapter to end; it was so sweet, interesting and transparently written with a wonderful sense of humor. They "met as students at Wheaton College; he was already an ordained Baptist minister. "I fell in love right that minute." (*Time* U.S. 2007). Rev. Graham says it like this in his autobiography, *Just As I Am*:

Two things I felt sure of: first, that Ruth was bound to get married someday; and second, that I was the man she would marry. Beyond that, I did not try to pressure her or persuade her—that is to say, not *overly* much. I let God do my courting for me (p. 86).

Gentlemen, let the Holy Spirit draw your woman to you as well. Allow Him to make her see your match made in heaven. Allow Him to align your hearts together.

Billy Graham goes on to write:

But as the months went by, I asked her to at least consider me. It would not have been right to let her assume that what seemed to be my heroic understanding of her concerns was a lack of interest or expectation on my part. We had lots of discussions about our relationship (p. 86).

Upon announcing his soulmate's passing in 2007, Billy shared, "We were called by God as a team. No one else could have borne the load that she carried." What a legacy she left when God called her home!

Scott and Connie

Scott and Connie met at the movie theatre at the tender ages of 18. He was a third generation pastor's kid and grew up in a Pentecostal church. She was younger in the Lord and lived in a troubled home. At that age Scott wasn't looking for a serious relationship. As he pondered life ahead though, he saw himself meeting and marrying a fellow Bible college student with a background more similar to his. Scott eventually enrolled in a Bible college, and then Connie enrolled there a year later. He continued to grow in his adoration of her and enjoyed her presence. He often tells our congregation of the times when the guys would ask him to hang out. He'd reply, "Uh, no thanks. I'm with Connie." Life changed for him; he didn't want to do the things he was doing before. He had someone else he would rather be with. "That's how it is with the Lord too," Pastor Scott tells us today. "When you are in love with Him, that relationship makes you want to live your life differently."

As they continued to date exclusively at college, Connie continued to grow spiritually and started developing her own spiritual perspective. Proceeding on, they realized that God had something for them together. They courted for three years, then decided that it was the right time to marry. Married 27 years now, and a *super* cool couple, Pastors Scott and Connie LeLaCheur are a well respected, strong, anointed, prophetic couple making big differences in the Kingdom of God.

That said, not everyone meets their mate in their church, place of employment or social circle with opportunities to see them regularly and get to know them. You may have to go somewhere with someone to learn more about them. But casual, sloppy dating is a no-no.

Casual, sloppy daters go on serial dates with whoever they meet, without discerning God's voice. Sloppy dating would be thinking every neat person you meet should be a coffee date. Sloppiness would be going into a relationship not long after the last one ended and holding down the Repeat button. Some females think every man is a potential husband, and they barely get to know a man before imagining their lives together. They want marriage more than they want to live their faith in a real and dedicated way.

As a rule, you find your mate (or they find YOU) when you're busy doing God's business. Listen to this story: A woman felt impressed upon by the Lord to ask a pastor's wife out to lunch. She had no idea why she was to do so; she was just following the promptings of the Holy Spirit. Afterward, the pastor himself told the woman he felt there was a man she should meet. They met and married. This woman followed God's leading, and fell into a holy hook-up!

Dan and Amy

And down in history goes the love story of Dan and Amy. They met at a weekly Bible study of single and married people. Amy saw that Dan was a fine man in the Lord. However, she did not even think twice about him as a marriage candidate for he was going through a divorce and was still legally married. Amy had never been married.

Dan was devout and was hoping to reconcile a divorce that he did not initiate. However, the divorce did become final and he was biblically free to remarry. He sought God on whether—and who—he was to remarry. Three months later, God showed Dan that he was to pursue Amy, for his former marriage would not be reconciled.

Dan saw Amy's wonderful Godly qualities, but Amy wouldn't give him the time of day. Dan had three young children (one with a handicap), and this was not the scenario Amy had dreamed of.

On a Sunday or Tuesday night service—Dan and Amy couldn't remember which—but whatever night...it was a "Thank God night!" "I was looking for anywhere to sit except in front of Amy," Dan recalls. "I didn't want to push my will. But there was nowhere else to sit."

Sitting a few rows behind Dan, Amy heard the Lord say like a lightning bolt to her spirit, "That is your husband."

She admired Dan because he took good care of his children, but told God, "I will fight you all the way on this." Three young children not of her own? But God, as cool as He is, began to work on her heart.

Meanwhile, Dan kept going to the Lord asking for confirmation, and God continued to show him *small* signposts that Amy was his future gift. They were not large signposts, but he held on to them in hope. He avoided smothering Amy in the meantime. They continued to participate in the same Bible study and fellowships.

Some three months later, Amy visited a church with prophetic ministry. The prophetess told Amy, "I feel you have passed your husband many times in the hallways." Immediately Amy knew who she was talking about. It was Dan and she had to give it all up!

Close to that time and just a few weeks before Easter, Dan was sitting reading the newspaper with an "Inside TV Magazine." He opened the magazine up to the front page where Hudson's was advertising a free, big bunny rabbit with a purchase. The ad read "Amy is Here!" Dan thought, "Yeah right, Lord." (This was just like the morning my [Denise's] own son was born; an inside magazine fell out of the newspaper with a picture of a baby that read, "You Arrive.") Who says God doesn't speak through media?

The following Tuesday after service, Dan saw Amy but was going to keep his distance and not make a big deal about saying hello to her. But Amy approached Dan and said, "Dan, could we talk?" They went for an hour's walk around the church neighborhood talking things out, sharing everything that had been taking place. Then, they began courting. Upon Amy telling her parents the good news, her father responded with, "Are you crazy!" But Amy's mother had already met Dan and took a liking to him.

I remember Dan telling me, "It's Amy. Now we just need to go back and get all the rest of the relational things known—the courting part." Six months after they began courting, Dan proposed. They counseled with their pastor and married nine months later. The only thing Amy ever panicked about from that point on was what she was going to cook. Dan and Amy knew they were God's match. Twenty-four years later, they have one of the most beautiful, successful marriages I know.

Are We Meant For Each Other?
You meet someone, your interest meter spikes, you feel a few flutters, you wonder. Hopefully you make it a point to pray; you forecast and ponder. One of life's biggest decisions is learning if two people should make a life-long commitment together. Some say God revealed their spouse prior to courting them. Some couples say they knew from the start they were the coffee and crème fit for each other. Some say they dated or courted to find out. Some were a surprising fragrant bloom from a friendship.

Some stay in a relationship for a lengthy time, their relational future uncertain. Some continue to date denying obvious and not so obvious shortcomings of the relationship. They date in irresolution becoming emotionally attached to each other or perhaps worse even falling into physical sin. This is mire. Good relationship principles should help in the selection and confirmation of a mate and avoiding this.

Like our Christian walk, I believe dating/courting should be a straight and narrow pathway. Avoid ditches (relationships that get you stuck not going to the point you want them to). Avoid cliffs (dangerous relationships that could cost you your purity, growth in Christ and dents in your heart). Avoid lengthy detours (long term relationships that go nowhere). At times, I have felt singleness and male/female relationships are as complex as the teenage years. Sometimes it seemed to be like a bewildering spaghetti blob in a bowl. It's a small world; someone's friend dated the new date somewhere else before type of thing. Sometimes it seems like a Christian soap opera without the sex. We need to get to a place of contentment and reward with less damage.

Mike and Cindy—Broken to Whole
"God works in different ways for people," Mike said. He started dating a woman when he was 18; they dated for one year and were engaged for two. She earned a scholarship in Texas, so Mike, engaged and in love, moved there with her. It wasn't an ideal relationship and after being in Texas six months, she broke up with Mike after deciding to be with their mutual handsome friend. OUCH!

Mike was "totally devastated…It was one of the worst experiences of my life. In hindsight, we should not have been together, but I did not know that at the time. I was angry and emotionally devastated. I was totally heartbroken. The rug was pulled out from underneath me. My girlfriend was gone; I was in another state. I was praying and repenting of everything to the Lord just to get her back. I thought, 'The Lord said He'd give me the desire of my heart and He's gotta' give her back to me.'…If not, I said, 'You're a liar.' And He didn't bring her back. I called Him on His own Word... And she didn't come back."

He continued, "So there was no reason for me to be there (in Texas). At the age of 21, I was going to go home. I quit my job. As I was backing out of the driveway to return, I was delivered 100% of all the sadness, depression and anger. I had been in agony; it was horrible, but I was delivered 100%! As I pulled out of my driveway, with everything in the trunk of my little car, all the grief was immediately lifted. I can honestly say, not one time from the time I pulled out of the driveway did I feel sad, look back or yearn for that relationship at all. I was joyful... *JOYFUL* coming home singing praises to God! It was night and day. I was delivered to joy and hope! I was anxious to come home and find another girl with no remorse trailing me.

"The interesting thing is this: While in Texas our mutual friend, who had become my former girlfriend's new boyfriend, acquainted me with classical music and I liked it. I had told my brother who was leading worship at a Michigan church filled with 150 college-aged single people, 'Larry, you should add a violin to your worship.' Larry prayed about it and made an announcement asking if anyone played the violin. A brunette girl raised her hand, said she played the violin in high school and she'd give it a try on the worship team."

That Friday after Mike arrived back to Michigan, he went to the church service with his good friend. Mike went in totally joyful, not on the rebound, being totally delivered. "There were single girls all over the place," Mike shared, "but I saw this beautiful girl standing in the front 30 feet away who stood out and I said, 'John, I'm in love.' And then she picked up the violin! I don't know. It could have been the Holy Spirit drawing me to her, but it didn't really feel like that. I just thought she was very attractive, but I do suppose that attraction was all part of God's plan." The girl's name was Cindy.

Larry, Mike's brother, said he knew her a little and gave Mike Cindy's phone number. Mike called her that week and introduced himself as they had not officially met at the church service. He figured this was okay since Cindy had trust built with his brother, and he asked Cindy out for coffee before the next Friday service. Mike spoke and chuckled, "Cindy had never seen me. I figured I was going to take her out for coffee with no pressure and could leave if it was weird."

But her parents instructed him to bring her home by ten. "I thought, 'What am I going to do with this girl for that long? I'm just asking her for coffee.'" Now before meeting Mike, Cindy had a few guys around. However, immediately before he asked her out, Cindy reformulated a plan of only dating one guy at a time. She had just arrived at this idea of "narrowing down" when Mike called. Perfect timing.

They ended up going to see a play at the university theatre. Neither of them recalls the name of it, but I guess it doesn't matter one bit. They had coffee afterward. Mike was open and told Cindy all about the break up and deliverance. Mike tells, "We just had a really great time and went out again." Cindy said, "I really thought he was good looking and I liked him. We got along well and it felt comfortable. I'm sure we laughed. It would have been pretty unlikely that we didn't. We've been laughing a lot since."

Mike stated, "Probably within two weeks of having met her, I knew I liked her but didn't know how she felt. But one thing I knew: she was so much better for me than the girl that broke up with me. I knew there's someone better for me. I think it was within six weeks of our meeting that I told her I loved her. She was 18 and I was 21."

Cindy added in, "When he told me he loved me I said, 'What do you mean you love me? What do you mean by that? Like, do you love me like you want to marry me?' My thoughts were if you love me, do you want to marry me? Otherwise it's time for me to move on to another guy because I want to marry. I have a plan."

Mike said, "Well if I asked you to marry me, what would you say?"

Cindy said, "I'd say I don't know, but at least I could think about it."

Mike said: "Okay. Will you marry me?" Cindy said nicely: "I don't know. I'll think about it." She prayed and came to the understanding that this was from the Lord. With fondness on his face, Mike said, "A few weeks later in a restaurant Cindy said yes, she would marry me. I said, 'If you marry me, I want to you to marry me this summer. I'm not asking you to marry a couple years from now. I'm asking you to marry me now.'"

Cindy also added that it would depend on what her parents would say. She felt that if they weren't in agreement, she would consider it a block from the Lord. Mike found favor with Cindy's parents. Six weeks after they began dating, they established a 4½ month engagement period.

"Mike was my favorite," Cindy beamed. "He was the first and the last in that new plan of dating one man at a time to find marriage. I remember saying once that the Lord would have to drop a brick on my head to let me know who to marry. Later on, Mike gave me a brick with 'Will you marry me?' inscribed in it. God promised the perfect husband for me and He brought Mike." (Mike jokes from the other room, "You hear that? Perfect!" Then Cindy says, "For me.") "I know if I were married to anyone else, I wouldn't be as happy, and that says something after 35 years! So blessed!"

Mike reminisced, "The interesting thing was that I was accusing God of not being faithful to His Word by not giving me the girl from Texas. But that's the exact thing He was doing, giving me *my* girl…moving me toward the girl that was the desire of my heart. God was true to His Word. Cindy is absolutely the woman of my dreams. I would never ever change the decision. She's the best Christian I know and we've been married 35 years. Husbands and wives know the faults of the other and I could still say Cindy is the best Christian I know."

Mike elated, "God connected two great people together. I would never have thought it. I'd have been absolutely crazy to pick someone else. There's nobody I'd get along so well with. She's the best girl ever for me. (Then Cindy winks at Mike). God had to break my heart to give me the desire of my heart.

"In the same month, I married a whole different woman; the right woman. Not to say anything bad about the former girl. She may have been a wonderful girl for someone else, but we weren't meant to be, in God's plan. I think God was directing our lives differently. I wouldn't have broken up with her. I wasn't that kind of guy. So God took me through some pain in order to be faithful to His Word and blessed me with someone and I can't believe how good she is for me.

"God used Texas to plant the woman I was going to meet standing in the front of worship with the violin. He set up the pieces of the puzzle, even while I was accusing Him of not honoring His Word and not being the God He is known to be. It was an appeal of desperation to God, a desperate cry. It was probably hard for Him to see me go through that and yet He knew 'If you don't go through this, I can't bless you.' It was the hardest thing I've ever had to go through, but the result is amazing."

When I asked them about the engagement and marriage relationship, Cindy said, "When you're both Christians, the core is right there for our decisions to a much greater extent. When you have an authentic relationship with the Lord, you should know a lot about them already."

Mike chimes in with his humor: "When we got married, the most important person in the world to Cindy was me and the most important person to *me* was me. But the thing I love most about Cindy is EVERYTHING. We're two peas in a pod, just two best friends."

Cindy chimes in, "I love his humor; it always comes in handy!" The Lord brought us together, even in the things that we would have never been able to figure out or know. But the Lord knew and He was able to bring it all together well."

Mike and Cindy, you're a great testimony of God's matchmaking. You are one of the best examples of God's love and marriage. Continued blessings!

Drawn Together
I believe God puts the desire for His specific woman into the man's heart first. After all, the rib came from the man's heart, and Adam first had the desire for Eve. He has to be strong enough and willing enough to find you. Women, allow the man to pursue you. *"The man who finds a wife finds a good thing"* (Proverbs 18:22 TLB).

There are many ways to discern God's will in choosing your mate.

> The Holy Spirit can lead through inner impressions. He can urge you toward the person. "He will give you sensitivity to what is right or wrong about the relationship. The inner promptings of the Spirit will be consistent with the truth and godly wisdom.
> ~Accessed 10/5/11, www.rbc.org

Sometimes it's hard to interpret what the Lord is saying from our emotions. For certain though, it is easier to hear Him more clearly when we avoid dipping into physical, intimate expressions. We confuse what our flesh is telling us with what God may be saying. Those emotions, fed by the flesh, cloud our judgment and snuff out our reasoning. We lose our objectivity in the relationship.

God does not want us to have so much pain in this area of single relationships. Date well and respectfully or court as you are discovering or discerning God's hand-made selection for you.

God showed Adam who his Eve was. The last few years I have asked the Lord to place me within a man's heart, and the man will call out to me from his heart. It reminds me of when Nehemiah was gathering the exiled families to come live within the rebuilt wall. He said, "So my God *put it into my heart* to assemble the nobles, the officials and the common people for registration by families" (Nehemiah 7:5). God will put me on the man's heart. I believe my man will see my inner and outer beauty and some of my flaws, and he will still need to have me. He should spot me through the lens of the Holy Spirit.

A woman's heart should be so hidden in Christ, that
a man should have to seek Him first to find her.
~*Maya Angelou*

Would this say that unless a man is wholeheartedly
seeking the Lord, God will not bring forth the woman or
show Eve to Adam?

Let me go to the fields and pick up the leftover grain
behind anyone *in whose eyes I find favor*.
~*Ruth 2:2*

Women should pray for marital favor from the right
man. Marital favor will allow him to see her in all her inner
and outer beauty as the woman God has for him. We know
that Ruth found favor with Boaz and they married. God
showed Adam who his Eve was.

Men, along with putting the Lord first in your life, also
pray for God to direct you to the woman. Pray that your
eyes and heart will be open to her. Pray that your ears will
be perked to her telling words.

Isaac and Rebekah: A Perfect Story of God's Leading

Consider the story in Genesis 24 of Abraham sending
his servant out to find a wife for Abraham's son Isaac. In
this case, it seems the Lord *showed* the servant who the
woman ought to be.

[Abraham speaking to his servant] The LORD, the God
of heaven, who brought me out of my father's household
and my native land and who spoke to me and promised
me on oath, saying, 'To your offspring I will give this
land'—he will send his angel before you so that you can
get a wife for my son from there.
~*Gen. 24:7*

God already had this union arranged and predesigned. It was set up and provided for. The servant took ten of Abraham's camels with him and went to the well in the evening looking for *Mrs. Isaac Right*. Abraham's servant was smart enough to go to the well in the center of town where most women congregated and at the common time of their visits By the way, men: Are you making any effort to go find your bride to be? And ladies: Can you be found easily anywhere?

The blessed woman had to be of the same faith as Isaac, not a Canaanite (or an unbeliever in today's meaning). The servant prayed that he would know who the right girl was by determining her answer to a specific question:

> May it be that when I say to a girl, 'Please let down your jar that I may have a drink,' and she says, 'Drink, and I'll water your camels too'—let her be the one you have chosen for your servant Isaac. By this I will know that you have shown kindness to my master.
>
> *~Gen 24:14*

God will let you know who your mate is! So, whoever loves my scrumptious banana muffins is the one. If he wants nuts, "I can adjust Honey!"

Notice what Rebekah was doing. You never know who you may be blessing. Are you a helper? A blesser? Water camels! Water all ten!

Even after the servant received the sign of Rebekah watering the camels, verse 21 says "Without saying a word, the man watched her closely to learn whether or not the Lord had made his journey successful." Even after you believe the Lord has shown you by the Holy Spirit who your mate is, continue to watch them and pray for confirmations. You want to make sure you heard right.

Until you meet, pray *for* your future spouse and pray *in* your future spouse. Pray for their life right now even though you don't know them yet (or maybe you do!). Pray for their walk with the Lord. Pray for each of you to be patient and of good cheer and productivity until God makes the right time to bring you together. Pray God will mold you into the people He wants you to be and who will complement one another. Pray for their spiritual, emotional, physical and financial protection. Pray for victory over sin. Pray for their strength to remain pure. Pray for good, strong fellowship and mentoring for them. Pray God would make the man a leader and the woman submissive. Pray blessings upon them. Pray for God to bring you together.

Often if the couple is ordained by God, it is not long after they start dating or courting that they "know." Three months seems to be a reasonable amount of time to get a good idea of how you relate to each other and whether you have deep feelings that will continue to grow. This does not mean you get married right then; keep walking the relationship out in wisdom and practical ways.

Yo-Yo Dating: More Dangerous than Yo-Yo Dieting
I'm not sure which is more difficult—individuals who want to receive more attention or be asked out or individuals who receive that attention and become disappointed again. I have found that going in and out of relationships (even short ones) is harder than refraining from wrong ones. It's the ups and downs that are difficult to handle and adjust to. Hope up...disappointment...hope up...dead end. It can be gut-wrenching. Enough of that! I'm not going to just take a swing at any decent pitch that comes my way. I'm going to wait for *my pitch*. How 'bout

you? How are you feeling? Are you ready to limit your relationships to courtships?

Have you seen the movie *Courageous*? Nathan takes his 15-year-old daughter out to a special, exclusive Father/Daughter Dinner. The father says, "Jay, if you'll trust me with your heart, I promise to take care of you and give you my full blessing when God shows us the right one." He asks for her to agree to trust him and submit to his guidance in the direction of marriage. Nathan presents his daughter with a purity ring to remind her of the commitment, which Jay joyously accepts. The ring would remain on her finger until being replaced by her wedding engagement ring. Jay feels loved and protected and offers her trust to a wise father.

Ladies, even though some of us may not have an earthly father to fulfill that kind of guidance and selection role for us, we have a heavenly Father who is the shaper of our mate and will bring him to us.

I am wearing a ring I call my Commitment Ring. It reminds me of my value to God. It is a statement that I am set apart for Him, and I don't mess around either physically or emotionally with men that have anything less than serious courting and marital intentions. If a gentleman desires anything worthy with me, he's going to have to go through Jesus. He's going to have to seek Him first in order for anything to happen. The ring is a symbol and a reminder to me that I am waiting only for God's man to come along, the one who's brave enough to have that devout marriage with Christ first and to ask for me. I am set aside for my Jesus and for one special man only. I am committed to waiting for the right relationship that will be carried out as God wants it.

Ladies, we determine our own value based on the value God puts on us. Our hearts are in safe keeping with Him, tucked away for the right gift.

Brothers and sisters, get together with God and let him cause your ordained get-togethers.

4
The Choice Is Yours?

Remember, there is only one of you. You were carefully fashioned by God to complement the man He knew He would place you beside. Many ask me if there is only one man for every woman. My reply is always the same, "There are many men you could settle for, but there is one that God knows is best for you." When He decided to give Adam a mate, he did not place Eve, Mary and Sue before him and allow him to pick. He designed one especially capable of meeting all of Adam's needs

~101 Ways to Get and Keep His Attention. Grand Rapids: Zondervan Press, p. 31. Copyright © 2003 by Michelle McKinney Hammond.

eHarmony says there are 29 dimensions of compatibility to a long-term successful relationship. They fall within four categories: Character and Constitution; Personality; Emotional Makeup and Skills; Family and Values. 29! Only God's ordained matchmaking design could bring two chosen people together with infinite combinations of these 29 idiosyncrasies, strengths, weaknesses, beliefs and values to stand the test of time successfully and beautifully. There are perhaps several people you *could* marry, but only *one* that was carefully designed by God and suited to be yours at your side for life. You are hand-cut special for someone, and someone special is hand-cut for you.

If your ordained spouse truly is your "one-in-a-million," then you are going to have to pass by the other 999,999 people. So try to keep things in perspective when nothing else is working out in your relationships. When you've found your one-in-a million, you can truly say they are your miracle.

> Though it linger, wait for it.
> ~*Habakkuk 2:2*

> Where is the man who fears the Lord? God will teach him how to choose the best.
> ~*Psalm 25:12 TLB*

That includes teaching you how to marry the best intended mate for you!

> Friendship with God is reserved for those who reverence him. With them alone he shares the secrets of his promises.
> ~*Psalm 25:14 TLB*

When you are that close of a friend with God, when you show Him the reverence that He is due, He will let you know who *your* someone is.

Some people believe that there are a number of people they could marry and live well with. While I would like to believe that because it makes the odds go up more in a single's favor for finding a spouse, it really does not set right with me. How would you feel as a spouse knowing that your spouse could have married someone else just as well? Does that make you feel unique or special? Wouldn't you rather believe that God designed your spouse specifically for the way you are made?

God has built within each person a spot that only He can fill. He has put in us a spot for one other particular person to fill too. Marriage is about giving someone that ordained spot. God wants to be in our ordained spot and not any other god or idol. It is a marriage specifically designed between us and him. Would he design His marriages any different? He said husbands are to love their wives as Christ loved the church and He designed us to have just Him. This is a principle of exclusivity to which we must pay attention. Would He go against that principle and leave you available to any one of several people?

So God has the plan, but we must walk in it. I believe He says, "All the serious people who want my ordained plan come over here in this group…Group "O" for Ordained. I'll pick and design your future marriage." Then He says, "All the other believers, you come over here and make yourself Group "C" for choosing your own mate. Since you want to do the selecting yourself, I'll go along with it because I know what you will do in advance and I don't want it interfering with my Group "O's" plans. You are allowed to marry anyone you believe could fit with you."

That's God's "Plan B" for you. Not His perfect will, but His permissive will—that is, what He allows you to do with your free will that is not submitted to His. He would rather you rest in His perfect will, letting Him take the controls, than to wander into Group "C" with a false sense of security. He wants all believers to live supernaturally with His best blessings.

As for some other answers, we are going to have to leave those to God's sovereignty.

I choose to ask and wait for God's pick. Do you?

What Are You Looking For?
Are you attracted to tall stature, blonde tresses, brunette locks, broad shoulders, long legs, tiny waist, toned thighs or small ear lobes? (And that's about all I'll step into.)

Some people have a particular physical appearance preference. What about being open instead to whomever God has reserved for you? How about paying attention to someone who is tall in character? God knows you need to have physical attraction (not animal) and chemistry with a spouse and He will set that all up with the right one. If you are attracted to one another, that's all that matters.

Men have shared conversation on this topic with me. I believe that because men are known as the visual gender, it may not be as easy for them to remain as open in the physical attributes category. Ask God to help you to stay open to His pick.

Destiny and Calling
Do not date anyone you know you would not marry. Don't sign either of you up for pain. It wouldn't be considerate. If you see certain circumstances or dynamics not desirable to you, don't go on one date. You are setting up the potential for settling into a marriage you don't really desire. This is where some people get off track and into a round-a-bout of limbo and anguish. There is the potential of marrying who you date. You are responsible for their heart as well as your own. They are your brother or sister-in-the-Lord.

Keep in mind, "No one can eat just one." If you go on one date...you may have a good time and go on another. You may have a decent time and go on another. But is there a situation, dynamic or trait you know you do not wish to marry into?

Some men and women are *fallable (fall-able...my own word)*. It's such an accurate word. Fall-able. I can sense your heart sighing right now. You know exactly what I'm talking about. Dreamy. Or real close to it. Fall-able. But despite your belief that God is telling you not to date this "not-quite-right" person further, do you continue on anyway? You don't even have to know why God is saying not to date them. His saying "No" is reason enough to leave it alone.

Beware of the clenching factor of sin. It's hard to break away and get out after some attachment. You may know in your heart you need to get out, but someone could end up hurt by that point. The word "entangled" doesn't even sound comfortable. It means caught among obstacles; enmeshed. You will only end up feeling like mushed mesh.

Your obedience determines your outcome in your life. Be obedient to the Lord if you believe He is leading you out of a relationship. Disobedience could change the entire course of your life and others on so many levels.

> Oh Sovereign Lord, you alone know.
> ~*Ezek. 37:3*

The Lord said he would establish Solomon's kingdom forever "if he is unswerving in carrying out my commands and laws." (1 Chronicles 28:7) *Unswerving*; there's not much wiggle room in that for error. We should be similarly unswerving in how we approach our dating lives. After all, on judgment day, we will have to give an account of everything we did. We will have to tell God, "But I wanted them. I loved them. I didn't want to live without them."

Won't we be sorry whiners then? With extra jewels missing from our crowns because we missed our calling. In essence, we may as well tell God, "I don't care as much about your leading as my own. My way feels better. I'm saved and I'll be with the Father in heaven. Thanks for the gift of your Son. I know you meant His bloodshed to bless each area of my life, but this is good enough for me. I am sorry I *couldn't* carry out all your plans." (Or would that be *chose* not to?)

What is your destiny? We should be alert to God's assignments, understanding that we will be measured according to the extent to which we fulfill God's destiny for us. Are you determined to do this with God or are you destined to make a poor decision based on your current behaviors and desires? "Don't try to fulfill a life that God never ordered for you," says speaker Tim Storey.

I know a woman who sensed the conviction of the Lord on a first date. She sensed the man was not God's choice for her, yet she didn't know why. Unfortunately, she was already smitten. She ignored and shushed the Holy Spirit and went on to date him further. She thought of the conviction she felt on the date: "No, that can't be. It must have been me. I must have just been nervous."

She now acknowledges it was the Holy Spirit giving her warning not to get into a relationship with this man. He had character flaws that would end up hurting her more than she could have ever imagined. Now this woman grew up in a very loving family with never an ounce of verbal or emotional abuse. She experienced this abuse in the relationship, though. No wonder God shook her with conviction not to get involved. She also felt strong conviction further into the relationship, which she ignored once again out of her love for the man. She put God in the back seat.

If you sense the Lord is leading you away from someone, but your flesh is undeniably desiring that person, get on your face and knees before God EARLY and OFTEN. Ask every strong, trustworthy Christian you know to pray for you that you will become willing and will carry out God's leading. You may be smiling or partially smiling with that man/woman now with fluttery feelings, but you may cry more than you could ever imagine later. Will you chose to ignore or follow the leading of the Holy Spirit? What are the costs or blessings of those actions?

> God only wants for us what we would want for ourselves, if we were smart enough to want it.
> ~Adrian Rogers. Accessed 8/15/11 from www.christianindex.org/2410.

Jesus is the perfect example of bowing to authority. He could have called down ten thousand angels, but He did not. He submitted to His assignment. "Do you think I cannot call on my Father, and He will at once put at my disposal more than twelve legions of angels? But how then would the Scriptures be fulfilled that say it must happen in this way?" (Matthew 26:53-54) How then will His will for your life be fulfilled if not by your listening for and obeying the Holy Spirit?

Consider Hebrews 12:1-3: *Let us throw off everything that hinders and the sin that so easily entangles* (It's easy to get caught up in the wrong person. Most people have at least some qualities that are very likeable. Put those together with some good memories, their accepting family, your desire for marriage and many people walk down the aisle with the wrong person.)...*and let us run with perseverance* (It may be challenging, but don't give up and marry the wrong person...)...*the race marked out for us. Let us fix our eyes on Jesus, the author and perfecter of our faith, who for the joy set before him endured the cross, scorning its shame, and sat down at the right hand of the throne of God.* (Endure a breakup so that you can succeed in having that joyous, meant-for-you marriage…) *Consider him who endured such opposition from sinful men, so that you will not grow weary and lose heart.* (Don't lose faith my brother and sister!)

> So be careful to do what the Lord your God has commanded you; do not turn aside to the right or to the left. Walk in all the way that the Lord your God has commanded you, so that you may live and prosper and prolong your days in the land that you will possess.
>
> ~Deut. 5:32-33

> Whether you turn to the right or to the left, your ears will hear a voice behind you, saying, "This is the way; walk in it."
>
> ~Is. 30:21

Take a look King Saul's wrongful actions in 1 Samuel 15. He was commanded by the Lord to attack and totally destroy the Amalekites including their king Agag. His army was to leave nothing in existence from that group. "But Saul and the army spared Agag and the best of the sheep and cattle, the fat calves and lambs—everything that was good. They were unwilling to completely destroy all things, but everything that was despised and weak they totally destroyed.

> Then the word of the Lord came to Samuel: "I am grieved that I have made Saul king, because he has turned away from me and has not carried out my instructions."
>
> ~1 Sam. 15:9-11

> "For my thoughts are not your thoughts, neither are your way my ways," declares the Lord.
>
> ~Is. 55:8

Don't do dumb things. You don't automatically think like God, so you cannot afford to act on your emotions or feelings. The very outcome of your life and others depends on it. The very plans God has for your life depend on your following through on His leading. You want your intended life! You cannot let your heart open up to the wrong person. Wisdom is godly knowledge applied. Don't decide to place Godly knowledge on the shelf. You spent much time acquiring it and God specifically had it delivered to you in one form or another. Use it.

> A simple man believes anything, but a prudent man gives thought to his steps.
>
> *~Prov. 14:15*

> In his heart a man plans his course, but the Lord determines his steps.
>
> *~Prov. 16:9*

> For wisdom is more precious than rubies, and nothing you desire can compare with her. I, wisdom, dwell together with prudence; I possess knowledge and discretion.
>
> *~Prov. 8:11, 12*

Webster's definition of "folly" is: Lack of good sense or normal prudence and foresight. Lewd behavior. A foolish act or idea. An excessively costly or unprofitable undertaking. Psalm 38:5 talks about this. "My wounds fester and are loathsome because of my sinful folly." Proverbs 19:3 again says "A person's own folly leads to their ruin." Only God knows what He wants for you and your future spouse to fulfill for His kingdom, separately and then together. So there; I'm talking higher standards than you and I may be thinking about when we are in love with the wrong person or fighting to stay together with them. Chose the one to meet God's purpose in your lives.

Can we choose who we love? Yes, if you catch yourself early enough. We can choose to redirect our affections and focus based on what we perceive to be a better, wiser choice. What or who we focus on is paramount. The sooner you can find out if you and your date should continue further into a relationship or not, the better. You will need prayer to understand this—and obedience. Get out quick and do not go back and back and back. Get in, get out, and nobody gets hurt—or hurt as much. Above all, don't disappoint the Father.

NO ONE falls in love by chance; it is by allowance and CHOICE... No one stays in love by chance, it is by WORK. And no one falls out of love by chance, it is by allowance and CHOICE. The very word "fall" means you must have made the decision to jump off in the first place.

Song of Songs 8:4 says "Do not arouse or waken love until it so desires." This is the third time in the chapter that this is said...that means it's triply important! Don't give in to the wrong relationship. Don't give your heart away to the wrong one or at the wrong time; guard it.

Have you had someone walk away from you? Instead of asking those endless questions that are so tempting to ask—Why isn't he interested in me? What don't I have? What am I missing? Say instead, "No, that's God." I have asked God to open and shut doors. He knows my man/woman. He has someone for me. I have asked him for a husband/wife. I am obedient. I have God whole heartedly first in my life and I still have the balanced desire to marry. He knows I would put my desire aside for Him if I need to. Take those negative, fiery arrow thoughts captive and NEVER take the lack of a man's/woman's interest personally. They are not intended for you. Blame it, instead on your good God. God knows your fine intricacies. He knows your kingdom callings. He knows your strengths and the weaknesses. He knows who will be well suited together with in order to meet His objectives. He knows who you belong to. Your Daddy will pick him real good! It's going to be one of those "When God Chooses Your Mate" testimonies for me. It's going to be that good!

Nothing occurs to God.

~*Adriane Rogers*

Were we not chosen by God to be placed into our mother's womb?

Before I formed you in the womb I knew you, before you were born I set you apart.

~*Jer. 1:5*

For you created my inmost being; you knit me together in my mother's womb.

~*Ps. 139:13*

He could have decided to place us with anyone, but He chose our parents. Parenting and marriage are amongst the biggest relationships we will have on this earth. Why would God not place us with a particular marriage partner? To me, free will means I can go against His selections if I am naïve, foolish and disobedient or not following closely. He has someone for me.

But you do have the choice to go around His plan. What if the man is called to be a pastor, but she is not called to be a pastor's wife? What if she is called to minister to the hurt and broken but he will never press into his calling? What if his calling will require him to live by extreme faith (which is really how we all should be living), but the Lord knows she will never rise up to the level that is required for him to carry out God's Kingdom plans? What if she is called to adopt six children, but he is called to be a missionary overseas? Even the incredible born-again believer you may be thinking about may not be God's one for you in light of your particular destiny and calling.

God knows in advance exactly how individuals will change over time. He knows how a potential mate will be able or unable to adjust to those changes. You could know an incredible man or woman in the Lord, you may find you have so much in common, and you can't believe there would be anyone better for you or them. But that does not mean God has ordained you for each other.

There seems to be is one select person for us. There was one selected man for Mary—Joseph. They had a particular high calling to carry out. God knew the kind of man needed to stand beside Mary to carry out the salvation plan of the world. Don't we all have a calling to carry out as well? We are not carrying the Christ child's birth, but we are supposed to carry the gospel to all nations and there are particular callings assigned to each of us if we will seek them. He will use us the way He made us and according to who He knows we will grow up to be.

It's not about me—my small, personal desires—but the grand purposes of God. It's about the child who doesn't have any food or know His name. It's about the nations being rescued from flames. It's about the Body receiving healing and rejuvenation. It's about what will bring His name glory. I surrender to His will.

Fasting For Your Mate
Fast your mate in. Fast for clarification; is this your mate? According to Pastor Christopher W. Brooks of Evangel Ministries in Detroit, Michigan, fasting is one of the most forgotten, powerful methods to getting closer to

God, getting breakthroughs and having your destiny come to fruition.

I strongly recommend two books on fasting by Jentezen Franklin called *Fasting* and *The Fasting Journal*. They are easy to read, can't-put-down books. My former boyfriend followed a Daniel fast (from the Book of Daniel), after which it was confirmed to him that we were not the ones for each other. God had then started to remove his emotions toward me. Oh, if only we had known to fast like this six years earlier. Who and where would we be now? But nothing passes to us before passing through the Father's hands. God will use everything for His glory still.

Desperate for relief, I later went on the fast to clear out all the longing for him that I could not clear by myself. It really peeved me to have to follow in my former boyfriend's footsteps, but I had to think higher—they were really Jesus's footsteps. I did find relief. I received an extra anointing and boldness in sharing the gospel and much more. I see how God has opened doors for me and my year is playing out with victories. Jentezen Franklin teaches:

> Every assignment has a birthplace. When God has placed a dream inside you that only He can make possible, you need to fast and pray. Good or bad, what's in you will come out only when you fast and pray (p. 4).

> When I feel myself growing dry spiritually, when I don't sense that cutting-edge anointing, or when I need a fresh encounter with God, fasting is the secret key that unlocks heaven's door and slams shut the gates of hell. The discipline of fasting releases the anointing, the favor, and the blessing of God in the life of a Christian (p. 4).

Every assignment, every call of God, every direction from Him starts somewhere. God has specific assignments for your life. But how do you discover them? How will you hear His voice? How will you know His will for your life, His plans for you? Whom should you marry? Where should you live? What job should you take? What mission field is calling your name?
(p. 46)

Every major Bible character fasted. They were given direction, guidance and protection as a result. You may have never really picked up on this in your Bible reading before; I certainly had not. I surely would not have *chosen* to see it; I like eating, sweets and drinking coffee all too much! Only when totally, totally desperate for a move of God in my life, did I go into an extended 26-day Daniel Fast. I was desperate for Jesus, His direction, release from bondage and wanted dreams to be birthed out of me. I needed another level of anointing. I had fasted for quick spurts before, but without the full knowledge of what fasting has done for others and what it could do for me. After that extended fast, I rose to a new level of trust and expectancy. I believe writing this book is a result of my fasting.

Jentezen says,

If Jesus could have accomplished all He came to do without fasting, why would He fast? The son of God fasted because He knew there were supernatural things that could only be released that way. How much more should fasting be a common practice in our lives?
(p. 14)

Along with fasting, we still need to use wisdom. Wisdom will never go out of style.

As I sit in the coffee shop, writing and people watching on an autumn Friday night, I find myself wanting to be the one walking into a coffee shop holding onto the arm of a wonderful man, meeting other friends and sharing fellowship over delicious coffee. And I want to share one of those incredibly scrumptious cookies they sell with someone! I want to walk through the crunchy leaves being adored and adoring. I want my Facebook profile to read "Denise DiDomenico Flynn is in a relationship with WONDERFUL MAN!" I want to soul dance with someone; that is how it will be when I and my man meet for life. I meet new people all the time at fellowships, church, ministries, work, school and all over. And one of these times I'm going to meet someone new or see someone in a new light and he's going to be the right one. One day…I will wait on you Lord. Only you know. Until then and ever after, I'm good…so good…so in love with you Lord. It's you and me. What a beautiful couple we make.

5
The Real Deal

While you're in the wait for a mate, "be single for a season, not for a *reason*" says evangelist Kate McVeigh in *Single and Loving It!* (2003). Do make sure there *is not a reason* you are single such as lack of character, issues, baggage, unhealed hurts, or spiritual/emotional lack. Make sure your expectations of other people and relationships are realistic and doable.

God will not give us a great gift we cannot handle. He will wait until we are ready to receive it and care for it with love. He is not going to give His precious son or daughter to an unprepared, immature daughter or son. He loves each one of us far too much. The Word says "no good thing does he withhold from those whose walk is *blameless*" (Ps. 84:11).

The Bible also says in James 1:17, "Every good and perfect gift is from above, coming down from the Father of the heavenly lights, who does not change like shifting shadows." ...and he's going to give a perfect gift to someone that is not ready for one? This says right here that the Father is not going to change His ways or mind to adapt to our wants. So we can either take the long way around the mountain or get to spiritual maturity by submitting our flesh to His higher ways right now. Become the blessing that you are believing God for. And remember, "I'm no better than my devotional life" (Adrian Rogers).

A Woman's Character
Boaz replied, "I've been told all about what you have done for your mother-in-law since the death of your husband—how you left your father and mother and your

homeland and came to live with a people you did not know before."

~Ruth 2:11

And now my daughter, don't be afraid. I will do for you all you ask. All my fellow townsmen know that you are a woman of noble character.

~Ruth 3:11

Boaz knew about Ruth's fine character. Her good reputation preceded her. Shouldn't the same be noticed and known about us?

Ruth got an entire book to herself! What does that say? The book talks about the character of Boaz and Ruth. It talks about the tough spot Naomi was in and her bitterness. It speaks of Ruth's devotion to Naomi, Ruth's hard work and her willingness to listen to Naomi's wisdom. It speaks about Boaz's tenderness and his availability toward Ruth. It speaks of his willingness to step up and take on the responsibility of marriage to Ruth and care for Naomi as well.

Now Boaz was "a man of standing." (Ruth 2:1) "Standing" refers not solely to his finances, but with respect to his reputation in society. He was well esteemed. The Hebrew transliteration of Ruth 2:1 literally reads "and [there was] to Naomi a relative, to her husband, a man mighty in substance." Boaz was noble and sturdy. There was real depth to his character; he was not superficial. He lived with honor, and high moral standards. His good character preceded him in the land. The English Standard version says he was a "worthy man." This is not pertaining solely to his finances. So, I'm waiting for a Boaz, not a "*beau AS IS!*" And any good Christian man is looking for an outstanding woman like an Esther…not an "I wish I had married her *instead* of you!"

God is putting together marriages where the man and woman are equally spiritually mature and strong. You will hear married men sometimes say, "I married up. I got way more than I deserved." But I see the man's respect, love and adoration for his wife right there. So again, I believe God is putting people together that both have enough goin' on with Him in their heart, character and life.

A Second Marriage—Made in Heaven!

Abigail has a powerful testimony. She had a no-good husband, Nabal ("surly and mean in his dealings," says 1 Samuel 25:3, and a drinker). After Samuel's death (Israel's spiritual leader), Israel's King David had moved to Maon and had sent his servants to speak to Nabal. In past times, David had treated Nabal's sheepherders and sheep very well and helped to prosper Nabal. David now however, needed a blessing back from him. It was custom for travelers through the land to have their servants (600 for David) fed by the property owner of the area (Nabal). Nabal was wealthy and David had a part in this prosperity because of his shepherding with integrity near Nabal earlier.

Nabal claimed no recollection of David's former help and refused to help David and his men. David then set out to wrongly take vengeance upon Nabal's crew with the sword to leave no man standing. Abigail had been notified of Nabal's rudeness by a servant and the servant also testified how good David's crew had been to them earlier.

The Bible says that Abigail "was a woman of good understanding, and of a beautiful countenance" (1 Samuel 25:3 KJV). Abigail immediately went to meet David on her donkey. (I'll never complain about my 10 year old mini-van again!) She brought to him all the food necessary for his crew. She called herself a servant to David. She asked him to withhold his vengeance against Nabal. David thanked her and said "Praise be to the Lord, the God of Israel, who has sent you today to meet me. May you be blessed for your good judgment and for keeping me from bloodshed this day and from avenging myself with my own hands" (1 Sam. 25:32). Abigail exercised further good judgment in telling Nabal what took place when he was not drunk. And…are you ready for this?!?! Nabal's heart failed him! He became like a stone on the spot and died ten days later. Look at God's intervention!

And…are you ready for this??? David asked Abigail to marry him! Who needs Harlequin romances?!

So let's look at Abigail. She had inner beauty and strength of character. I'll call her "Abi*girl!*" She had it goin' on! The King James Version says she had a beautiful countenance—her aura. Because of her inner beauty, she had a beautiful peace about her and a beautiful facial expression. Isn't it our peace that can be alluring and attractive to someone, believers and unbelievers? Isn't it our peace that can be persuasive to someone? She was not lax in stepping up to her calling in preventing a body of people from being wiped out through bloodshed from David's people. She was giving and hospitable. I imagine she probably packed a pretty mean sack lunch for the guys. She knew well to wait to tell her husband of the events. Abigail served this man David even before he became her husband, even before there was any kind of romantic relationship between them.

And so, ladies and gentlemen, what have we learned today? Serve each other. Don't serve to get a blessing. Don't serve to get a man or a woman. Just serve him or her because he or she is your brother or sister in Christ and it is the right thing to do. We honor our family. Honor them in place of all the people that never honored them before in their life. But you never know, you may both just get an even bigger blessing out of it. Look for someone with a servant's heart, good integrity and judgment. Look for one who does what is right in the eyes of God. Not a perfect person, but one who more often than not takes the higher road.

As in any Bible story, this story really has a lot packed into it. We see that it is better to wait on God and not seek our own vengeance in a situation. We see that the Lord can step in and take control of the situation better than any man, including David, could possibly do. Much bloodshed and much more damage would have occurred otherwise. We see also that a godly woman's insight and input can be very persuasive to a godly, wise man. (Take notice of that, men.) We see that the unjust will eventually be put to shame. (Take notice of that too!)

Study these other verses about character:

Prov. 11:16   "A kind hearted woman gains honor."

Prov. 11:17   "Those who are kind benefit themselves."

Prov. 12:4   "A wife of noble character is her husband's crown."

Prov. 31:10   "A wife of noble character who can find? She is worth far more than rubies."

Prov. 31:29   "Many women do noble things, but you surpass them all."

The Ten-Cow Woman—A Love Story

In a small village in Hawaii it was the custom for the men to propose to a woman by offering his future father-in-law a cow.

For an "average" girl they would offer one cow, and for a particularly striking woman they would offer three cows. In fact, no one had ever offered more than three cows. Then a rumor began to spread that a young man named Johnny had given eight cows to a particular family. The bride to be was a woman named Sereta who was seen by most as plain and ordinary.

The eight cow gift became so well known that a reporter wanted to interview the families involved for a human interest story. He began asking people about Sereta. He found that everyone was stunned at the groom's gift because Sereta was just the average girl next door.

When the reporter went to Johnny's house a beautiful woman answered the door, introducing herself as Sereta. The reporter was struck by how attractive and graceful she was, especially in light of the statements the townspeople had made.

Sitting down with Johnny, he asked about the eight cows, wondering if he had been taken advantage of by his bride's father. Johnny assured him that he gladly offered the eight cows for his wife to be. He then further explained, "Imagine several of our wives are sitting down for tea and they begin to share about the gifts their families received for the marriage. One shares her family received three cows, and another received one. How would you feel if someone gave one cow for you?"

The reporter then asked, "So you gave the extra cows for her hand in marriage?" To which Johnny replied, "Not at all. I gave eight cows because I wanted an eight cow wife. I want her to know that I value her that much, and now you see how beautiful she really is.

I want to be a "ten-cow" woman of God, valuable to my beloved. So for reasons that transcend the marriage motivation, I took an intercessory prayer class. I wanted to bring something powerful to the marriage union. I want to be the biggest blessing I can be to my husband, my son, our family, our church, our community, the nation and the Kingdom. I want to be able to change the environment, our lives and the lives of others through prayer. I want to be the woman a man would willingly pay ten cows for. I don't want to just *look* like a ten-cow woman—I want to *be* that woman of value.

Paul and Jan Crouch, the married Founders of Trinity Broadcasting Network, the world's largest Christian network of 38 years, testified of all the great things and miracles God has done in their ministry. Jan said she would ask God one day why He thought them worthy to choose them for the mission. Paul said that a good and successful man has to have a tenacious praying woman behind him as Jan has been to him.

What's Inside?
The crown of a man or woman is godliness. The distinction of a man or woman is godliness. There is just no substitute for Jesus, integrity or godliness. Women believe that there are not enough single men available who are pursuing God with a fire, the fire that makes a person truly whole. Just as a candle cannot burn without fire, man cannot [unfold] without a spiritual life (The Buddha). Pursue God running. Pray for the single body of Christ around you to arise to their fullness in Jesus.

A church gave an award to their "Best Married Couple" of 20 years and the "Best Male and Female Single" and others. It was explained that the wife of the winning couple originally had broken up with the man while they were dating because he was not going after the Lord as she was. The victory story is that the man decided to fully sell out to the Lord. The man had a spiritual awakening, grew in his walk, the rest is history and now they're thriving in marriage and getting awards publicly! After calling the "Best Male Single" up to receive his reward, the preacher quipped, "We better pray for you right now. I can see all the single ladies lookin' at you."

What does a man have way down in his sub-Q layer (subcutaneous tissue, the deepest layer of our skin)? What does he have way down in his heart, the seat of identity? What is he made of? Does he have deep strength from God in his inner most soul? Do integrity and love make up his fibers? Any other kind will not do.

The subcutaneous tissue is a layer of fat. Most people don't think we need fat. It has a negative reputation, but we do need it; it's not an option. Subcutaneous tissue (fat) "insulates the body, absorbs trauma and is a reserve energy source" (Answers.com). My strong God within the deepest part of me (my soul) insulates me, absorbs my traumas and is my energy source! I need a man who has Jesus deeply within his sub-Q. Into the subcutaneous layer is where the injections go to get people better—to make a real difference for someone. Jesus can make a real difference in someone if we let Him into those deep places of ourselves. I think a great t-shirt would say, "Got Jesus in the sub-Q?"

Ditch having obnoxious, dominating, controlling or attacking attitudes and personalities. Take these ways to the Lord; let Him refashion you and crucify your flesh so that these become the old you. Shift! Get pleasant. With Jesus, get a grip on mood swings and emotions. I am not talking about those with psychological or mental disorders, although we should seek a physician's assistance for that as well. I am more so talking about becoming more stable in the Lord and disciplining our flesh better. There's nothing better, sweeter and more promising than two nice, pleasant and emotionally stable people coming together.

6
Gender Similarities...A Short List

We're born.
We breathe.
God loves us; we're meant to serve Him.
We eat.
We love.
We die.

And that about says it huh? Point made?

Gender similarities…a short list.

7
Gender Differences...
"Male and Female He created them."

~Genesis 1:27

While we love to be in love, it can be challenging. "Male and female He created them" (Gen 1:27), and ohhh, did He create them different! Let's look at, appreciate, marvel and say "Oh yes, I know that!" at some of the inner workings God put in each gender. Dr. J. Vernon McGee taught in his broadcast, "I take my watch to one repairman and my car to another. The watch is a more delicate mechanism and needs the attention of a different mechanic with a different technique. Woman is made finer than man."

He then goes on to quote Alan Beck's definition of a little girl:

<u>What is a Girl?</u>
by Alan Beck

Little girls are the nicest things that can happen to people. They are born with a bit of angel-shine about them, and, though it wears thin sometimes, there is always enough left to lasso your heart—even when they are sitting in the mud, or crying temperamental tears, or parading up the street in mother's best clothes.

A little girl can be sweeter (and badder) oftener than anyone else in the world. She can jitter around, and stomp, and make funny noises and frazzle your nerves, yet just when you open your mouth, she stands there demure with that special look in her eyes. A girl is *Innocence* playing in the mud, *Beauty* standing on its head and *Motherhood* dragging a doll by the foot.

God borrows from many creatures to make a little girl. He uses the song of a bird, the squeal of a pig, the stubbornness of a mule, the antics of a monkey, the spryness of a grasshopper, the curiosity of a cat, the speed of a gazelle, the slyness of a fox, the softness of a kitten. And to top it off, He adds the mysterious mind of a woman.

A little girl likes new shoes, party dresses, small animals, first grade, noisemakers, the girl next door, dolls, make-believe, dancing lessons, ice cream, kitchens, coloring books, make-up, cans of water, going visiting, tea parties, and one boy. She doesn't care so much for visitors, boys in general, large dogs, hand-me-downs, straight chairs, vegetables, snowsuits or staying in the front yard.

She is loudest when you are thinking, the prettiest when she has provoked you, the busiest at bedtime, the quietest when you want to show her off, and the most flirtatious when she absolutely must not get the best of you again. Who else can cause you more grief, joy, irritation, satisfaction, embarrassment, and genuine delight than this combination of Eve, Salome, and Florence Nightingale?

She can muss up your home, your hair, and your dignity—spend your money, your time, and your patience—and just when your temper is ready to crack, her sunshine peeks through and you've lost again. Yes, she is a nerve-racking nuisance, just a noisy bundle of mischief. But when your dreams tumble down and the world is a mess— when it seems you are pretty much of a fool after all—she can make you a king when she climbs on your knee and whispers, "I love you best of all!"

So these are the beautiful and possibly debilitating effects that a little girl and a woman can have on a man. How will we behave realizing this, women? Hopefully we will carry ourselves maturely and walk only in the ways God would have us to. God built an intrinsic attraction into the man for the traits of a woman and the woman for toward the man.

What is a Boy?
by Alan Beck

Between the innocence of babyhood and the dignity of manhood we find a delightful creature called a boy. Boys come in assorted sizes, weights, and colors, but all boys have the same creed: to enjoy every second of every minute of every hour of every day and to protest with noise (their only weapon) when their last minute is finished and the adult males pack them off to bed at night.

Boys are found everywhere—on top of, underneath, inside of, climbing on, swinging from, running around, or jumping to.

Mothers love them, little girls hate them, older sisters and brothers tolerate them, adults ignore them, and Heaven protects them.

A boy is *Truth* with dirt on its face, *Beauty* with a cut on its finger, *Wisdom* with bubble gum in its hair, and the *Hope* of the future with a frog in its pocket. When you are busy, a boy is an inconsiderate, bothersome, intruding jangle of noise. When you want him to make a good impression, his brain turns to jelly or else he becomes a savage, sadistic, jungle creature bent on destroying the world and himself with it.

A boy is a composite—he has the appetite of a horse, the digestion of a sword-swallower, the energy of a pocket-sized atomic bomb, the curiosity of a cat, the lungs of a dictator, the imagination of a Paul Bunyan, the shyness of a violet, the audacity of a steel trap, the enthusiasm of a firecracker, and when he makes something, he has five thumbs on each hand. He likes ice cream, knives, saws, Christmas, comic books, the boy across the street, woods, water (in its natural habitat), large animals,

Dad, trains, Saturday mornings, and fire engines.

He is not much for Sunday School, company, schools, books without pictures, music lessons, neckties, barbers, girls, overcoats, adults, or bedtime. Nobody else is so early to rise, or so late to supper. Nobody else gets so much fun out of trees, dogs, and breezes. Nobody else can cram into one pocket a rusty knife, a half-eaten apple, three feet of string, an empty Bull Durham sack, two gum drops, six cents, a slingshot, a chunk of unknown substance, and a genuine supersonic code ring with a secret compartment.

A boy is a magical creature—you can lock him out of your workshop, but you can't lock him out of your heart. You can get him out of your study, but you can't get him out of your mind. Might as well give up—he is your captor, your jailer, your boss, and your master—a freckled-faced, pint-sized, cat-chasing, bundle of noise. But when you come home at night with only shattered pieces of your hopes and dreams, he can mend them like new with two magic words, "Hi Dad!"

Thoughts flow to me of Jesus and his mother, Mary. How many times she must have been intrigued by Him and the cute little things he did. How many times she must have caressed His cheek as He grew. How she would have done anything to stop His crucifixion if she should have. From a selfish point, I am glad she couldn't.

And this boy and girl are created in the image of God. I do not know which gender is more mysterious. I guess it just depends on which gender you ask. Perhaps if we want to learn more about why an S.O. (Significant Other) acts in some particular, mysterious ways, we should ask them about their younger days—their roots. Maybe then we will learn why they are the way they are in their thoughts, feelings, desires, needs, emotions, and habits. Perhaps they will be flattered and touched we took the time to dive deep in getting to know them.

8
Bless Fest

"Friendship? Yes Please." *~Charles Dickens*
"Please Pass the Grace." *~Denise Flynn*

Chic' Up Your Chivalry Gentlemen!

I asked a brother-in-the-Lord his thoughts about single men performing chivalrous actions like opening doors, etc. for single women. He did not think it was a good idea. He thought that if he was to open a friend's car door, she would perceive it as a romantic gesture and if another gentleman was interested in her, he would think she was already being pursued or taken.

While I respect my friend's selflessness, I disagree. ("Ron, I've been sitting here in the car for hours now! Let me out!... ...) It seems to me that if another man is really interested in her, he will watch her for awhile, ask others about her or even ask her directly what her availability status is.

Male or female, we deserve to be treated nice as singles! Why should only the married folk get all the blessings?

> Love each other with brotherly affection and take
> delight in honoring each other.
>
> *~Romans 12:10*

Gentlemen, "Chic' up your chivalry!" Opening car doors, lifting heavy items, letting her walk in first, walking on the outside of the sidewalk next to the curb, letting her order first, helping her put her coat on, helping her with difficult tasks...those areas are all within brotherly affection and honoring her as a person and sister. And just think of it! If a car swerves recklessly up onto the sidewalk you'll be the one hit and see Jesus! See? There's always a blessing in blessing!

If you are really concerned that a woman will take your honoring in the wrong way, why not say to her, "Would you mind if I was a chivalrous friend? As a sister-in-Christ you should be honored and treated well." Believe me, your ratings will skyrocket in the singles group along with that fine godly character you are developing! And the same goes for women who are not afraid to bless men in similar ways.

I talked with a woman who was spending time with a man going different places and doing different things. She said that he always called her when he said he would. He opened up car doors for her and I saw him extend his hand to women to help them up or down from different ground levels. (I know this man; his character is not that of a flirt.) She said she was not used to that as her face delighted— "You don't see that too often." I could tell she really liked the treatment, as she deserved. See what I mean?

Some people may say chivalry is from the old school. But that "old school" has a lot of great values that many of us women admire and want in a courting and marital relationship today. Some of us women believe that there was something about the WWII generation; they had a devotion, dedication and gentlemanly quality that are so missing today.

I have single, platonic male friends that bless me in chivalrous ways, and it makes me only want to bless them back and honor them more. I don't think there are many singles that couldn't use a blessing every now and then. Chivalry, help, respect, honor, words of affirmation or even gifts distributed throughout the single Christian community can go a long way towards eliminating loneliness and purposelessness, and will help the Body of Christ function the way in which it was intended. It lets singles know they don't have to settle for bad romantic relationships just to get some nurturing or care.

My friend brought me yellow "friendship" roses next time he came to my fellowship after our chivalry discussion.

My editor's husband went home to be with the Lord in the middle of a wonderful marriage. He and his male, married friends had made a promise to each other beforehand that if anything was to happen to any of the men in their circle, the remaining men would see to it that the wife remaining would be taken care of and blessed. One day Diane was told that she was going to be taken out to a fine dinner by the team. She was given roses with honor. She felt the love her husband could not give to her in his absence. She was touched beyond measure with their sincerity and knew she was special in God's eyes.

There are men and women who have been neglected, rejected or abused (sexually or emotionally) by the opposite gender. They carry wounds within and walls around themselves. God can use the intentional blessings from healthy and mature persons of the opposite gender to begin or continue a healing process for them, setting a standard for their ultimate selection of a mate. Sometimes after a divorce or break up we tend to want to swear off any connections or communications with men or women because we have been hurt by them. I have felt this way at times in the past. But I encourage you to keep a little door open to keep relating or learning to relate to men or women. Don't lose your relating skills. Keep improving on them. Learn the ways of love, honor and submission now.

Women can learn to submit to a man even in friendship. I was planning a celebration that included cookies. My friend suggested having a cake instead. I originally decided against cake because I thought it would have been more difficult to eat standing up and I was trying to keep things simple (no plates or forks). But my friend had a special idea for the cake which was to put a photo related to the event on it. I knew he was going to feel special in helping and the idea was cool so I said, "Okay, cake it is! Good idea!" He then called back that there was much more involved in the cake ordering...had to have the rights to the photo desired on it. So he said, "How 'bout cookies; too complicated." I said, "Cookies will be fine. Thank you for your idea and willingness to help!" Then I realized, "Hey, I submitted to a godly man even in a friendship!" and patted myself on the back. I know this is just a little example, but start learning and practicing submission even in little things ladies. And that friend...he honors me.

My friend did some home repairs for me. He went out of his way, taking extra time and energy from his hectic schedule and responsibilities. I was so very thankful. I wanted to bless him back, but in a way that he could not ordinarily or easily do for himself. So I made him a really big, fat gourmet sandwich with healthy snacks in a lunch sack for his next day of work. As a busy, single father, I knew this is something he couldn't easily do for himself. Jesus did something for us we could not do for ourselves— rescued us with a special blessing. My friend was very appreciative. He said it had been years since anyone had done this for him. "Mission Return-Blessing" accomplished!

Ask yourself, how can you make this day unlike any other day for someone? What can you do to show up like an angel in someone else's life today? Be a blesser in life; you reap what you sow. So what are you gonna' do?

Say It Is So!

Did you ever want to give a single brother or sister a compliment, but you are afraid they will think you are flirting or want to marry them and have their seven children? In the past, I have held back on complimenting gentlemen. I did not want them to think I was flirting. I didn't want to inspire them further if I detected they had romantic feelings for me and I didn't for them. Or I didn't want them to feel I had romantic feelings for them if I thought they would be uncomfortable. Over the last year, I have begun blessing single, Christian men with compliments more. Encouragement is one of my spiritual gifts and I felt like I was not letting it flow in this realm. If I think a man may perceive the comment the wrong way, I say to the man, "I am not flirting with you; I just want to bless you and compliment your good qualities. I really like the way you....I really appreciate the way you....I've really seen you growing in the area of...You are really good at..." The practice seems to be going well; I have good nurturing friendships and I'm not married with seven other children...yet.

Socially Speaking: Some Tips

To give the most and get the richest fulfillment out of the community Bless Fest, one does need to use good verbal communication skills. You would be surprised at the number of individuals that struggle in this area. Some will admit their anxiety over it and some you can see their uneasiness within.

When you withhold yourself from others due to shyness or communication deficiencies, others don't get blessed. They don't get the blessing of knowing YOU! And God made you cool! So don't be selfish; allow your coolness to come out and be drawn out with some prayer and technique. Share yourself with us, OK? Here are some tips to make you more comfortable:

Things your communications coach would teach: (my Mom was mine)

- Listen carefully to whomever you are speaking with. Resist the temptation to interrupt. Men especially hate this. Sometimes when there is much good conversation to share between two people, they start out talking at the same time. Back off of your sentence and let them continue with theirs. Interrupting is really about pride. The interrupting person thinks their information is more important than the other person's. Give way to your conversational partner. You just might learn something. If you both start talking simultaneously, stop and say "You first."

- Keep the conversation balanced. Try to even up your talking time versus theirs. People dislike not being able to get a word in edge—wise either in person or on the phone. Don't corner someone in a conversation where they feel like they have to look for a way of escape.

- Vary your conversation in terms of topics.

- Ask questions about the other person and their experiences (keep this in balance with the following).

- Tell about yourself and your experiences (keep this in balance with the above). You don't have to wait for a lull in the conversation to do this, but it is a life raft when you need one. Ask another question about a piece of information the other person has already shared. Dig deeper into the topic you are already on. It deepens the conversation and keeps it going. Picture the tennis ball or conversation volleying back and forth. Think interactive communication!

- Ask a combination of open-ended questions (that require a more in-depth, extensive answer) and closed-end questions (that can be answered with a simple "yes" or "no").

- Ask God to give you a sense of wit and humor. He really will! And it will be tailored just to you cuz' you are unique and fearfully and wonderfully made my friend!

- Ask God to help you with small talk. Help yourself, too, by keeping up your reading of a good mix of Christian and secular publications and websites. In order to have conversation, you have to know something!

Finally, all *of you be* of one mind, having compassion for one another; love as brothers, *be* tenderhearted, *be* courteous.

~1 Pet. 3:8 NKJV

9
Snazz It Up!

Snazz it up ladies and gentlemen! Physical chemistry and attraction is still a key ingredient in a marriage relationship. It's no different in the Christian dating world—Christians are human too! Be at your best inside and out. We are carrying the Holy Spirit; He deserves to live in a kept up and holy place.

Common Tips for Men and Women:
- Be sure to give your body enough water and nutrients from good foods and supplements.
- Exercise your temple. Keep fit. Let God know He is worth the effort to be housed in an honorable way. Let the man or woman know they are worth the effort to impress.
- Wear colors that look best on you. Ask a wardrobe/color consultant about this. Particular colors look best with certain skin tones and hair and eye colors. The right color can look like "Wow" on someone! The wrong color can look like "Oh, hi." Color looks good on men! Don't be afraid to wear bright colors. You'll not only look good, but you will feel good. You'll look your best and a man or woman's eye will be drawn to you. You would be surprised how affecting color is! Women love color on men too! There was once a pressed, celery green and white long sleeve, checkered shirt and an orange shirt that drove me nuts!
- Demote those old tattered shirts that look tired (the spotted, faded and pilled ones).
- The best stain remover is Jesus!

- Freshen up your wardrobe annually. Purchase a few new shirts each season and new slacks when needed.) This is an investment in "you" and you are worth it! And he or she is worth it too!
- Keep updated with styles. It's just a fact of life. We have to spend some money on what we wear. Seek a wardrobe consultant for expertise. Men, women can tell when you are wearing a sport coat from 20 years ago. My favorite, fantastic wardrobe and image coach is Penelope of Penelope's Principles. www.penelopesprinciples.com
- Own dress jeans as well as casual jeans.
- Get some jeans with some fit to them. Anything too baggy tends to look sloppy and makes one look even overweight. If you need the waist to be larger or smaller, seek the services of a tailor. You may be in between sizes. Men tend to overlook the importance of tailoring, but it is very important.
- Know a tailor and don't be afraid to use the service. Proper fit is important.
- Make sure clothes are lint and fuzz free. Adhesive rollers work best.
- Keep teeth white with a home or a dentist's whitening system.
- Keep that breath fresh with regular dental cleanings, floss, mouthwash and breath mints. I'll never forget the young man who sought me out in a coffee shop while his date visited the restroom. He assertively asked me if I had any mints (to kill coffee breath), which I shared for the cause of young love. She then returned and they left in the sunshine of the day. How totally cute.
- Use good posture. Number one, you look 10 pounds thinner. Number two...you are standing tall with the confidence of Christ inside of you and it has a

subtle, unconscious alluring effect. It's the way you carry yourself. Men and women love God-confidence.

More Tips for Gentlemen

Gentlemen, women go just as crazy over you as you do over them. Perhaps we control it or hide it better though. The way you move, your leg crossed or not crossed, the hair on your wrist above a glove line…you never know…whatever she prefers. A crisp, striped shirt; your masculine hands, your hair, cologne…My! If you take more notice on these things, she will too. I guess it's just plain, old fashioned chemistry. Oh, and men's shoes can be very alluring!

- Make friends with your iron.
- White socks with jeans or khakis? Really? Blinding. Go gray or with a colored sock.
- Have well groomed hair. It's usually best to avoid comb-over hair. I've never heard anyone say anything positive about it. Ask a modern hair dresser for alternatives.
- Keep facial hair neatly trimmed (nose, ears, eyebrows, mustache, beard).
- Use a skin care system. You can pick one up from almost any pharmacy store. This would include a cleanser (other than a bar of green soap in the shower), a facial scrub to remove dead skin cells, a toner and moisturizer. Women are attracted to soft, kind faces without looking worn, dried or peeling. God's woman will want to touch your face; it should be smooth.
- Sport neatly manicured fingernails and toes.
- Use manners when eating. No shoveling—go a little slower—a little gentler. Use utensils for scooping. No fingers.

- Do not snort. I know this sounds funny, but snorting is unattractive. Blow your nose instead. Only little kids are allowed to snort.
- I'm not suggesting you be someone else, but do be a well presentable *you*!

More Tips for Ladies

Oh, where does it ever end? It does seem like women have the brunt of having to look good placed mostly upon them.

As you have no doubt heard, men are physically wired differently. They are visual people; something attractive catches their attention and many cannot help but look…and think. Men are plagued with sexual images throughout every day. Pornography is an issue, even in the church. It is a constant threat to many men and those in a relationship with them. Because many men are plagued with this, the least we should do is to dress in a godly yet attractive way. As a general rule of thumb, we should take care of ourselves; spend the extra time and money to look well. Men are held accountable for the things they should have control over though, refraining from and avoiding stimulants.

Ruth was instructed to put on her best clothes to see Boaz. Ester prepared and prettied herself with beauty treatments, special foods and royal robes for King Xerxes. Honestly, in my former marriage I used to believe that my husband should have been physically attracted to me because he should naturally love me for me, because I'm loveable. But the real truth ladies, is that they are wired differently and we should help them because of that. Men now days are up against a lot. Every advertisement, check-out counter and billboard has pre-pornographic images; it's ridiculous and frankly I feel compassion for men. I believe it falls on us women to help them as much as possible. Our dress should reflect God's values to give them a beautiful, spiritual refreshing alternative.

Feminine Tips

The best beauty treatment is Truth Serum, the blood of Jesus Christ! "He is the way, the truth and the light"!

- Do the best you can in the way you've been blessed physically and make peace with the rest.
- Do not show cleavage. No shadows or a crease showing either. Wear a fitted camisole underneath your blouse or top. Use broaches to prevent low necklines. Or, check out the latest, clever snap-in concealer called Cami Secret.
- Avoid wearing fabrics that are revealing or too sheer. Wear a camisole or slip underneath.
- Do not allow your undergarment straps to show out from underneath your tops. It's just downright tacky! Purchase a strapless undergarment or the plastic pieces that gather the straps to the middle of your back.
- Do not wear short skirts. It's the truth. Don't make it hard for the brothers! Just above the knee is really about the shortest one should go.
- Today's swimsuits…not much fabric there. Yet there are still some good, appealing choices available. Two-piece bikinis and string bikinis should be saved for your private backyard tanning. Tankini tops with reasonable bottoms are fine. Just make sure the top covers and supports you well.
- Dress stylish, but conservatively. Don't be the cause for a brother lusting. You can be very fashionable, sophisticated or cute yet modest. Call Penelope's Principles.

- Wear a great hair cut! Check with a stylist to see if it's a really great style and color you have.
- Use a skin care system. This would include a gentle cleanser, a facial scrub to remove dead skin cells, a toner and moisturizer. Men are attracted to soft, kind faces. God's guy will want to touch your face when it becomes appropriate; it should be soft.
- Make sure your eyebrows are trimmed and shaped. Ask your beautician if you should have any facial hair removed. Men notice this. "Threading" (facial hair removal) is the latest technique.
- Yes, use make up. Very few women can go without. Draw out your good features and minimize or camouflage the rest.
- Manicure your nails and toes. They do not need to be long or false nails, but filed, shaped and clean. Use clear nail polish at least for special occasions.

I'm not suggesting you be someone else, but do be a well presentable *you*!

10
Relationship Status

How far is it from here to there? Where am I in the
"here to there"? Closer to here? Or there?

Is It Friendship or More?

Gentlemen, when women say they want to be just friends, they usually mean it. They don't *not* mean it. Take it at absolute face value. Drop it. They have come to a place and they have made their decision inside. Don't wait with false hope that she will change her mind. If she does, it is likely not to be a true formation of the right, authentic kind of love.

Ladies, your challenge is to make sure you don't "fall in love" before you find out you actually do not like the man you've been seeing. Soul ties and attachments can form from the sheer dint of time you spend with someone. That makes it very, very hard to distinguish between a "habit attachment" (that is, you are used to the person being around and so feel uneasy when they are not around) and genuine love.

If you actually do have an interest in a man, but don't know whether he's interested as well, just sit tight. You don't want to be in a situation where you have more interest than him and believe me, if he is that motivated, he will eventually make the first move. Sometimes, when the woman makes the first move, the man goes along for the ride until he is no longer interested…not good for you. Not to say that you can't drop hints. Sometimes men are a bit slow. As a woman, you can help him to "get a clue." Throw a gentle softball pitch like "I enjoy your company." See if he takes a swing or lets the ball go by. Let him know you think highly of him. Pay some attention to him, smile, take a slight interest in his life, ask questions, or invite him to a group event. Like Hansel and Gretel, litter the pathway to the house with rose petals of interest. Light the runway and give him permission to approach. Just know when to change directions if he is not responding with signs of interest.

Women, after having taken the above steps—giving your time, conversation, compliments, leave it all in his court to ask or suggest anything further to you. He is supposed to be the leader. If it happens that he does like you, but doesn't have the guts to ask, do you really want that in a man's personality or character?

Look at how Ruth made her interest known to Boaz. She followed Naomi's instruction to tip Boaz off of her interest by following the *moral* Israelite custom and law of the time. Ruth let her interest in Boaz be made known to him by 1) Coming alongside him and moving his garment, uncovering his feet; 2) Asking Boaz to spread the corner of his garment over her. Then she left the rest in God's and Boaz's hands.

Sometimes it's difficult discerning the nice things the opposite gender says or does. The ministering men and women are nice, sweet, friendly people regardless. While it is an absolute blessing to be in the healthy company of the opposite gender as opposed to being in the company of those lacking the ability to bless, it can have its other set of frustrations. Turn your frustration into wisdom here. How is one really to know if the person you have an interest is mutually interested?

Two men once asked me if I thought of them as friends or more. They could not discern my intentions. I respect them so much for coming out and asking me that. They're the men, and that's their role.

Time spent together is not necessarily an indicator of romantic interest from a man—at least enough interest to go the whole marathon of life together. Men get lonely for companionship too. They may spend time with a woman because they like doing things they would not ordinarily do with their male friends. They may enjoy a feminine presence. They may be going through loneliness and struggling for a little attention themselves. They may be lonely, but not your *one and only*. I do not want to be the "in the meantime" girl or the "pacifier" close friend. It could be costly to be in a friendship with a man who is lonely, likes my company and companionship, but who doesn't really see me as "The One." I feel myself to be a godly, sweet, attractive and fun female, a good listener, even soothing and sensitive. Men do seem to appreciate those traits. As such, it would be easy for me to fall into a dead-end, semi-romantic relationship. This requires that I guard my heart. I don't want to be the "in-between, time killer" while they are waiting for their Mrs. Right. I'm not Ms. Almost.

The man should be the initiator of a date and of a relationship. He must be the stabilizer and maintainer as well. Women, don't take up that role! It's simply not right. Men do not pursue women who are pursuing them. You might get attention for a minute, but it will fade. Women in the leading role violate God's natural law. Deep down they won't have respect for you. In the movie *Gone With the Wind,* Scarlett O'Hara longed for Mr. Ashley Wilkes who was about to propose to Melanie instead. Her Pa said to her, "Have you been making a spectacle of yourself running about after a man who's not in love with you when you might have any of the bucks in the county?"

Ruth's destiny was that she was brought to Boaz through her devotion to Naomi and by working diligently in her situation. Ruth did make herself beautiful and visible to Boaz and did as custom said at the time, but **Boaz made the suggestion to Ruth** that he could be her kinsmen-redeemer, not the reverse. We as women should keep our dignity.

It has been told to me, "Trust man through God." I am not sure which gender has it more difficult—the man having to lead and take the chance to ask a woman for a date or a relationship, or the woman having to wait and see if the man shows interest. I have sympathy for both roles. But when we operate in our perspective roles with men as the leaders and hunters and women as the patient, pursued ones, there is a peace and a healthy sense of pride and productivity—regardless of the outcome.

That said, it is okay to ask a gentleman to attend such events as weddings or other ceremonies where you may need an escort. Make sure you communicate when you are asking him to go that you "would prefer a companion for the evening" if that's your intent. If it is a dating relationship you desire with him, after that event, leave it all in his court. If he wants anything further, he will ask you.

If a man really wants you, he will make time to find and be with you. He will consistently and increasingly come around you and stay in touch with you. He will not be able to keep silent. It will come out. You won't have to wonder. That's what real interest consists of. That's what it should look like. If he likes you enough for a date or relationship, he will find determination to get something going *and keep it going*. If he desires a relationship, he WILL be talking about it with you, about you. Remember that old Motown song "Ain't no mountain high enough to keep me from you"? Apply that here. If he is not doing those things, he is not sincerely interested or interested deeply enough and the truth will set you free.

Here are a few more tip-offs of platonic friendship. When a man addresses a woman as "Kiddo," that's a flashing signal he is only interested in platonic friendship. It is a fun, chummy title. It is a polite title, but says you are a friend who they have no romantic feelings for, yet there is a mutual respect and appreciation between you both. This is used when people have no interest, time or desire for a romantic relationship. I know a man means no harm when addressing me that way, but it makes me feel belittled because I actually am a grown woman with character. It makes me feel like an unaccomplished teenager. Brothers, even though you mean well, it may not be the best way to make your sister's day.

"Take care" is another term holding up a pink flashing signal. It is something one would say to an aunt, neighbor, college buddy or work associate. Should you hear it as the conversation closure, the heart connection probably is not happening.

On the flipside women, when a man says, "You're the only one I can talk to," "You are so easy to talk to," "I feel like I've known you for a long time," "You are so stable," "I love your laugh" or lets you know you can call him even in the middle of the night (unless he is offering to physically protect you from harm)...that very likely means you are finding a special way into his heart. You'll have to decide to be really responsible with what should and will happen next. Pray and decide. Do you really like him or not? If not, you may need to pull back from spending so much time together. Thank him for those compliments. Tell him you consider him a good friend and brother in the Lord. Or, you can pray and continue to move forward, thanking him for the compliments.

The Dance

The trouble we have is when our emotions get the best of us. Hope indeed is a wonderful thing, as is being confident in ourselves that we are a good catch! But hope and real life can be confused.

Here is a common dance among singles: Boy likes girl. Girl does not share the same feelings. Boy is sure she does have a romantic interest in him though, or that she surely will come around to that real soon. Boy feels frustrated that his romantic interest in her is not being reciprocated. Girl feels a little suffocated from the extra attention of his words and actions she cannot reciprocate. She feels guilty, and explains they are platonic friends. Boy says okay and backs off from pursuing her romantically, continuing in fellowship. The pressure is off of her and she starts to act nicely to him again thinking he understands the terms. Boy starts to have romantic feelings for her again. He thinks she's changed her mind and now has feelings for him, but she has not. Recycle! Ladies: stay back, and then give the friendship *six more months of space*. Men can misinterpret friendliness. Women can too. It takes some refocusing and realigning to keep our hearts on the real track—the track of truth—that is, what is really or is not really going on in the other's heart. It sometimes takes a good friend to say, "Didn't you just tell me last week he/she's not interested in you? What changed?"

Resist the temptation to hope for the "come around." It usually does not happen. It is better to take the strong medicine and move on with life rather than get frustrated over unrequited love. You may have to keep saying to yourself, "Lord, help me not to hallucinate! It is only *platonic* friends!" Most of all, at this point, don't beat yourself up because your heart got stirred up again over the person. It's just how we are. It's natural to unintentionally hold a candle for someone. We're human. YOU ARE LOVED BY GOD AND OTHERS! Keep your eyes and focus fixed on God, His glory and the works we should be doing. My pastor always reminds us of the old, true hymn:

> Turn your eyes upon Jesus
> Look full in His wonderful face
> And the things of earth will grow strangely dim
> In the light of His glory and grace

Keep your eyes on Jesus and your knees on the ground. Try it…it really works. He really fills you up.

Setting and Keeping Emotional Boundaries

If you want to keep things parked at "platonic," and keep things operating in the best functional shape—even your heart, you have to set boundaries and live within them. It's not easy; only in certain situations do I believe this can actually occur, but let's say you've got one or you want to try to accept this platonic friendship. It takes two very mature people to make platonic work. As the one who would prefer to have a romantic relationship with the other, it's an odd thought but, "Hey! I'm committed to not being committed to you!"

Ask God. Ask God to give you worthy and sustainable boundaries to curtail the heightened or hopeful emotions, then discuss those boundaries together. The difficulty occurs when either party has unmet expectations. As long as you can manage each other's expectations, you'll be alright. If the other person will not agree to live by an important boundary, then you may have to decide if you should stay in any kind of relationship with them. Mature and respectful people submit to boundaries. And yes, you can give someone an ultimatum if they repeatedly violate those boundaries. Those are the controllers, the prideful; neither of these characteristics makes for healthy relationships.

If you are trying to pace a relationship or keep one at a certain level, here are some examples of boundaries to set in place:

- Don't talk over the phone in the late night hours. This is "pillow talk," a time when we typically want romantic closeness, a time when we are more vulnerable. Pillow talk creates verbal intimacy perhaps when a relationship should not include that. These late night phone calls are a definite nicety and an opener for feelings to begin or flow. It's not like you have to do your talk from 9 to 5, but consider this theory.
- Limit your phone calls to so many per week, perhaps one or two.
- Limit your one-on-one texting.
- Limit how often you see each other, including how many times you each go out in the same friendship circles.
- Limit the types of discussion you share in. Scale down in sharing so many of your feelings, needs, desires or problems. This develops depth and connection.
- Limit the amount of favors you ask of each other.

Make sure you stay committed to your boundaries. Emotions toward the other person may lighten after a week or so depending. Leave that space between you to focus yourself in other directions, further reducing pressure or desire. When you get some release from the intensity, keep the boundaries to keep the relief or you'll end up right back where you started.

If not, you'll be like the patient who stops taking their medication because they feel better. When they cease the meds, they relapse or have an outbreak. The very reason their symptoms had declined was because they took the medicine. Consider the thin person who is told "You're so slender; why do you diet?" Well, the person is slender *because* they diet and operate in discipline.

Stay in tune with your emotional "checkbook." After all, your treasure is where your heart is (Matthew 6:21). Your money goes where your God is or where your affections lie. Likewise, check your texting histories and saved voice mails. If Andy's or Tiffany's messages are stock piled in the memory, that's a dead giveaway there's more than a platonic friendship going on in someone's heart. Re-reading those texts? You're so busted!

Competition
Women, I know there seems to be a shortage of Christian men. If competition comes onto your prospecting scene, don't even stay involved in it. Don't even worry about it. Diplomatically bow out and defer to the other female. If it's God, the man will choose you either now or later. If it's not God, then you just saved yourself from stooping to some humiliating levels. There should be no convincing someone to like and love you.

Men, if competition comes to your block, well…I think the rules are different. We women do like to be fought for a little bit. We want to see we mean something to you. So, I'd say, go the extra mile and don't give up that easy. Bulk up on your godly character. But don't do anything wrong to win her or that you won't be willing to do to keep her. And do not do wrong or evil to your brother.

"When;
A girl is in love,
You can see it in her smile.

When;
A guy is in love,
You can see it in his eyes"

~*www.wittyprofiles.com 2011*

An Ace is an Ace

Call an Ace an Ace. A common point of confusion is whether the man and woman both consider the event a date or not. Someone once asked me if I was dating a particular gentleman. I answered, "I don't know." What kind of a ridiculous answer is that? But I was afraid to incriminate him. I didn't know how he would feel about that term "date." I am a confident woman, but how would he feel about that? Would he be upset? Would he feel pressured? Does he prefer to remain private?

Consider these levels to help you locate where you are with someone:

   a) We've been on a few dates together
   b) We are dating
   c) We are dating each other exclusively
   d) We are courting

Gentlemen, let me say this boldly (since you can't return my book after you've already purchased it): if you are trying to spend time with a female for the purpose (hidden or otherwise) of getting to know them to see if you desire to date them…IT'S ALREADY A DATE! The deciding factor is the *intention* of the time spent together.

God is not a god of confusion. He is a god of order. So if we are spending time with someone, going places with someone, *kissing* someone and you don't know where you stand in the relationship—then title the relationship "confusion." One or both of the participants are not going about the direction of things correctly.

Status Updates
Men, I understand that being a leader in the relationship involves risking your heart. Women experience their own equally unsavory form of risk as well. We experience LIMBO—(no emotions on my part here) —(that waiting and not knowing where we stand in a relationship. We sometimes don't really know how the man really feels. And if you have several potential relationships over time, this can really become the "I can't stand" part of dating (when you like the guy that is). Women need and deserve to know where they stand in a relationship. The sooner a gentleman can let a woman know where he and she stand, and as often as he can, the fairer, nicer and more respectful he is treating his sister in the Lord. **D-T-R…**Define The Relationship. It's like a job; people are much more comfortable knowing their titles. They then know what tasks to do and what tasks not to do. They know where they fit; they know what the story is and what the expectations are. How much more important is that with matters of the heart?

So how would a man do this updating of the relationship status? Here are some sample conversations:

Asking to court:

> Jenson: "Kristen, I have been enjoying getting to know you. You have fine qualities. You love the Lord. You are kind and personable just to name a few. I have feelings for you that are beyond friendship. I have prayed about this. How do you feel about me? Would you have an interest in courting me for the purpose of seeing if we would be right for marriage? Could you pray about this and let me know your thoughts?"

From within a dating or courting relationship status:

> Jenson: "Kristen, this is difficult for me to say this. We have been getting to know each other and I have enjoyed the time. However, I don't feel that we should continue pursuing that type of relationship. I am led to keep our relationship as a platonic friendship. Please forgive me if I have done or said anything to cause you any hurt. God has good things for each of our lives."

Understanding what is going on and what is not going on with regard to the status of a relationship and being honest with it all to God, ourselves and each other is a point of integrity. It's speaks to our character.

11
Heart in Pocket

"Above all else, guard your heart, for it is the wellspring of life." ~Proverbs 4:23

One thing's for sure. It's wiser to wear your heart in your pocket than on your sleeve in singleness. You've got to keep using those relationship principles. You have to have a well thought-out strategic plan for relationships. Be mindful and intentional. Cautious relationships will protect hearts. That is our responsible calling. Being careful, fun— what a needed and delicate balance! It's self-protection, but not fearful. It's being careful not to open up one's heart too soon, too much or to the wrong one. Pray, pray, pray. Oh…and pray! You have to be sensitive to the Holy Spirit.

Guard your heart, but do not put a protective wall around yourself so high so that no one can get in to see you or you see out to anyone. Like the Kay Jewelry commercial of the open hearts pendant, "With an open heart, love will find its way in" (Jane Seymour, 2000). Don't hide the Christmas gifts *too* well. You know, when you wrap the gifts, hide them well and then forget where you hid them. If you close yourself up and hide yourself too well, you won't be able to find your own way out of that hiding spot.

Here are more of those principles of wisdom:

You are not married 'til you're down the aisle and have said "I do." Imperfect people make comments and ask questions when they're emotional, when the sun is out, when it feels good to have a date somewhere, even Christians. We're not perfect; you know that. People ask hypothetical questions. A man/woman can pay a very special compliment about your personality, temperament or walk with the Lord, but that doesn't mean they will marry you. They're figuring it out. Don't believe everything you hear right away. Watch. Keep your feet planted on the ground. Keep hold of your emotions and imaginations. People are learning and assessing one another. They did mean that comment, but as things unfold, each of you may realize you are not God's match for each other. Some comments you're just going to have to strike from the record and your memory that they said something special. People can think one way one day, and another later. Emotions change. They can take those emotions back into themselves and close up their heart again. They have to balance out over time to find the true stable point. Situations change. Situations don't change. They see things later they didn't see in the beginning. Don't count on the relationship ending in marriage until you've blended at the altar. Even engagement is not marriage, it's a step—a pre-trial period with physical boundaries and limitations.

The older we get, the more caution we should employ in dating. We attach more quickly with age. We share more. We have more experiences and interests to share. We talk about our children, homes, jobs, experiences, emotions and faith. There are not as many "biggies" to share about at earlier ages. We go more diverse places together, all building memories and depth. Break ups as we are older can be more of an emotional setback. After all, we may have had several tough break ups underneath our belt already. Losses can tend to mound and become heavy. We don't rebound as quickly. At an older age, we may be more concerned of being alone if the relationship doesn't work out. Maybe we want a mate more by that time. We need to be cautious and conscientious and wise in the first place though in our relationships. Take heed. People's hearts are fragile. Handle with care.

Wear that beautiful heart of yours in your silk-lined pocket. This may seem obvious, but let it serve as a reminder. Be careful in sharing events or happenings that are emotionally bonding until you can see that this may be someone you have strong potential of staying with. Don't expose your delicate heart on your sleeve. Keep those emotional ties to a minimum. Time spent plus experiences, equals bonding—a deep equation. You don't want to create a wonderful relationship that you'll hate to leave if it doesn't have all that either of you need or are called to. I don't mean to sound harsh, but you can fall in love with a *gorilla* if you spend enough time with it. You'll see they have a soft side too.

One of the most important times to wear your heart in your pocket is when a person is still hurting over a former breakup. One may think they are ready for a new flame, but they really aren't. They are still processing hurts and questions from the former relationship. They still have the other person in mind and heart. They need time to heal and to resume or build their own confidence through Christ. I would not want to be used as a plug for a man or woman with a hole in their heart. God has to heal that hurt first. There needs to be a time of recovery and re-stabilization.

I reattempted love too soon in my past and I see others wandering and wanting another partner before their hurt has gone away from the former. I strongly do believe God will not bring your mate to you before you have healed. So don't allow Satan to tell you there is something wrong with you as a person or there is no one out there for you. It may truly just not be your season yet. You need time to heal. I know that stinks. It's not what we want to hear. It's not the quick, happy fix. But you can still have joy and fun even going through the healing. Watch and see all the things God will do through you if you let him; while you're on the trip, see the countryside!

In the classic movie *Gone With the Wind*, against protocol, rebellious Scarlett O'Hara accepted a dance with Rhett Butler at the ball while she was in mourning over her second husband. She was too insensitive to truly grieve him. As was customary, she wore a black dress, but it was not customary for a woman to dance during mourning. While all the other women twirled with colored dresses on the ballroom floor, there too was Scarlett in her black ball gown swirling with Rhett. It even *looked* totally out of place and time. It was a visual picture of how it is out of sorts to date someone new when you are still mourning another. You've not given a chance for your emotions to heal, stabilize or grow from the experience. When we mourn, we wear an emotional sackcloth. How can we cover up our loss with another's love besides that of Christ's? When we try to cover up sackcloth with clothes or another relationship, all we get is bulk.

I keep my heart cuddled in my pocket around the holidays. I am reluctant to meet someone or get to know someone when people tend to be lonely and may be unknowingly looking to fill a void. Any time someone is vulnerable to the warmth of a new relationship with an unrestored heart isn't the right time. We would think ourselves wiser and in control, but the heart is always at risk for bad judgment. They may like you in their season of need, but when they regain their confidence and stability, they may come to terms that you are really not their true cup of tea. What are some of the less optimal times to begin a relationship? Depression, sickness, immediate post break-up, times of uncertainty and fear, just to name a few. And, of course, yo-yo dating—that is, going back to an old relationship.

Same goes for the season of birds chirping and freshness in the air. The old saying goes: "In the Spring a young man's fancy lightly turns to thoughts of love" (Alfred Lord Tennyson, 1842).

Worldly Sayings Exposed

Worldly Saying	Truth
Love at first sight	Infatuation or lust at first sight. You don't know enough about someone to have it be love.
Head over heels in love	Better dig the heals in before I get in over my head.
"Tis better to have loved and lost than to never have loved at all." (Lord Alfred Tennyson)	'Tis better to have had a million dollars and lost it too. What a feeling! Eh-hem…no thanks! According to Dr. John R. Buri of *Psychology Today* (2011), Tennyson wrote the statement at the death of someone whom he had a healthy love relationship with—not a dysfunctional and hurtful one. People try to justify a hurtful relationship experience. But misusing the quote, Buri says, is "like finding a great deal at a restaurant, only to get brutal food poisoning for the next 3 days, and announcing, 'At least I was able to enjoy the food as it was going down before I got deathly sick for 3 days.'" Buri

	says, "For such love, I suspect Tennyson would have said: "Tis better to have refrained from love / Than to have experienced such a destructive love at all."'
Opposite personalities attract	But they form strenuous marriages. There is a difference between the attraction of opposites and the compatibility of opposites. What you are initially drawn to is something you yourself do not have in your own life, but would like to. This may be something you do not have the means (either in your personality, circumstances or finances) to do in your life at the time of attraction. It's like having a little excitement brought into your life, but then you are left with differences. Choose someone with whom you also have enough activities, likes and passions in common (even beyond the things of the Lord). Then there won't be arguing, debating or making deals about who gets to do what activity; You'll just enjoy it together and truly be on the same wavelength.

Sharin' Prayer

As a female (I have seen this in and heard this from males also), I find that praying and reading the Word alone together with a date or boyfriend to be intimate and bonding—something to be careful of. Our hearts are humbling before the King of the universe. At that time, we are open. Our hearts yearn to share the beauty of Christ and devotions with a mate. We long to have that type and degree of close connection. And, experiencing spiritual oneness can only lead to the desire for physical oneness. Hard to give that up once it starts. This may be something you wish to curtail in your relationship until you are well on your way. If you do pray alone together, it is not necessary to hold hands for prayer if you have not decided yet that he or she is "the one."

It is said that the family that prays together, stays together. So prayer is a binding thing. That's very good in marriage but needs caution in relationships.

Make sure to pray by yourself or with someone else before you go out on a date though. Ask people to commit to praying about your relationship and its direction.

Pray to see what each of you needs to see in each other—aspects that would be complementary or otherwise to a relationship. Pray for emotional and physical purity, respect for each other and to glorify the Lord on your dates and in courting. Pray that you would be a blessing to each other and that you would enrich each other's lives and learn something new about God and life even on just one date. Pray to be a blessing.

Worshipping and ministering together are also creators of the strongest of stirrings within our hearts towards another. It is when we see the other believer in their most beautiful and appealing of states as they honor God. This beauty can draw us in unbelievably. Unfortunately, this spiritual attraction still does not mean the man and woman are for each other. So, you may wish to curtail, or find a good balance that enables you to hold onto your own emotional hat when it comes to worship and ministry together.

12
Keeping Hope Alive

The afternoon knows what the morning never dreamed.

~Swedish Proverb

You understand. It rains a little on every field. But beyond those showers, keep your hope alive in God for a blessing of greenery and flowers. You never know when God's "Suddenlys" are going to come.

Temporary Disappointment

"How did I get here? said one person I interviewed. "I haven't even been seeing anyone! How do you get hurt when you're not even in a relationship? How could this have happened?" But this is how it happened. It was a friendship with an amazing godly man with uncovered mutual interest toward each other that God had not sanctioned. The friendship had been nothing but a complete blessing—provided spiritual growth, godly, honoring, respectful, fun and helpful. The girl's attention got got! He was amazing. It seemed like they had much in common and would have created an increase of good to the Kingdom. She got a sample of Priest, Protector and Provider—all the things we as Christian women are taught to look for in a man. She was sidetracked by a shiny, gold penny on her path.

But sometimes even a great female or fella isn't the right one for us and only God knows the deep reasons why. Strong feelings are not the leading of the Holy Spirit. Not every good thing is a God thing. Bitter-beautiful.

Romans 5:3-5 says "we also glory in our sufferings, because we know that suffering produces perseverance; perseverance, character; and character, hope. And hope does not put us to shame, because God's love has been poured out into our hearts through the Holy Spirit, who has been given to us." When the suffering happens, say to yourself, "Character increase occurring."

My interviewee understood how she got here; what was she going to learn this time? She learned to rest with the discomfort for a little bit. She stretched out to minister to others even in the midst of her pain. She realized that she'd been through this enough to know that Jesus would heal her. She knew not to let it steal her joy and that God will always bring her out. She knew that in a few more days, she would be back up and running again. She encouraged herself in the Lord as David did. And while this man was not the one, he was a fine, fine example of God's best. And she can now see in the flesh what her man will be more like in character. He may not be this particular man, but he will be *like* that man. Her eyes have been opened.

Tim Story says, "The longer the left, the bigger the right." Sometimes the longer the wait, the better the design. Give God the time to work His design. Don't spoil His surprise. God must have something *really big* for you if this is not it. Wait for it patiently. "If this awesome man or woman is not the one, then I can hardly wait to see your gift to me! They are going to be incredible!"

I once applied for two different sales positions. I interviewed and did very well on one, but was not hired. I was stumped and disappointed. Sometime later, I was hired to sell a different service that was a much, much better fit for me. It was something that I had a sincere passion for and excelled well in. When I looked back, I could see that those other positions were so not me! God, your plans and timing are always RIGHT!

Priscilla Shirer shared, "He's (God) not trying to keep you from things; He's trying to keep you for *some*thing" (2011). My pastor, Scott LeLacheur, mirrored this: "He's (God) not trying to take something from you; he's trying to get something to you" (2011). My eyes have been opened.

So don't cry for me Argentina! The truth is, God's got His best *for me*! God, I am open to your plan even though there are disappointments along the way. Your plan is really what I want.

Hope With God
Sometimes it can be discouraging to see secular couples in relationship. You know, they look so happy. Sometimes it seems easier for secular couples to hook up. They don't seem to care about as many dynamics as Christians do. And the truth is…they are blinded…they just don't know, so how can they care about anything greater? They choose what and who they want without any regard to God and who God may have had designed for them in His plan. Don't fall for watching them and thinking how good they've got it—not even for a moment. With your spiritual heart and mind you KNOW that that is not all it's cracked up to be. You have God and heaven before you–in this life and the next!

I witnessed a man and a woman appearing to be in their late 40's to early 50's on what seemed a first date at a coffee shop. I wondered what was going on in their minds as it transpired. The date looked like it was going well. They both seemed to have the same level of "niceness." There was no mention of Christ at all; how empty. I quickly got over my jealousy. They talked a lot about chickens.

Be still before the Lord and wait patiently for him;
do not fret when men succeed in their ways, when they
carry out their wicked schemes.
                                                    ~Psalm 37:7

Peace I leave with you; my peace I give you. I do
not give to you as the world gives. Do not let your hearts
be troubled and do not be afraid.
                                                    ~John 14:27

Don't copy the behavior and customs of this world,
but be a new and different person with a fresh newness
in all you do and think. Then you will learn from your
own experience how his ways will really satisfy you.
                                                    ~Romans 12:2 TLB

Sometimes looking at other Christian couples can get a little frustrating. Why does God bring some people a mate much sooner than me? How come they got to get married at a young age? Were they more deserving than I? More perfect than I? How come they were only single again two years and got remarried and I've been single again nine years now? I think it may be easy to wonder those things at times. Again, nip those small, burgeoning thoughts of jealousy in the bud. If you are walking obediently with the Lord and seeking Him first in your life, He knows what He is doing for all the right reasons. God is too wise to create error, and too kind to not care about you becoming your best and giving you His best. God is never late—11:59pm, and equally important, He is never early either! If He was early, the bread dough would be sticky in the middle or the steak would be overly pink inside creating possible poisoning and negative outcomes. It would be like flipping the pancake before the right amount of bubbles surface; you would feel the "Ohhhh" as it's thrown half way up the side of the pan and half on the bottom—messy, sloppy and distorted. Stay in trusting, blind faith. God's timing is important.

You may feel the odds are against your favor to meet your someone special. Perhaps you are saying to yourself "I'm 52 (or 63). No single men or women in my church. I see nothin' nowhere. There was only one of him or her. How will I ever find another?" But my brother or sister, God does not care what numbers are or are not in your favor. His plans go beyond numbers. God's promises trump life's problems.

Look at Abraham and Sarah. They were too old, yet they conceived! Sarah had passed 90 and Abraham was 100! You are never too old for a blessing.

Consider Gideon and his army of men as they overtook the Midianites. God did not bring them to victory according to the few number of warriors they had. In fact, "The Lord said to Gideon, "You have too many men for me to deliver Midian into their hands. In order that Israel may not boast against me that her own strength has saved her, announce now to the people, 'Anyone who trembles with fear may turn back and leave Mount Gilead.' So twenty-two thousand men left, while ten thousand remained" (Judges 7:2-3). And the number of the men in the army kept decreasing until God allowed only 300 as fighters! But Gideon's army won the battle because the Lord gave it to them. God cut the numbers down, making the natural statistics worse! And it says that the enemies were as "thick as locusts. Their camels could no more be counted than the sand on the seashore" (Judges 7:12). It looked really bad out there. Does it ever really look bad to you out there?

You may be thinking, "I've dated three men or went through three cuts already. I see no one else on the horizon or in the interest zone." Remember, Gideon's army was cut down three times. It doesn't matter how few or how "nothing" your choices are.

Do you see? God does not work by good or favorable statistics. He is not limited by the natural. His plans and purposes are not limited by numbers and circumstances or what you see or what you don't! Keep your hope up in God.

It will not do any good to keep complaining about being single. In fact, it will drive you further down. Whatever you do, you will get more of. If you complain about things, more negative things will come upon you. If you praise even in the midst of trials, more good will come upon you. The dog you feed wins. Feed the negative dog, he'll rip the finish line down growling. Feed the positive dog, he will cross over the finish line with friends cheering and applauding with a yummy reward bone.

Sure, many of us go through times of feeling sad or lonely that we are single, but I have matured in my trust in the Lord. I try to nip that type of thinking and feeling in the bud. It is way too costly! I do not want to go down into that pit, cuz' it's a long way up if I allow myself to slip down into it. I try to limit myself to the acknowledgment of what and why I am feeling that way. I admit it to God and ask Him to give me His joy. I thank Him for all His blessings in my life and those yet to come. I ask one or two close friends to pray for me. I worship. I go to the altar for more prayer.

Paul said, "I know what it is to be in need, and I know what it is to have plenty. I have learned the secret of being content in any and every situation, whether well fed or hungry, whether living in plenty or in want" (Philippians

4:12). I know what it is to date and be in a relationship. I know what it is to be single and be in a relationship with my Father. I am content in either situation. It may have taken me some adjustment to get here, but I did. Changing my thinking changed my heart. The Bible changed my thinking.

The single life must be a full life—one with a rich relationship to Christ, community, connection, care and service to others for satisfaction. We may go through a season of aloneness and growth with the Lord. But as a lifestyle, we should not stay isolated. Many singles cook for one, eat alone, ride to places alone, grocery shop alone, run errands alone, drive to church alone, go home alone, travel alone or not at all and more. So in order for these types of things to not continually feel like a loss to us, we need to be rich in those other blessings.

Try this: Do a little bit of life together with someone else. Plan a day to go grocery shopping or run errands with a friend. It may take you longer in order to complete both household's needs, but you will have fun doing it! Stop for lunch in between!

Just to remind you during the times when you cannot think clearly for yourself, God has not forgotten you. Delay does not necessarily mean denial. It may just mean "No for now." He is not endeavoring to torture you with waiting. He could be aligning things in the natural for a relationship. He could be growing you both in your walk with Him. He could be transforming you so that when you come together, it will be a better fit. Your spouse may not even be saved yet. It just may not be the right season yet.

"Timing: The control of the time or speed of an action, event, or other, so that it occurs at the proper moment."

(Author Unknown)   Later doesn't mean less; it should mean more as we do it God's way. We will be richer and fuller of Christ to treat and appreciate the marriage with tenderness.

God's delays are not God's denials.
                                         ~John Hagee (2011)

Right now you have been given the gift of time. It's time to pursue other hopes and dreams. It's time to be involved with different kinds of things than you may be able to do later with a mate. Think ahead in faith. Take time to gather tools for creating, operating in and fixing a future relationship and marriage now, beforehand. You will learn tools and tips that will bless all other relationships as well. You may even share information and have an effect on someone else's marriage!

Your objective now is to be holy and wholly single in contentment. I believe that if we pursue the first, the second will be established.

13
Right Click If You Like Me
Press Escape If You Don't

One of my most embarrassing moments with technology happened a year out of my divorce. I became friends with a man from Bible study and took an interest in him. I emailed my little gushy sentiments to my girlfriend. Much, much to my surprise…I received an email back from HIM saying "Oh?" I must have been thinking about him as I sent the email…'cause I mistakenly sent it to him! I wanted to crawl under a rock! The friendship survived well and years later we are dear, dear friends. Right Dwight? I still laugh about it.

So that there story (nope, I'm not from the south) reminds me of the coffee maker at night. At night I prepare the coffee maker so all I have to do is just hit the brew button in the morning. (I don't want a fancy maker with a timer.) But after the grounds are set up and the water's been poured into the reservoir, I have got to restrain myself from hitting the "Start" button! "Don't hit it. Don't hit it. Don't hit it." It's just a natural reaction to proceed to.

Similarly, to this day, I experience anxiety when texting or emailing concerning a man I may be mentioning with interest. It's like the old email story. I have to consciously refrain from accidentally texting it to the man I'm writing about! Anxiety! No more embarrassing moments! Perhaps we…or *I*…shouldn't put anything into technology that would embarrass me in the wrong hands or inboxes. If you have something private to say, do it the old-fashioned way: call.

The world is always changing. The movie "He's Just Not That Into You" shows that now you can be avoided or let down by someone through different technology portals in addition to face-to-face: cell phone, home phone, text message, email, Facebook, and MySpace. Eee gads! Relationships and break ups just get more complex with each decade. You have to decide who to add to your Facebook "friends." If you add that guy or girl before there is a committed relationship and it doesn't work out, you'll feel bad deleting them. I guess the younger set, who grew up with social media, is OK with that, but I'm not!

And Facebook social media allows people to establish themselves as couples! Yes! Dating and break ups just got more complicated! And you can post that too as a "Status" on your Facebook account! "Candy is in a relationship and it's complicated." Gosh, talk about airing one's laundry! Or you can invite someone to accept your "relationship request," and your profile says, "Candy and Josh are in a relationship."

I'm just curious: How many people have snooped out their ex's Facebook account? If *I* was really super spiritual, *I* wouldn't have done it! Felt real snoopy and foolish doing it, but the trail was right in front of me…and I followed it! Depending on their account settings, you can see some information. Just curious if anyone else has done this…

Here's a list of Facebook postings that will surely bring your "ex" back if they scope out your wall:
- The new puppy I got is just so cute! So loving! Great for cuddling and hugging!
- Just got back from the mall. New black skirt, red blouse, hosiery and heels!

- Skiing in the Alps is great. And the ski lodge with the fireplace has so many Christians here! Am I so blessed!
- Worshipped at church. Altar call was great. God is answering all my prayers just the way I want.

Really now...I'll stop.

Don't bash or state anything negative about the person you were dating in your postings. Typically, too many people see these postings. This is not how the Lord would want us to react, ruining someone's character even further. If you have something negative to share, share it in a personal, private message between you and one other person.

And...don't forget to "Like" "Marry Me!" on Facebook!

And now we have the emoticons to determine too! Can anyone really tell me if they got this texting symbol from a male/female, friend/date what this means?? :-C or XD or ÷

Internet Dating

Has anyone tried Internet dating? I personally have. I know some frown upon it for different reasons. One viewpoint is that we live in a busy society and do have this technology available and God allows us to use technology in a non-sinful way just as we use Facebook to meet and relate to people. God expects us to do our part in locating a job using the Internet as well. Could possibly finding or being found by a mate be any different?

As with any "live" meeting of a "prospective relationship" person, you should first be healed from any former romantic relationship(s). And, you should not be pursuing online dating if you are lonely. You are ready when a relationship will be the "icing on the cake" for you. Relationships are no place for desperation—either for replacing the last love you are heartbroken over or to fill your life. You're picker is not working accurately then and you won't be the best pick for someone else either.

I would advise against utilizing free websites since the integrity of some users is questionable. Before you post your profile to a site, know within yourself these things:

- What are you looking for? (Friendship, dating, marriage)
- What kind of time do you have to commit to corresponding, meeting or dating? Is this a good fit?
- What is the furthest you can travel regularly with time and budget constraints?
- Are willing to relocate to marry?

Whatever your decisions are, make them fully known in your profile. Save people the energy of getting into something that either of you cannot fulfill.

Complete your profile accurately and honestly. Ask a friend to tell you if it really sounds like you. Don't exaggerate but don't downplay your beauty either. Showcase your personality and character, not just the qualities that you are looking for and things you like to do.

Include updated, accurate photos at least from the midsection up. And please don't take the picture of yourself with the camera in your extended arm in front of you—it's tacky. If this means anything to you at all, ask a dear friend to take a real photo of you. Places like Wal-Mart and Meijer even have photography studios starting at about $15. You may be thinking, it's carnal to have to include your photo to receive more communication on line. As mentioned earlier though, physical attraction is important and an entire purpose of online meeting is to cut to the chase avoiding wastes of time. So depict yourself attractively, yet accurately.

Women, if you participate in online dating, fill out your profile with enough information, then sit and wait. Do not make the initial contact to a man. Create your profile and let it sit and attract incoming mail. Women should not be the initiators of the interest. Let the man pursue you.

Naturally, there are some dangers to meeting online. Some participants are not genuine; some are even dangerous. There is the opportunity for game playing because people are more anonymous not being in clear view. You cannot see their facial expressions nor see their life before you. It is sometimes said in the marketplace "do business with someone locally," but understand: game playing and hidden identities can occur with someone living in your own area too. You could meet someone wacky anywhere or from anyone, not just from the Internet. Any way you meet someone, you have to ask questions and LISTEN to the answers. Pray for extra discernment. Do not ignore red flags.

As with any "getting to know you" situation, be a good interviewer. ALWAYS...ALWAYS ask the four most key questions kindly but directly in the beginning of communicating with the person. If you wait till you've gone on a date, you've waited too long to ask. Ask these questions: "How long have your last relationships lasted?

Have you ever had a serious relationship? When did your last serious relationship end? Do you still communicate with that person?" You want to find out the availability of their heart. It is not enough to let them tell you they are ready for a relationship. This is your involvement and your heart on the possible line.

Here is an example of what I am sharing: A woman was communicating with a man from the Internet as well as by phone and frequent texting. They went on one date that went well and they continued in the communications afterward for some time. She really liked the man, but he wasn't coming around to her. Mind you, she did not outright ask him the questions in the previous paragraph. Come to find out through some investigative work (you can find out just about anything via the Internet) his former wife had died just months prior. This man was in no way ready for another relationship! Had the woman not searched this out on her own, she may have been mislead for sometime by this man. Understanding that he must have still had ties to his late wife took the weight off of her shoulders. She didn't have to take it personally then. Be proactive; it's your life too.

Internet dating sites were not intended to sustain a relationship, but only to meet other people. After meeting online, carry the getting-to-know-each-other part and relationship that may develop out in the physical, tangible world, not in cyberspace. If someone is not asking to meet you after a reasonable period or they put off meeting you, there's probably something fishy going on. Move on quickly with your heart intact in your chest cavity.

Don't give out your phone number or address until you feel comfortable. **Meet in a public place. Meet in a public place. Meet in a public place.** Meet at church. Let your friends know who you are going out with. Give your friends your date's contact information before going. Be discerning of the person just like you would anyone else you met somewhere else.

I met several strong Christian men of very high quality and integrity online, even though I was online prematurely looking for a replacement to erase the pain I was still in from the breakup of the man I loved. Kevin was a dear friend. We would email, talk on the phone and he'd call me and play his instruments over the phone which I loved. The mini-concerts were an absolute treasured treat for me. His friendship was a cool blessing and helped me heal by giving advice.

Another man, Ben, was an absolute blessing—the absolute finest of Christian men. I wrote to him:

> I washed a favorite pillow of mine this morning. The back covering of it was torn already from repeated washings and I wondered if it would make it through another vigorous cycle. When I opened the washer afterward, I was blessed seeing large mounds of pure white, soft fluff deeply covering the other items. It was almost like Christmas! The pure white, soft fluff reminded me of YOU. Your heart is pure and holy and of the Lord. I just need to tell you how beautiful you are.

When we prayed over the phone, his prayer brought me to tears. He said, "Your prayer brought me to my knees." There are solid, good believers online.

We had the perfect first date. Upon checking my email that morning before Ben's arrival, I had received a message from someone else entitled "Angel at the door." This still all blows me away. Ben picked me up a short time later and we went to my Sunday church service. Ben was indeed an angel at my door. I had no character concerns about this gentleman.

Good men are online. And good women are online, because I was and I know of others. It just wasn't God's plan. Ben and I were a strong blessing to each other; he was a blessing to my son as well. We encouraged each other in the faith and life. We both taught each other things and grew. He was and still is an incredible man. All my discerning friends raved about him as well. Marriage just wasn't what God had for us. Ben will go down as one of the best people I will ever meet in life and I think of him with the finest sentiments always. Ben met a man at one of the singles events I took him to and they have become best friends! Through the small world of singles, Ben is now also close friends of one of my best friends. I know that his fine character is still shining forth for two years now. You can find good, stable people online too.

Ben gladly drove 2.5 hours one way to see me on weekends. I was in school full-time and could not travel. He first stayed at his cousin's home in my area. At my suggestion, other times he stayed in my home while my son was away; I in turn stayed at my girlfriend's. My bags were packed and ready to go in my car in advance, leaving no chance for something to go foul. A good relationship is worth the drive. You have to look at the drive as a temporary stretch if it leads to marriage.

And as for the musician gentleman, Kevin, I wrote of above, listen to his online dating praise report. He remained online on a particular Christian site for three years consistently. He mingled in the chat rooms, met friends and set up local fellowships with them. He acquired thirty-four dates, eight of which went beyond the first date. Kevin tried not to email too long before meeting a woman. He did not want an emotional bond to develop before meeting to only to find out there was no interactive or physical chemistry between them. His heart was to alleviate hope, then disappointment for both. Some people could think that he was a pick axe murderer or something though, trying to meet rather soon. Kevin is indeed a very admirable Christian picker, both on the guitar and in meeting his wife!

So Kevin met Katie online and because of her schedule, they emailed longer than he preferred. He was attracted to her heart and her devotion in trying to reconcile her former marriage.

Kevin decided within his heart before meeting Katie, that if there was a social and physical attraction when they met, he would ask her to marry him. Their first date was at The Rib Cage and then to the Bass Pro Shop (they both love to fish) for nine hours. They spent time at the outdoor park area of the store with a waterfall and obviously had a great first date.

Kevin plays four instruments like crazy and sings. He is active in music ministry at his church and is a member of a bluegrass group. Katie sang in church years ago, but never received the positive input she deserved from her former spouse; she felt discouraged by that. Before they were even engaged, Katie sang with Kevin at his church. Kevin blessed her with compliments and his pride. Katie's father and brother are bluegrass musicians! How is that for God bringing a quartet together by matrimony! So now we have Kevin, Katie and their three children combined. They are God's handiwork. They look lovely together. And I watched all the Facebook congrats flow in after their wedding.

For six years, Kevin had struggled being a single parent as many of his contract jobs were out of town. He relied on his parents to take his daughter into their home while he did this on and off. This meant transferring schools for her and all. It wasn't easy, but what a testimony of endurance, waiting in faith for his bride, and a blessed ending. Now that is what a match made in heaven (that connected online) looks like.

It is true. People do not grow up saying "I want to meet my wife or husband on an Internet dating website!" It is not the way we dream of the meeting, but that is how it can happen sometimes.

One man shared with me that he wants the Lord to *present* his wife to him. He wants to see her in his church. Yes, that would be a beautiful way to meet your spouse. That is how it happens sometimes, and maybe that *is* how it will happen for you. But trust me, when Kevin saw Katie for the first time, he felt *presented* with her. When he saw her coming down the wedding aisle to him, he felt *presented* with her.

Use your judgment, but I think it is appropriate to only write or communicate with one person at a time on or from a site. I do not think dating more than one person at a time is admirable, nor writing or talking with more than one at time either. If someone contacts you, a pat answer would be "I am currently communicating with another individual at this time. Thank you for your contact. God bless you." Then, if something goes no further with the other person, you can contact them back. If you are on a dating site, it is assumed you are there to meet someone. Therefore your communicating has implied meanings. I would not hesitate to write this into my profile: "I only communicate with one person at a time. I prefer the same from you. If you are communicating with others simultaneously, please contact me later should something not work out with them. Thank you and God bless you." **God isn't interested in you getting your money's worth from the amount you are spending for the service. He is interested in the proper treatment and respect of people's hearts.** Don't worry that you may miss the right person. If it's of God, He will bring you together at the right time. Don't let your online dating communications be an excuse for lower standards than in-person communications.

I am not encouraging you to find or be found on a Christian internet dating site, but I am saying not to necessarily exclude the possibility. Pray about it. The success stories noted here are not the only ones.

14
Party On!
Single's Fellowships, Games & Ice Breakers

If you want to get to know people so you have a rich relationship life, show yourself friendly to others *first*. Your smile and friendly eye contact are excellent greeters for connection. Host a fellowship gathering yourself! You don't have to wait for other events to come along. You can invite people personally at first and after people get in the habit of knowing you host gatherings, invite them easily by email, texting or Facebook. Maybe it needs to start with you!

Here are some ideas for games to play at your gatherings. They ease introductions and help make new friends.

"Fellow-Feld" Game

There are two versions to this game of Seinfeldish type questions.

<u>Version 1</u>: You pick a question out of a hat and answer it aloud to the group.

<u>Version 2</u>: You pick a question out of a hat and the whole group takes turns answering the same question.

<u>Version 3</u>: You pick a question out of a hat and have the rest of the group discuss and come to a conclusion of how they think you would answer the question.

Sample Questions

Q: Which would you be more likely to make for dinner for yourself?
- o Salad
- o Homemade chocolate chip cookies
- o Pot of chili
- o Trip to Little Caesar's
- o Bowl of cereal
- o Phone call to mom
- o Eat or order out

Q: Would you kill a spider in your house by:
- o A slamming shoe
- o Crushing it with a tissue
- o Bug spray
- o Calling the neighbor
- o The sound of your shrill scream
- o My home is too clean for bugs

Q: Do you close the lid on the dish detergent bottle?
- o Yes & why
- o No & why not
- o I don't do dishes, pots or pans

Q: You lose a button on your shirt. What do you do?
- o Pass the shirt by each time you go through the closet for two years
- o Re-sew it on yourself
- o Call 9-1-1
- o Use a paper clip or binder clip
- o Use two-way tape
- o Donate it to a community store

Q: Do you think people have control over how loud they sneeze and their style of sneeze?

Q: You could live anywhere you wanted. Your job would still be available there. Where would you live?

Q: Name three things you love to find on sale and where!

Q: What was the biggest foot you ever put in your mouth? (The most embarrassing or worst thing you ever said.)

Q: If there was one descriptive word to put before your name beginning with the same letter as your first name, what would it be?

Q: You're playing a completive game with a friend. If you win, they donate to your favorite charity. If they win, you put in service/help time at their favorite charity. Who do you hope wins?

"Scripture Scramble" Game (Christmas version)

of players: Minimum 4

Everyone in the game receives a piece of paper with a book, chapter and verse, and *part* of a scripture verse on it. We'll use the verses below:
- Matthew 1:21-22
- Matthew 2:10-11
- Luke 2:11
- Luke 2:14
- Isaiah 6:6
- Isaiah 6:7

Example: 3 people will have the first part of Luke 2:11 on their paper. 3 other people will have the second part of Luke 2:11 on their paper. Those 6 people will need to find each other in your crowd because they will all have Luke 2:11 written on their paper. This will bring groups of 6 people together. The group will need to decide how the sections of the verse fit together properly. When everyone has found groups, each group will select 2 members to recite the scripture verse aloud in proper arrangement to the group at large.

Verses

Matthew 1:21-22
"She will give birth to a son, and you are to give him the name Jesus, because he will save his people from their sins.' All this took place to fulfill what the Lord had said through the prophet: 'The virgin will be with child and will give birth to a son, and they will call him Immanuel'—which means, 'God with us.'"

Matthew 1:21-22
"She will give birth to a son, and you are to give him the name Jesus, because he will save his people from their sins.' All this took place to fulfill what the Lord had said through the prophet:

Matthew 1:21-22
"The virgin will be with child and will give birth to a son, and they will call him Immanuel'—which means, 'God with us.'"

Matthew 2:10-11
"When they saw the star, they were overjoyed. On coming to the house, they saw the child with his mother Mary, and they bowed down and worshiped him. Then they opened their treasure and presented him with gifts of gold and of incense and of myrrh."

Matthew 2:10-11
"When they saw the star, they were overjoyed. On coming to the house, they saw the child with his mother Mary, and they bowed down and worshiped him."

Matthew 2:10-11
"Then they opened their treasure and presented him with gifts of gold and of incense and of myrrh."

Luke 2:11
"Today in the town of David a Savior has been born to you; he is the Messiah, the Lord."

Luke 2:11
"Today in the town of David a Savior has been born to you;"

Luke 2:11
"He is the Messiah, the Lord."

Luke 2:14
"Glory to God in the highest heaven, and on earth peace to those on whom his favor rests."

Luke 2:14
"Glory to God in the highest heaven, and on earth."

Luke 2:14
"Peace to those on whom his favor rests."

Isaiah 6:6
"For to us a child is born, to us a son is given, and the government will be on his shoulders. And he will be called Wonderful Counselor, Mighty God, Everlasting Father, Prince of Peace."

Isaiah 6:6
"For to us a child is born, to us a son is given, and the government will be on his shoulders."

Isaiah 6:6
And he will be called Wonderful Counselor, Mighty God, Everlasting Father, Prince of Peace."

"Ice Breakers" Game

Write the below statements on a piece of paper and place them in a bowl. Each person shares how they would fill in the rest of the statement.

Version 1: Each person in the group comments on the same statement.

Version 2: Each person in the group comments on a different statement.

- "Truth is……."
- "When I grow up, I want to be…"
- "I just couldn't believe the time when…"
- "So I think…"
- "But if I ___?___, then ___?___..."
- "The last time I tried a new food…"
- "Given the choice of 90 degree weather or 32 degree weather, I'd choose…"
- "When I see a puddle of mud, I…"
- "Given the choice of a revolving door or a push door, I…"
- "The funniest sign I ever saw was…"
- "I'm dreaming of…"
- "I love…"

"Pass The Bowl" Game

Pass a bowl full of three different candies of any sort (perhaps mini candy bars, chewy items and hard candy). Ask each person to take one item and to hold onto it—"No Eating!" After players have chosen their candy, explain that depending on which candy they chose, they will have a specific task or statement to share with the group.

Candy = Sing part of your favorite song aloud

Starburst candy = The strangest Christmas gift you ever received

Carmel candy = Share one wish you have

Hard candy = A most embarrassing moment

"The Sugar Tale" Game

Pass a bowl full of two types of candy (perhaps mini candy bars and Starburst Fruit Chews). Ask each person to take a piece or pieces of candy and to hold onto it. No eating! Do not tell them how many pieces to take or why the number of pieces matter. After players have chosen their piece(s) of candy, explain that for each piece of candy taken, they must tell the group one interesting fact about themselves, i.e. 3 pieces taken = 3 facts to tell.

"Sweet Greetings"

This is a simple ice breaker game. Once enough people get to the gathering, pass out different pieces of candy to each from an assortment of perhaps four kinds. They must not eat it yet. Then tell each one to trade their candy with someone new and introduce themselves.

Yes, I realize most of my games have to do with candy. Pray for me!

15
Frankly Speaking
Physical Affections

Are you Frank? Is your name Frank? Probably not, but let's talk like him. I mean...let's be frank in this chapter about physical affections. Let's clear the air and discuss things not everyone talks about, either because they do not want to incriminate themselves, it's awkward, they do not want to face truth or just don't know how to feel about the subject.

Yes, it is all together possible to remain a virgin. It is the best way and it shouldn't be any other way. Contrary to popular belief, not everyone is "doing it." There really are people who want to live upright in every area of their life.

It is better if both you and your date are both highly committed to this area of purity. If one of you is not all on board with the importance, it could be *much* tougher; maybe not even possible. I can't even imagine. I would not be in a relationship with someone who does not hold the same level of high commitment that I do. I don't believe in taking chances. That's being unequally yoked in a deeper meaning of the commandment. My Lord and my brother mean too much to me to fall in this area.

One must crucify physical desires and deal with it one day at a time. It is all together possible to keep ones clothes on and keep hands out of inappropriate places. James 1:21 tells us to "Therefore, get rid of all moral filth and the evil that is so prevalent and humbly accept the word planted in you, which can save you." Here is how you crucify your flesh—those sexual desires. Here is one way you do not delve into those temptations as one may cave for a bowl of ice cream with hot fudge sauce. James said it right; you "*humbly* accept the word planted in you." You humble yourself to the word (the scriptures regarding instruction for moral behavior) that are planted and deeply rooted within you. You humble yourself or bow to the word (Jesus—Jesus is the Living Word) that is within you—to be holy, for His holiness in within you.

Romans 12:2 tells us not to conform to the pattern of this world, but be *transformed by the renewing of your mind.* Then you will be able to test and approve what God's will is." We renew our mind through the reading of God's Word—planting it down within us.

Get on your knees. There is an extra measure of grace given when you humble yourself on your knees. You have minimized yourself to ask and receive God's great power.

One woman I interviewed shared that there were a few times she was tempted like crazy (I told you we'd be talking frankly here). She had a pure conversation with a godly, attractive single man in a suit that surprisingly bowled her over. Later, she literally got on her knees to ask for strength to think differently and flee the tempting thoughts and desires in her mind. God will beckon to your call, my saved and sanctified friend!

Sometimes women allow physical interaction because they want to feel physically appealing to a man; it makes her feel attractive and desirable. Some women dress, act or influence in ways specifically and intentionally to get that attention and affirmation. Would we honestly rather have our feminine egos boosted than honor and encourage our brother's Christian walk? Men may allow inappropriate physical interaction in a relationship to flatter their egos as well, but it is not right; it does not honor God.

I don't know how long you—or I for that matter—will be single and tempted. But His grace will be new for us each time! He is worth it! And your living holy and blameless, receiving blessings and favor and eternity in heaven, is worth it. He sees your worship to Him even of your physical body. Nothing eludes His watch and knowing.

> For *the eyes of the LORD* range throughout the earth to strengthen those whose hearts are fully committed to him.
> *~2 Chron. 16:9*

Be careful with your body—all of it. Do not sin and develop physical, soul ties. Conduct yourselves as God would have you. God is not a kill-joy, but has established guidelines, boundaries and laws to protect us—our bodies, emotions and soul. His directions are to give us results of increase, blessing, joy and good outcomes, not decrease, guilt, shame, sorrow and repercussions. Many a sorrow and regret set in when we go out of bounds from God's ways. Acting out of bounds in the area of physical interaction causes scarring. I have heard the hearts and cries of the regretful in this area. It is seemingly easier to ask for God's forgiveness than to be obedient when you don't want to be, but you will be blessed if you do. Since I do not know where each reader stands in their understanding of God's guidelines for pure relationships, here are some scriptures to tell of how we are to be moral with our bodies and actions.

> Flee from sexual immorality. All other sins a person commits are outside the body, but whoever sins sexually, sins against their own body. Do you not know that your

bodies are temples of the Holy Spirit, who is in you, whom you have received from God? You are not your own; you were bought at a price. Therefore honor God with your bodies.

~1 Cor. 6:18-20

The King James Version states the above verse 18 as "Flee fornication." (Fornication is sexual relations outside of any marriage. Flee means to run from or leave abruptly.) So the firecrackers you feel when you are intrigued by the flesh are the firecrackers telling you to get the quick out of that situation! Sex and sexual type interactions outside of marriage dishonor the participants, God and the gift of marriage itself.

Now concerning the things whereof ye wrote unto me: It is good for a man not to touch a woman.

~1 Cor. 7:1

· This means keep your hands off and away from all personal places. All private areas. You know what I'm talking about. This means momentary touches and/or short and lengthy caresses. Your hands should not even be in those vicinities.

Daughters of Jerusalem, I charge you by the gazelles and by the does of the field: Do not arouse or awaken love until it so desires.

~Song of Solomon 3:5

Do not go down that hot, steamy passion road that may cause sexual arousal for some individuals. That causes soul ties that are hard to break. When your soul is tied to another, you develop an attachment that perhaps you shouldn't have. That attachment can cause you to think you're in love when you're not. It can cause you to pursue a relationship that is not God's best for you, or in the extreme to do things that you would not otherwise do, from allowing yourself to be used or abused to falling into obsessive behaviors with this person that you think you love.

> Therefore, I urge you, brothers and sisters, in view of God's mercy, to offer your bodies as a living sacrifice, holy and pleasing to God—this is your true and proper worship.
>
> *~Rom. 12:1*

> If ye love me, keep my commandments.
>
> *~John 14:15 KJV*

> Since everything will be destroyed in this way, what kind of people ought you to be? You ought to live holy and godly lives.
>
> *~2 Pet. 3:11*

> Be holy, because I am holy.
>
> *~1 Pet. 1:16*

> Rather, he must be hospitable, one who loves what is good, who is self-controlled, upright, holy and disciplined.
>
> *~Titus 1:8*

> He has saved us and called us to a holy life—not because of anything we have done but because of his own purpose and grace. This grace was given us in Christ Jesus before the beginning of time.
>
> *~2 Tim. 1:9*

> For God did not call us to be impure, but to live a holy life.
>
> *~1 Thess. 4:7*

Postpone hand holding and putting arms around each other. Consider waiting for these things until you are so, so, so sure the relationship is the one God has called for. But how can you really know that you'll make it to the altar for sure? Maybe the kiss should be reserved for the altar? It is not unheard of. Some couples choose this. I'm just sayin'. I think kissing (beyond a peck) is highly under-rated. It is beautiful. It is blissful and let's just admit—it could very easily make you want more. The flesh is never satisfied. And gosh, that is your mouth—that's a personal place. Shouldn't even kissing be saved for "the one"? May the only kissing I do be giving an honest answer to someone. "An honest answer is like a kiss on the lips" (Proverbs 24:26). Passionate kissing is clearly setting us up for possible/probable failure of some sort. It puts you in a position to use all your holy wits about you to turn the flesh off and stop. It's like playing with kindling and matches with gasoline nearby. Run! Flee temptation!

The late Art Linkletter reminisced during his Chick-fil-A keynote speaking engagement. He talked about his and wife Lois's courting season some 72 years earlier while floating around in a canoe. Art said, "I got romantic under the moonlight one night and I said to her, 'We oughta' get married or something.' And she said, 'We'll get married, or nothing.'" I like her.

I can only speak for women in this, but our hearts are open while kissing. You lose a lot of yourself in it and you give a lot of yourself through it. Men, you need to know this and respect a woman even in this area of kissing. If she likes you, the act means more to her than you may realize. We were made emotionally. If she doesn't like you, then you shouldn't be letting her kiss you anyway. I think kissing should really mean something to men as well. "Out of the overflow of the heart the mouth speaks" (Matt.

12:34). I know the scripture is certainly not written about kissing, but when your heart is out to someone, the mouth tells of it here too. I'm sure no pastor has ever spoken on that scripture this way before!

I love the Lord with all my heart, soul, mind and strength, but I don't want to test my limits, or that of my date! But let's be frank: saying "no" to passion and keeping hands in appropriate places can be difficult. And face it, if you are in that euphoric mental state at that point, you have entered lust and are in sin.

> Put to death, therefore, whatever belongs to your earthly nature: sexual immorality, impurity, lust, evil desires.
> ~*Col. 3:5*

I am a firm believer that even passion should not be entered into before marriage. You risk wading into deep, drowning waters. Where can you go from there? Nowhere! It is too natural and the flesh would want more each time. When you dabble, you tend to travel. Once you travel to the island destination called "Soft," next time you will want to travel to the island destination called "Sensual." The next time you will want to travel to the island destination called "More please." And once you get into sin, it's like ground flaxseed meal stuck on the inside of your blender— REALLY, REALLY hard to get out! Yes, I know people that have their convictions not to fornicate and have good brakes because of their convictions. I am saying according to the Bible that even passion (lust) outside of marriage is sin. You can't just take a night off from the Holy Spirit.

Avoid intercourse, outercourse and foreplay. The two are just as emotionally bonding. I know women that even feel cheapened after cuddling or kissing a male when the relationship has ended. The attention was fulfilling at the time they received it, but left them feeling hollowed out and used afterward. "Wisdom always chooses to do now, what it will be satisfied with later on" (Joyce Meyer, 2011).

"Warn your readers about the power of sensual touch," said one of my interviewees. He does not want to see others go through the pain he is still going through regarding former errors. He wrote:

> You may think you can control the emotions, but they are like a tidal wave, so intense and hard to stop when the emotions are so intense. I felt I betrayed God and my values. I had to live with guilt and it took me a long time to forgive myself. I had to ask God to forgive me. When you really love someone you respect each other and setting limits on touch is a must (2011).

He also urged that men need to protect the woman they date. Women are sensitive and even soft touch is stimulating and dangerous. Soft, gentle touches should not be downplayed at all. They can develop into an inferno. The more touch, the more difficult it is to stop. Singles need to be responsible with that knowledge.

Let's resolve that we will continue to crucify our flesh, seek continued growth in the Lord and be ever changing from glory to glory. It is not a time for business as usual. Only when His light exudes from us, can we change a darkened world.

What I have come to know is this. You will never be sorry that you obeyed the Lord, but you will be sorry at some point for having disappointed the Lord. It may be the next moment, the next day, the next month or the next year, but righteousness or sin will always show forth. It's just a matter of time. Which do you want?

In fact, this is love for God: to keep his commands.
And his commands are not burdensome.

~1 John 5:3

"Discipline says, 'I need to.' Duty says, 'I ought to.'
Devotion says, 'I want to. '"

~Adriane Rogers

Out of your heart you should want to honor God and
His commands. You don't know when God will bring your
mate. You don't know how many more people you will
date before marriage. Do you want to be holding hands and
caressing all those arms and shoulders before your mate's?
Do you want to be kissing indiscriminately? Consider the
discomfort of you and your future spouse in the same room
with someone else you shared physical affections with.
Eww! Honor and give your future mate a commitment of
physical purity before you even meet. They will thank and
respect you highly for that purity.

Friends don't kiss. Friends don't hold hands. Friends
don't share those connections. If you are involved in this,
be honest, you've moved beyond friends. You need to
change the title of your relationship to dating. If putting a
title on the relationship makes either of you uncomfortable
or wishing to hide it from others, something is wrong and
you should not be dating, OR kissing.

Friends with benefits? WHAT?! The last time I had a
benefit cut that came with my job, I felt like I was going
backwards. The last time I had a benefit from health
insurance that was removed, I was really bummed. A friend
that you've become physically active with to whatever
degree (cuddling, kissing) isn't necessarily going to meet
you at the altar and be your mate for life. So at some point
that benefit will change, or go away and one or both of you
will be left empty-armed again. How's that really going to

feel? Why get yourself into something you may just have to get yourself out of later? Why complicate?

In addition to that, you may have been romantic with someone else's God ordained spouse. You are causing them to give out places of their heart that should be reserved only for their saved future spouse. Really, you are taking from them, not giving affection or care to them. Remember, real Christian love calls us to higher places.

One can try to justify physical interaction with another because we are human and have physical needs. They think, "It's been a long time since I had that attention or I've never had this opportunity before." But engaging physically with someone can merely be using one another to satisfy fleshly desires. I know that sounds really ugly, but frankly it is. Your emotions and energized body may be feeling like, "THE SHOES ARE FINALLY ON SALE AND THEY'VE GOT MY SIZE!" or "THE FISHING POLE I'VE ALWAYS WANTED IS IN STOCK, NOW!" as you're considering going for and risking blowing it all in this physical opportunity. Don't do it! It's a bad deal!

We are called to a higher calling in Christ than that. We can control ourselves.

According to Virginia Satir, family therapist, "We need 4 hugs a day for survival. We need 8 hugs a day for maintenance. We need 12 hugs a day for growth." Perhaps we need a group of friends that are sanctified huggers (side huggers) to add some of the human touch that we need. The balance of any physical desires will have to be worked through in the Spirit.

So more than committing to "I'm not going to do anything I don't want to do," I'm suggesting you don't do things you *do* want to do. Don't act on emotion. We are called to be different than the world—self controlled. "Offer your bodies as a living sacrifice." (Romans 12:1) That means ALL your body.

Affections cause fractures of the soul. When couples begin those physical attachments, then break up, it becomes more than a parting, but causes a fracture—something is physically separating. A tie or a connection is made between the man and woman through intimacy (not limited to forming by sexual fornication). This is called a soul tie and it is a linkage between the people's souls. These are positive such as in marriage when the two shall become one flesh or in the deep friendship of Jonathan and David. But in unhealthy, temporary soul ties the two hearts feel like they have a piece being torn away from it. Read Gen 34 for an example of a sexual soul-tie between Shechem and Dinah. It is said that Shechem raped Dinah, then came to love her. Now I don't call that REAL, agape love—far from it—but something happened in the physical relationship that at least made Shechem think that he was in love.

Given even one or multiple break ups of that physical nature, and enough fractures, your strength is weakened or compromised. By the time one actually finds their true mate, the blessings of any physical activity short of sex have been cheapened or tarnished.

Know your commitment and make your decision with regard to physical affections before getting into a relationship or situation. Plant the decision in your heart while you are strong. The older are just as vulnerable as the younger in this. You should also share your unmovable boundaries with the person you have entered into relationship with. If you want to have a shot at keeping those boundaries, you have to be very proactive about it. It's not ridiculous; it's what a winner does.

I realize I've written some big words on these pages that I will have to live by as well one day. I am sure it will be tempting for me to veer off this straight and narrow, but I resolve to keep the lid on the box rather than have to fight off more passion. My convictions are such because I love Jesus.

Affections are not a way to develop love or create love. They are to show love that has already been built. Love must grow first through true agape care and concern. You can show your love through that language after it has been developed, seen, tested and tried. At that point, and only at that point, do I believe someone may be worthy of my deep non-sexual, light affections which in me create further devotion and attachment. As a Christian, you can't legally have sex or sexual touch. Therefore kissing, hand holding, caressing and touch take on a much deeper meaning even creating possible soul ties and attachments between the individuals. When those things are all you've got to toy with, the level of meaning and weight they carry deepens.

If you do not plan on going the route of waiting to kiss at the altar, I think it is proper for a man to ask a woman if he may kiss her for the first time. Respect her. Don't be selfish. Do you really think she and the relationship are ready for that step? Let her be a part of that decision.

If you are wondering if outsiders will think your love is really true should you decide to delay physical affections, believe me, they will still see the love in your eyes and the whites of your teeth as you smile with your significant only if it's the real deal. They will see your respect and godly treatment for each other. Adoration is bright, really bright. That stuff shows brighter than you can ever imagine. They will see you moving toward marriage when the time is right if it is really a true God connection. If the relationship is not the real deal, then you don't want to be sharing physical sentiments anyway.

Professionals talk about bringing baggage into a relationship. Christians teach that having pre-marital sex brings baggage into a marriage (sin, memories, bondages, visions, possible comparisons). I believe the other smaller degree affections may produce the same effects. Satan opposes marriage and he will use anything to create trouble. Flashbacks...of former relationships—you will have them, even when you are married; they will flash before your mind and eyes. Now, in this single season, give yourself less to "flash back" on one day.

Affections are like a stove or electricity. They can bring warm, comfortable and enjoyable treats. A stove can cook us up a scrumptious, tasty meal, but touch the burner and you'll feel pain. Electricity can bring us light and working appliances or it can surge through a body and leave it motionless and breathless...deadening. We must know the power affections carry and respect them for their capability and intensity. We must know what affections do and their damaging effects. We need to only apply them cautiously if at all when dating or possibly when engaged.

There was a woman who was strongly attracted to a man's character and friendship, yet there were some things different than she was looking for in a mate and she was not having a physical attraction to him. A few God-fearing female friends suggested she kiss him to find out if there could be any attraction built. They said, "It's in the kiss."

No! It could be the kiss of death! The kiss gets in the way! Either of the below scenarios could then happen:

1) Perhaps there are larger circumstances, situations or dynamics preventing either man/woman from moving forward. Maybe it's a God thing. Now they've attached affectionately and may continue further. Once those warm fuzzy experiences start, it could be hard to shut them down—hard to break away from that once it has begun. The kiss creates a false sense of acceptance.

2) Perhaps the kiss is just a form of lust and not an outward expression of phileo love.

3) Say the woman still does not have a physical attraction for the man after the kiss, but his heart has been opened up. Now he may be hurt.

No, it cannot be in the kiss! That is a worldly saying. The kiss is like an arm coming out from one person to the other taking you hostage. Meaningful love should already be in place before a kiss. You would know if you really wanted to kiss someone. One can fall in love without any kind of physical touch or kiss ever having taken place yet. If physical attraction does not occur in a reasonable time frame, it likely is not going to.

Are you unsure if you are physically attracted to someone? Chip Ingram, Founder and Teaching Pastor for Living on the Edge, an international ministry, says someone can look attractive or alluring in the right sweater or the right jeans and the light hitting in such a way. I branch out to say that you may have attraction at particular times, but the attraction may not revisit often enough. It is frustrating, but honest, that one can be attracted to someone's character and personality, but the physical attraction does not come.

People can definitely become attractive from their inner beauty, but sometimes this does not happen. My guideline is that if you are in a close relationship with someone, enjoying each other's company, knowing their good character pretty well and you feel no physical spark by the end of three months, it probably will not come. There are exceptions, but exceptions they are.

Each of you has to have a physical attraction/chemistry for one another. God meant for the marital sexual relationship to be steamy hot! I'm not sure how a couple could enjoy it as God desires us to if there is not the natural physical attraction between them. It does not mean that we allow the physical allurement to supersede other aspects of the relationship, but there must be some kind of "liking" goin' on. A wise mother of the church shared that it's that physical passion and "liking" toward the other that will keep you coming back together even when times are not easy in the relationship. Sexual intimacy in marriage isn't just about "feeling good." It's about serving the other's desires as well. How can you do that if that "wow" is not there from the beginning? You have to go to bed with the person every night. As we age, we will get more of something and less of something else on our bodies. The "liking" will be built in from the beginning though. And with true love, we should only become more beautiful with age to the other.

Pure and Simple
Instruction to men: The popular word out is that you are highly affected by visual images. I have compassion for you because the world is so full of lust—everywhere from billboards, to commercials, grocery store check-out lanes and the way women dress. Sometimes you do not have an option of what comes into your view, but it is what a man does after that first site that is their choice and should be

dealt with in godly behavior. That sentence carries heavy instruction to men. Men need to train their eyes to look away. Job in Job 31:1 declared "I made a covenant with my eyes not to look lustfully at a girl." That's the ticket.

To men and women: Habits like pornography, lusting over women or men, masturbation or worse need to be repented of and taken care of before go into a dating relationship. There are ministries that minister to these very specific issues. Reconciliation Ministries *(www.recmin.org)* has a division called Living Waters. New Life Ministries *(www.newlife.com)* is another. You will not be able to function wholly in a relationship with this sin present. These sins will catch you sooner or later. A man admitted that willpower was not enough to kick the habits. He tried to get a little help here, a little help there. Not until he attended an Every Man's Battle weekend through New Life Ministries did he finally realize that he had a much bigger problem than he understood on his own. His life was then changed for the better.

Masturbation seems to be an undecided gray topic to some. I do not believe it belongs in a glowing Christian's life. Let's look at these points: 1) Masturbation is an act of *self*-love. It is not serving the needs of a marital spouse.
2) What types of thoughts is one thinking about during the act? They most likely are not pure thoughts. 3) Who are they thinking about or envisioning during the act? This would be lusting over someone. 4) If the act were holy or right, it would not bring shame if another person or a community was to learn of it. 5) The act itself may bring a sexual release, but quickly afterward one senses shame or ugliness. God's holy ways do not bring about shame or ugliness. 6) When you feed the flesh, it is never satisfied. It will want more. Masturbation could be the beginnings of ending up caught in the trappings of a sexual addiction.

One could end up looking at pornography or worse when their own thoughts cannot bring the stimuli any longer.

Be pure. Save sexual fulfillment for the pleasure that it is meant to be between two God-adoring spouses. Wait to give your spouse the honor of blessing you. Give them the honor of experiencing the unknowns or forgottens and the beauty of sexual pleasures as God intended for them to be. When you think about it, no matter how tempted you are...how fun is a sexual act with yourself? Where's the love? Masturbation is a fraud and fallacy. It depletes your self-respect—and God's respect of YOU.

Now, let's talk about something else. Remember this. We are not responsible for when a bird lands in our hair, but we are responsible for letting the bird nest there. And you are not responsible for when a sin thought enters your mind, but you are responsible for dwelling on those thoughts, discussing those thoughts with others and acting on those thoughts. If you should have a dream of intimacy or sexual activity while sleeping, you are not responsible for that. However, you should ask for God's forgiveness in case you did anything that may have brought that on. However again, one is responsible for what they do with any lingering images or thoughts from such a dream. Do you dwell and fantasize about them? Do you have long, excited discussions about the fantasy to others? Those types of responses would be letting the dirty bird nest in your hair—and that you are responsible for.

> All who are prudent act with knowledge, but fools
> expose their folly.
>
> *~Prov. 3:16*

We can't really help hormones and how intense they make us feel; they can add to the occasional maddening.

Exercise is a good prescription for working off accumulated energy. Root yourself in the Word of God. Keep busy with good things and people.

Fences for Our Fancies

Affections are like saccharin. People use saccharin to get that sweet taste they love so much without gaining weight. They think saccharin will help them get a little of what they want and satisfy them without blowing all the calories. But actually, saccharin stimulates the appetite and can cause cancer (an aggressive killer).

Similarly, some people may think if they kiss or caress, those expressions will satisfy them enough to go no further physically. But in reality, kissing or whatever actions it is for *you*, stimulates everything else! Then you've started an aggressive killer rolling! In this area, I don't consider myself a stoic. On the contrary! I don't want the struggle to even begin!

Joshua Harris' book *boy meets girl* is an excellent resource. He shares physical expression guidelines he and his wife followed during courtship. He stresses the importance of specifying beforehand what each of you agree is appropriate and not. Then have your accountability partners ask you how you are doing which each of the expressions. Their guidelines:

1. We will not caress each other. For us this excludes:
    - rubbing each other's back, neck, or arms;
    - touching or stroking each other's face
    - playing with each other's hair;
    - scratching each other's arms or back.

2. We will not "cuddle." For us this excludes:
   - sitting entwined on a couch watching a movie;
   - leaning or resting on the other person;
   - lying down next to each other;
   - playfully wrestling with each other.

3. We will guard our conversation and meditation. for us this means:
   - not talking about our future physical relationship;
   - not thinking or dwelling on what would now be
   - sinful;
   - not reading things related to physical intimacy
   - within marriage prematurely.

4. We will not spend undue amounts of time together at late hours. A specific area of concern for us is time together late at night. We're more vulnerable when we're tired. Even if we haven't compromised, please ask if we're spending too much time together at late hours.

5. Appropriate physical expressions during this season include:
   - holding hands;
   - Josh putting his arm around Shannon's shoulder;
   - brief "side hugs."

~pp. 157-158

We don't want to stimulate our appetites. We may not struggle as much with desires creeping up when avoiding triggers, but they still will; nothing will solve all that. Ask yourselves, "What gets your motor running?" PUT THAT ON THE "DON'T" LIST! You need guard rails to stay on the straight and narrow. If you don't have guard rails, which are these types of plans in place, it's sure harder to control your hands. God gave physical intimacy, foreplay and sex as natural, fabulous gifts in the place of marriage only.

It is good to communicate to your significant only when you are feeling weak regarding physical touch/intimacy. But the other person has to have enough true love and integrity not to capitalize on the other's time of weakness. When one person is weak, the other should take the lead of strength. If both of you are in a weak intimate stage simultaneously...run and flee from each other till the feelings subside and you are surely in God's strength. Communicate briefly what and why you are fleeing or staying apart for a bit so the other person does not attribute it to being angry with them or otherwise.

If both of you are not on the same page about what is right and not right to do physically in dating or courting, perhaps you should not even be dating. Both of your hearts need to be understanding, wanting and pursuing what is completely holy and right in God. It would be wise to have one or two accountability partners who you are honest with in regard to this area of physical behavior. The male and female in the relationship may have different accountability partners or the same ones. These partners must be people that already understand the importance of holiness. They would ask you questions about behaviors in the relationship every week that each of you will answer honestly.

Examples of accountability questions:
- Have you kissed?
- Were you alone when you kissed?
- How long did you kiss for?
- Have you reached a point of passion?
- Have you kept your hands where they ought to be?
- Have you kept your clothing on?

- Have you participated in foreplay?
- Have you participated in sex?

It takes humility to set up accountability partners and bear answers to private questions, but holiness can be attained with such. Holiness has high standards. You will be positioning yourselves individually and the relationship for greatness. God will bless you for it!

> If you should stumble in sin, confess it to God. "If we confess our sins, he is faithful and just and will forgive us our sins and purify us from all unrighteousness.
>
> ~*1 John 1:9*

Confess it, receive it and move forward. If you continue to struggle, talk to a pastor or a professional Christian counselor.

Rightly withholding intimacy does not lessen your value as a single person as the world tries to make it out. It increases your God favor!

Do not spend the night or weekends at your significant only's or fiancé's house. This develops strong emotional ties. Even without sexual conduct, this develops ties and attachments. It's just a few steps back from living with each other.

It's okay to have your sibling spend the night. It's okay to have your best friend or buddy spend the night. It's okay to have your cousin or niece/nephew spend the night. It's okay to have your mother/father spend the night. But it is not okay to have your boyfriend or girlfriend spend the night! These are different types of relationships! You are not married.

I am aware of couples spending the night at one another's house but in separate beds to be more moral. I am aware of the evening, lying down, side by side, tuck-in snuggle times. I am aware of the morning, sneak into the other's bed, wake-up, snuggle times. This may seem a better decision to some than having sex or sleeping together in the same bed, or some may be questioning its propriety deep within themselves. You are not married. Even those types of behaviors are not right. Do you want to be a boyfriend or girlfriend that is wanted because you're a teddy bear or because you are truly loved for being you and they desire to marry you? Do you want to be the company or be *in* the company—the corporation you would make once married?

Do not spend the night in the bed or out of the bed. Don't fall for the excuses: 1) They live too far. Driving home just to return the next day would be a waste of gasoline, energy and time. 2) Someone is too tired to drive home. While each of those reasons may be true, you've just *got* to work around them. They offer a temporary comfort with a long range emotional and spiritual punishment. God will bless you for honoring Him. Nothing we ever do for God that costs us more is a waste of time. Perhaps the home owner could stay at a nearby friend's house instead, so at least you are not together in the home overnight. Perhaps you'll have to start or end date nights earlier. See how long your relationship goes on for. If it ends because of distance, it probably wasn't the real deal. Real love cannot stay away. Real love can't help but go extra miles to be with "the one."

Spending the night also creates witnessing issues for the neighbors. Most would not believe sexual relations are not going on. So your witness to them of Christ could be blown.

Additionally, even if not spending the night, I am aware of dating couples lying in bed together (clothed) having snuggle, holding or kissy time. The bed is a personal place and it's like a lit burner—don't touch it. One person should get to share it with you till either of you dies—that's it—no one else, ever. How can God honor what is honorless in your relationship? These kinds of behavior will catch you sooner or later. In Hebrew the word "ahurite" means "the end result." We have to think about what the ahurite of our actions may be. All these types of inappropriate interactions…you pay whole units of pain for this kinda' stuff in a break up!

If you believe in taking a vacation alone with your significant only, I believe the man and woman should sleep in different hotel rooms. This view may seem strict, but I believe in keeping things fresh and new for marriage. I feel the same way about premature blended family vacations; the man and woman should stay in different rooms, not merely in the same room but in different beds.

So what about a dating couple staying alone in a cabin with separate rooms? It seems then we are back to the scenario of staying at each other's house in separate rooms, which I am not a proponent of. There's a degree of closeness and warm, fuzzy connecting feelings in those settings which should be saved for your mate upon marriage only. The same goes for a pre-marital blended family as well.

It's like not opening or peeking at a Christmas present early or playing with it then putting it back in the box for Christmas morning. It's about not even picking up the box and shaking and listening to it. Personally, I don't think I will travel alone with a significant other even in separate hotel rooms. It's just something I want to save for marriage.

What about a dating couple traveling alone to stay at a parent's house in Chicago for the holiday and staying in separate rooms? If the purpose is to meet the parents or spend time getting to know the parents to establish a good basis, maybe yes, go ahead. But if the purpose is to merely see Chicago, I would not. It's about keeping boundaries that do not allow so many emotional and memory ties to be created. It's about keeping things special for that one special person after a wedding.

As we end this chapter together and hopefully bringing an end to any chapter in our life that is not pleasing and holy unto God, know that God's forgiveness always abounds to a repentant heart. It is never too late to "go right."

16
Living Fruit:
Being One and Picking One

But the fruit of the Spirit is love, joy, peace, forbearance, kindness, goodness, faithfulness, gentleness and self-control. Against such things there is no law.

~Gal. 5:22-23

Where do you get the best fruit? At the grocery store? The fruit market? The fruit stand? Home grown? Weren't we taught which fruit was in season and ripe for eating or rotten? Don't date or marry a banana; know what their fruit is and whether their character seems ripe for a relationship!

A Christian psychologist once said, "Make sure your picker is working right." Once your picker is working right, it's time to "move up the food chain." The single person's selection of dates or relationships should be improving each time with learned knowledge and discernment. Know what to look for. Go for character—someone who can love like 1 Corinthians 13: "Love suffers long *and* is kind; love does not envy; love does not parade itself, is not puffed up; does not behave rudely, does not seek its own, is not provoked, thinks no evil; does not rejoice in iniquity, but rejoices in the truth; bears all things, believes all things, hopes all things, endures all things. Love never fails."

Chose someone who exhibits the fruit of the Spirit of Galatians 5:22-23: "But the fruit of the Spirit is love, joy, peace, longsuffering, kindness, goodness, faithfulness, gentleness, self-control." *Safe People* is an invaluable read by Drs. Cloud and Townsend. It examines how the fruit looks played out in real life situations and relationships.

I truly believe that if we live out those commandments and love as we love ourselves (Matthew 19:19), and commit ourselves not to correct others until we have corrected ourselves (Matthew 7:5 NASB), so many offenses and hurts could be minimized, even eliminated. Ephesians 4:1-3 instructs us to "live a life worthy of the calling you have received. Be completely humble and gentle; be patient, bearing with one another in love. Make every effort to keep the unity of the Spirit through the bond of peace." Romans 12:10 admonishes us to "honor one another above yourselves."

Part of this love is shown in our communication. We make a decision to honor or dishonor God with it. Teacher and evangelist Shane Willard says "you are saved, but are you saved when someone upsets you?" How do you react? How do you respond? Sharply? Rudely? Shaming? Or do you respond with patience, kindness and a soft or respectful tone in a way that honors God and His people? There's a difference between being a believer in Christ and being a follower of Christ. Taking the name of God in vain is not just verbally abusing His actual title of God, but defaming His name through our actions or words of disrespect to others as well. "The Lord is compassionate and gracious, slow to anger, abounding in love" (Psalm 103:8). We should be the same. When a woman makes a bad decision, how does the man respond? When a man makes an error, how does the woman respond?

Do everything in love.

~1 Cor. 16:14

Marriage was created by God to be lived out His way. You can only experience the gift of marriage the pure intended way if you are like Him. *The Love Dare* book (2008) brings it home so poignantly:

Love is built on two pillars that best define what it is. Those pillars are patience and kindness. All other characteristics of love are extensions of these two attributes...

Love will inspire you to become a patient person. When you choose to be patient, you respond in a positive way to a negative situation. You are slow to anger. You choose to have a long fuse instead of a quick temper. Rather than being restless and demanding, love helps you settle down and begin extending mercy to those around you. Patience brings an internal calm during an external storm...

The irony of anger toward a wrongful action is that it spawns new wrongs of its own. Anger almost never makes things better. In fact, it usually generates additional problems. But patience stops problems in the tracks. More than biting your lip, more than clapping a hand over your mouth, patience is a deep breath. It clears the air. It stops foolishness from whipping its scorpion tail all over the room. It is a choice to control your emotions rather than allowing your emotions to control you, and shows discretion instead of returning evil for evil...

Patience stands in the doorway where anger is clawing to burst in, but waits to see the whole picture before passing judgment...Kindness is love in action. If patience is how love reacts in order to minimize a negative circumstance, kindness is how love acts to maximize a positive circumstance. Patience avoids a problem; kindness creates a blessing. One is preventive, the other proactive. These two sides of love are the cornerstones on which many of the other attributes we will discuss are built…

Love makes you kind. And kindness makes you likeable. When you're kind, people want to be around you. They see you as being good to them and good for them.

~*The Love Dare*, pp. 1-6

Love is more than giving money to the needy or ministries. It's when I mess up and you act and speak in love toward me when you could have flared up at me. It's when you give me what I don't deserve—kindness and mercy.

The Love Dare then breaks the character of kindness into four other basic core categories: gentleness, helpfulness, willingness and initiative. I strongly recommend this book for anyone. We need to learn and do the traits of our Master.

Is your date patient and kind, as described above? Do they value other people? How do they treat others? That's how they'll treat you later. Pay attention. Minister Dr. Ken Stewart writes,

The problem in most relationships is that you don't see the true character of the person until you're so deeply involved that it hurts to get out…What is so sad about that is that many of these people go ahead and marry anyway. They think that will hurt less than getting out of the relationship. It always hurts more…Real love is constant giving. Givers make good lovers. You don't want somebody who's stingy.

~Dr. Ken Steward, *Choosing a Mate*, pp. 63, 66

The story of Rebekah tells it beautifully. Abraham directed his servant to seek a wife for his son Isaac (Genesis 24). He prayed, "Lord, lead me to the woman who will offer water, not only to me, but to my camels too." Here is the passage:

> Before he had finished praying, Rebekah came out with her jar on her shoulder. She was the daughter of Bethuel son of Milkah, who was the wife of Abraham's brother Nahor. The woman was very beautiful, a virgin; no man had ever slept with her. She went down to the spring, filled her jar and came up again.
>
> The servant hurried to meet her and said, "Please give me a little water from your jar."
>
> "Drink, my lord," she said, and quickly lowered the jar to her hands and gave him a drink.
>
> After she had given him a drink, she said, "I'll draw water for your camels too, until they have had enough to drink." So she quickly emptied her jar into the trough, ran back to the well to draw more water, and drew enough for all his camels.
>
> *~Gen. 24:15-20*

Rebekah was a giver. She was a person who saw others as valuable and precious.

~Stewart, p. 67

We have heard to watch men to see the relationship they have with their mother, but the converse is true as well: watch the relationship she has with her father. If you can't do that, watch them interact with people that serve them (waitresses, home repair people, customer service representatives). How polite and kind are they then? How respectful are they then? Are there demeaning undertones in their voice? Are they thankful? Do they bless and not tear down? Are they patient?

Author Ptolemy Pruden of *Building a Beautiful Wife* says, "Trust is the most important factor affecting how your wife relates to you because she is entrusting her weakness to your emotional strength" (p. 20). He also teaches that men can "develop healthy emotional stability if we use wisdom in our responses and utilize proper wife-based knowledge in each circumstance" (p. 21, 2010).

While Ptolemy is speaking to those who are already husbands, the same encouragers are for those honoring their single brothers and sisters in Christ. A woman is contemplating or has already given her delicate emotions, flaws and thoughts to you. What will you do with them? In what temperament will you respond to them? In what character will you respond to them? How much will you be like Jesus? In the movie *Courageous,* Nathan teaches his daughter Jay about men: "They want to win your heart, but they don't know how to treasure you" (2011).

And what about YOU? How much will you be like Jesus? Spend plenty of time with Jesus so that you can become like Him. So that you will bear good fruit—living fruit. Then, once you are in order, pick living fruit.

17

Mirror This Radiant Marriage

One day I came across aged, yellowed photos of people I did not know. I studied a photo of a man with a straight, stern face and formal suit. I pondered over a photo of a woman with hair up in a hat and fitted, formal attire. And as I wait for the good relationship God has for me, I couldn't help but wonder about these former real people, their lives and relationships.

- Was he respected?
- Was he honored?
- Was he cooked for?
- Was he prepared for?
- Was he prettied for?
- Was he delighted in?
- Was he spoken highly of?
- Was he spoken kindly to?
- Was he done for? (Some men would say that with a woman in his life, he was!)
- Was he told he's the best?
- Was he given his role to lead?
- Was he prayed for?
- Was he accepted?
- Was he encouraged?
- Were his passions exalted?
- Was he told he would become everything God wanted him to be?

- Was she loved?
- From her head to her toes?
- From her inside to her outside?
- From her heart to her soul?
- From her riches to her deficits?
- From her strengths to her weaknesses?
- From her smile to her tears?
- From her writing to her speaking?
- From her rising to her resting?
- From her giving to her receiving?
- From her birth to her going home?
- From her serving to her praying?
- From her succeeding to her failing?
- Was she loved as Christ loved the church?

Were this man and woman adored by each other? Did they value each other as God wanted the other valued? The kind of spouse we should seek to be and to find is someone who has the ability of character (fruit) to create the kind of marriage written about below here. Someone who has the desire to love you like this...bless you like this. Someone who has the passion to continue growing into this kind of marriage through Christ.

A Marriage Prayer

O God of love, Thou hast established marriage for the welfare and happiness of mankind. Thine was the plan and only with Thee can we work it out with joy. Thou hast said, "It is not good for man to be alone. I will make a help meet for him." Now our joys are doubled since the happiness of one is the happiness of the other. Our burdens now are halved since when we share them, we divide the load.

Bless this husband. Bless him as provider of provender and raiment, and sustain him in all the exactions and pressures of his battle for bread. May his strength be her protection; his character be her boast and her pride; and may he so live that she will find in him the haven for which the heart of a woman truly longs. May his soul be so wide a sea that she may launch her all on its strong tide.

Bless this loving wife. Give her a tenderness that will make her great, a deep sense of understanding and a great faith in Thee. Give her that inner beauty of soul that never fades, that eternal youth that is found in holding fast to the things that never age. May she so live that he may be pleased to reverence at the shrine of her heart.

May they never make the mistake of merely for each other. Teach them that marriage is not living for each other; it is two uniting and joining hands to serve Thee. Give them a great spiritual purpose in life. May they seek first the kingdom of God and His righteousness, and the other things shall be added unto them. Loving Thee best, they shall love each other the more, and faithful unto Thee—faithful to each other they will be. May they not expect that perfection of each other that belongs alone to Thee. May they minimize each other's weaknesses, be swift to praise and magnify each other's points of comeliness and strength, and see each other through a lover's kind and patient eyes. Give them a little something to forgive each day that they may grow in the grace of longsuffering and of love.

May they be as forebearing with each other's omissions and commissions as Thou art with theirs.

Now make such assignments to them on the scroll of Thy will as will bless them and develop their characters as they walk together. Give them enough tears to keep them tender; enough hurts to keep them humane; enough failure to keep their hands clenched tightly in Thine; enough of success to make them sure they walk with God.

May they never take each other's love for granted, but always experience that breathless wonder that exclaims, "Out of all this world you have chosen me."

Then when life is done and the sun is setting, may they be found then as now still hand in hand, still very proud, still thanking God so much for each other. May they serve Thee happily, faithfully, together, until at last one shall lay the other in God's arms.

This we ask through Jesus Christ, great lover of our souls. Amen.

"A Marriage Prayer" expresses by Dr. Louis H. Evans Sr. the radiant marriage as God himself designed it and intends it to be. Spoken over a new bride and groom, this prolific writing and prayer is meant to inspire them. The couple is making a marriage promise to adore, cherish and love each other till death do they part. The wedding day may show a promising future, but without this prayer acted out can the future end up desirable or will the couple keep the vows given? God, the designer, intends for the enchantment to continue as well as improve. The institution of marriage is a work of art. There is a method set out to making it so, which "A Marriage Prayer" sets forth. It makes sense for us to follow the Designer's techniques to create a radiant marriage.

I learned later that Dr. Evans, Sr., pastor of First Presbyterian church of Hollywood, California during the 1940's and 50's, influenced such great evangelists as the founders of Campus Crusade for Christ and Rev. Billy Graham. Dr. Evans, Sr. wrote "A Marriage Prayer" for his son Dr. Louis H. Evans Jr. upon marriage to Colleen Townsend. One would imagine that the senior Dr. Evans intended that through the prayer, a strong marriage and loving family heritage would be passed down from generation to generation.

What if "A Marriage Prayer" was promoted around the world? How many marriages and families might be impacted forever? The piece begs a challenge to have it widely distributed.

Every line of "A Marriage Prayer" is laden with power packed wisdom and benefits that applying biblical principles should bring to a marriage, one that you and I are aspiring to. It is highly impactful, much more than even some marriage sermons. It explains the beauty and depth that a marital relationship should grow to and all that it should offer and become by the way we treat and respond to a spouse. And it cannot occur for the weak or character-challenged.

"Thine was the plan and only with Thee can we work it out with joy."

A spouse who lives out this calling will be blessed and multiplied with joy from the union.

Now our joys are doubled since the happiness of one is the happiness of the other. Our burdens now are halved since when we share them, we divide the load.

Pastor Evans asks:

Bless this husband. Bless him as provider of
provender and raiment, and sustain him in all
the exactions and pressure of his battle for
bread.

How much more difficult this provider role has become in these overly competitive and expensive days since the 40's and 50's. This is a great reason for the devotion of a praying wife. The groom needs wisdom, perseverance and favor to thrive in the trampling workplace.

Evans further asks:

May his strength be her protection, his character be
her boast and her pride, and may he so live that she will
find in him the haven for which the heart of a woman
truly longs.

Wow. This husband sounds like a very balanced person, trustworthy, incredible…like a rock…one who would bless and draw commitment from his wife. He has her best interests in mind. The bride's heart wants to go where she is treated kindly and she wears a proud smile because of this.

Evans prays:

Bless this loving wife. Give her a tenderness that
will make her great, a deep sense of understanding.

"Great" is an excellent rating to acquire; You get a great rating by supplying tenderness—something so needed. With this caring love and the strength that comes from it, couldn't the man have an easier time providing? This echoes "behind every good man is a good woman."

With an attentive listening ear and encouragement from his loving wife, daily issues and the hardships of life could be consoled. This attentive wife would certainly be easy to come home to and fold into his heart.

Give her that inner beauty of soul that never fades.

After time erodes a woman's outer youthful beauty, she can continue to give to the man from her tender heart, zesty mind and passionate soul. She should bring continued delight, fascination and contentment to him. Excitement need not fade.

May they seek first the kingdom of God and his righteousness, then the other things shall be added unto them.

In these fast-paced days of such need and disarray, the biblical promise that seeking God first will ensure all other needs will be taken care of, will reduce anxiety, worry and lack, and minimize marital arguments and strife. Would not the absence of those hindrances help make a marriage joyous? And wouldn't spouses who seek the kingdom of God first be kept from co-dependence on the other for *all* emotional needs and fulfillment?

May they not expect that perfection of each other that belongeth alone to Thee. May they minimize each other's weaknesses, be swift to praise and magnify each other's points of comeliness and strength, and see each other through a lover's kind and patient eyes.

This is a chance for patience to work into true love. God is the ONLY perfect One; we should not expect that of each other. What an intimacy that could develop from such a mindset! What a rose that could blossom in the bride and groom's personality and life as their pluses are accentuated and minuses given grace! When your spouse accentuates your positives, you simply want to do more. What a soft place of life to lay one's head on.

> *May they never take each other's love for granted,*
> *but always experience that breathless wonder that*
> *exclaims, "Out of all this world you have chosen me."*

Oh, how gratifying and gladdening this would be. What captured a man or woman's heart in those first months of relationship would continue to be found and felt until the end of life. What deep reward for making the effort to live out life "with Thee!" To still feel, "I'm in awe of you"—doesn't that make you want to work this prayer's requests? One can imagine in this comfortable, respectful, admirable marriage the husband and wife still calling their spouse "my bride" or "my groom" 20 years into marriage. Finally, Evans confirms:

> *This we ask through Jesus Christ, great lover of our*
> *souls.*

All we have to do is ask Jesus Christ for His way and to do it "with Thee" for this relished outcome. After all, the great "Lover of our souls" would only want *good* things for us—a radiant marriage and life.

As a single desiring marriage, deepen your character by deepening your relationship with Christ. Then you will have prepared yourself to be this kind of a blessing to a spouse…in His timing.

18
Necessary Devotion

*"A successful marriage requires falling in love
many times, always with the same person."*
~Mignon McLaughlin

Someone once asked a longtime husband, "How did you stay married for 71 years?" The husband simply replied, "We didn't get a divorce." Pure and simple. (*Accessed 11/15/10 from* www.kimbettieshow.com)

Let us take hold with sobering regard the degree of commitment required to honor God's marriage vow. In the book *Straight Talk (What Men Need to Know, What Women Should Understand)*, Dr. James Dobson's father (Dr. James C. Dobson Sr.) expressed these words to his future wife:

> I want you to understand and be fully aware of my feelings concerning the marriage covenant which we are about to enter. I have been taught at my mother's knee, and in harmony with the Word of God, that the marriage vows are inviolable, and by entering into them, I am binding myself absolutely and for life. The idea of estrangement from you through divorce for any reason at all (although God allows one—infidelity) will never at any time be permitted to enter into my thinking. I'm not naïve in this. On the contrary, I'm fully aware of the possibility, unlikely as it now appears, that mutual incompatibility or other unforeseen circumstances, could result in extreme mental suffering. If such becomes the case, I am resolved for my part to accept it as a consequence of the commitment I am now making, and to bear it, if necessary, to the end of our life together.

> I have loved you dearly as a sweetheart and will continue to love you as my wife. But over and above

that, I love you with a Christian love that demands that I never react in any way toward you that would jeopardize our prospects of entering heaven, which is the supreme objective of both our lives. And I pray that God Himself will make our affection for one another perfect and eternal (Dobson, p. 43).

Are you really willing and prepared to take on the covenant of marriage? Often people think about the vow "till death do us part," but may not consider what those words really mean. People either take the vow lightly or let fear stop them from marrying at all, when they could work on their own character and chose one with good character to make a radiant marriage. Marriage is not for the faint of heart, but with the increase of effort comes the increase of blessing!

19

Make Your Shopping List

We all have that shopping list: that list of desires in a mate. "I want him to be tall, dark and handsome." "I want her to sweet and petite." Or, at a deeper level: "I want him to be spiritually strong," or "I want her to be pure."

But what about YOU? Are you seeking "first his kingdom and his righteousness," so that "all these things will be given to you as well" (Matt 6:33)?

We need to check ourselves. Men, if you want the Queen...be the King. Women, if you want to be treated like a Queen...honor him like a King.

Below are comments from an informal poll from mature, strong Christians when asked what they are looking for in a mate. Use this to begin a checkoff list of qualities for you to develop, instead of a checkoff list of what YOU want in someone else.

What a woman is looking for in a man:
- Strong character
- A man who will encourage her to the high levels of God
- A man who does not talk negatively about anyone or gossip
- A man who does not embellish facts or tell white lies to anyone. How could you yourself trust him?
- Sensitive, gentle and tender but not overly so
- Protector—physically, spiritually and emotionally
- A confident man

- Someone who is willing to help her with tasks/favors
- A persevering, non-quitter
- A good listener and communicator
- Someone who really cares about her and her family
- Your undivided attention and non-wandering eyes
- A loving, frequent smile
- To be free to be herself around you
- She is looking for character...not a character

Myself, I want a crier. A man whose adoration and appreciation for the beauty of Jesus moves him to tears. A man whose own sins make his face wet in repentance. A man who is sensitive to the loveliness and presence of the Holy Spirit.

Did you notice? Jesus is all these things listed above.

The very heart of a woman, whether she realizes it or not, is looking for a man who resembles her heavenly Father. This is just something that is built into the fabric of a godly woman.

What a man is looking for in a woman:
- She loves Jesus
- A woman with a passion for the Word of God, to encourage each other with
- A prayer partner
- Respect
- Best friend and confidant
- Trustworthiness
- A woman who truly likes him (not just loves him)
- A woman who does not bombard him with all her problems

- A woman whose eyes express softness, kindness and love
- A woman whose facial expressions convey gentleness, peace and pleasantness
- Equal expectations for family, finances and faith
- A woman who is not flirtatious with other men
- Someone who can laugh, joke and have some fun
- Physical attraction to each other

My friend boasted on the woman he takes great interest in with, "She is as decent as the day is long." Wow. What a statement about that lady!

What non-material blessings and strengths will you bring to a union? Can you line up with these expectations? Check yourself.

20
Flip It

I have felt for years that the church has the order of wedding engagement and pre-marital counseling in the wrong order. I strongly believe the church should hold courtship pre-engagement sessions before engagements occur. Many engagements, and hence divorces, could be avoided if people followed this.

If you're thinking to yourself, "But, I don't want to avoid engagement with the one I want," trust me—you definitely don't want to experience what it feels like to call one off.

Pre-engagement is the time to make triply sure you are going to ask the right person to marry you or say yes to the right person. It is the time to learn as much as possible about each other's thoughts, expectations, goals, values and feelings. Once a couple is engaged, it is extremely difficult to look at the relationship objectively without rose colored glasses. The grand excitement has already been stirred as the news of the engagement has gone out. Talks, dreams and visions are cast forward. Wedding parties are forming; dresses are being selected and bought. All the hoopla has begun. This is too late for open, wise eyes, counseling and questions. It could be extremely (and that's putting it mildly) difficult to halt and call off the marriage at that point. The dreams of a future together are too close. It could be devastating to bring that to an end. The loss, humiliation and embarrassment, not to mention money expended, could be too much for some to fathom.

This will take effort, manpower, rethinking, and reorganization on the church's part, but it would change the face of society for the better.

If your church isn't available to you for this type of help, go over some of my *500 Questions* on your own together. Seek a mentoring couple you respect to help navigate subjects you and your S.O. (significant only) may not see eye to eye on.

500 Questions Anyone?

Five hundred questions anyone? 20 Questions was a game from the 1940's held live on weekly radio. A group of questioners asked questions to one answer person. The answerer could only answer with "yes," "no" or "maybe." The questioners needed to use *deductive reasoning* and *creativity* to arrive at the correct answer. Deductive reasoning and the Holy Spirit are certainly needed in the courting phase of relationships to arrive at the correct perceptions and matchings to the other person. However, 20 questions don't cover anything in this arena, so I bumped it up a bit, to 500. The total 500 will be in my next book.

Couples wanting their marriage partner confirmed should ask questions and have open discussions about marriage. Make some dates where there is good opportunity for real conversation. This Q & A time may is an ideal "courting" activity—a purposeful, deliberate and mature way of deciphering if you are meant for each other by the guidance of the Holy Spirit.

What do you think? Doesn't this make more process sense? I think couples should keep the horse before the cart...or the "relationship fit" before the ring. Save the ring and excitement of an engagement until it's really time.

Here are few samples from *500 Questions*.

- What does "being there" for your spouse mean to you?
- If you felt you and your spouse had grown apart, what would you do?
- Throughout the marriage, would you both agree to your electronic communications being public between you? Would you agree to share passwords with one another?
- What do you see married life being like in 5, 10 or 20 years?
- What are some traditions you anticipate keeping or starting after marriage?

Study each other's verbal communication skills. See the strengths and weaknesses as individuals and as a couple. If rough spots are revealed regarding communication skills or otherwise, work to be as healthy as possible—spiritually, emotionally and circumstantially before marriage. The more you settle on prior to marriage, the better. Amos 3:3 says "Can two walk together, except they be agreed?"

Pray, pray, and pray more while you find out answers before engagement. Ask God to reveal what needs to be known. Observe whether your significant one's actions match their answers over time. Ask in-depth questions and listen with empathy and without judgment for the answers. Deceive no one—yourself included.

"The first rule of love is to listen." This means I don't just hear you...I HEAR you with all my ears, eyes and an open heart. Of all places, I bought a plaque with that saying from the dollar store...and it still works! The message and the plaque! Listen sharply; don't speak sharply.

It's okay to occasionally disagree on a topic you may not see eye to eye on. But does your intended respect your answers? There is great power in "For where two or three are gathered in my name, there I am in the midst of them" (Matt 18:20 KJV). That is the place where a couple can really make things happen—in Christ. Ultimately, God will bring you an answer that is better than what isn't working for you now. "A home filled with strife and division destroys itself" (Mark 3:25 TLB).

As you truly listen to your partner and move through a relationship consider this: men work with the left side of their brain; women work with the right side. In In *Tale of Two Brains,* Mark Gungor delivers the message that there is a physical difference between the thought processes of men and women. Men compartmentalize all their different thoughts inside topical mental boxes. Each topic has a box of its own (work, kids, church, golf, girl). They can only think about one topic at a time. They open up only one box at a time to think about. And…they have a "NOTHING BOX!" Yes, men can actually think about nothing! I can't comprehend that as a woman. I only wish I could do that—have a "nothing box!"

Women's minds are like spaghetti wire or the World Wide Web—every thought is connected to every other thought. It's all important all at the same time. We are always thinking about something, sometimes in the style of frenzy. So sometimes, we can overload the males in our lives bringing too much up at once. We need to manage the delivery of information better for them.

Even if you seem to match up well according to the interrogations…eh-hem…or questions rather, it is still wise to take your time. Spend a reasonable amount of time in either the courtship (preferably) or in the engagement. You need time for each other's qualities—good and bad—or showstoppers to come out. You must match up on paper, in hearts and by the Holy Spirit! Do not ignore any checks or red flags in your spirit. Ignore…is that short for Ignorant in this realm?

You may wish to find a mentoring and accountability couple (a wise couple you respect that can help guide you through your singleness and dating/courting/getting to know someone). It's great to watch a godly couple doing marriage well and learn. You could meet with them before and after someone special comes in your life. And when you do meet someone special, both couples could then meet for some fun dates and some serious times of helping you explore the direction of your relationship. Your honest discussions with them may help you avoid pitfalls and spot things you cannot. The couple may help keep you on track to where you actually want to go.

While you are courting, legally the woman does not biblically have to submit to the man yet, but you should practice. The woman needs to ask herself, "Is this a man I *could* follow and be content?" Does he make sound decisions? Do you both generally come to the same conclusions? Or do you shake your head frequently and surprisingly wondering how he came to his decision? Does he ask your opinion? Do you feel comfortable giving it? Does he respect it? A wise man will always seek, listen carefully and consider the woman's views. Can you actually picture this man leading you through life? Can you serve each other in love? It he ready to take the role of the husband, and continue to grow in that role?

The man needs to see that the woman is capable and willing to be submissive to his leading. Does she have an attitude about doing so? He should ask himself, "Does life with her get difficult when we end up taking the road I choose?"

So...flip it! It's better to rearrange the sequence of counsel and engagement events and "flip-it" than to flip out later when the emotional investment has been made and the hurt is so great.

21
Stepping

Whether you are a single parent or a single without children planning to date/court, you should know something about relationships when children are involved. Read books on blended families before you step into a relationship with children and mess it or them up.

I've heard of a church that teaches a step-parenting class right along with their divorce recovery class. They understand that a high percentage will remarry and encounter these situations. That's pretty smart. Even if you don't end up using the information, you can share it with someone else one day. God doesn't give us everything just for our benefit.

First things first: It is not wise to involve your date's children, or have them involve yours, early in the relationship. If you are established as a couple, however, the new person should come in as a friend to the child(ren), not as an authoritarian. They should not try to fill the role of a biological parent. Once married, the step-parent should fill the role of a spiritual mentor to the child(ren). Don't push yourself on them, just let your light be seen and speak when God tells you to speak. Be a godly example and be available to them.

If the other biological parent is in good relationship with the child, the new person should not expect to have the same level of bonding with the child. Do not think less of your relationship though. It does not mean the child does not like you or care about you. Don't try to go against the natural grain of their devotion to their biological parent.

Don't try to compare relationships; that's apples and oranges. You have the beautiful role of being a blessing "supplement."

Let the biological parent do the disciplining. Yes, it is still all on you, biological mom or dad. This will not go away. I was so disappointed to learn this, because I was looking for relief and envisioned it all working like a first-time marriage. But the role of the step-parent is to support the biological parent from behind the scenes with prayer, encouragement, other types of help, ideas and love. This will be the blessing to the biological parent and to the child(ren).

Just like an "original" married couple, you must discuss parenting/step-parenting issues behind closed doors away from the child. When the step-parent has concerns or ideas, they should share them privately with their mate, but the final decision should be the biological parent's. If it seems in dating you do not generally share or arrive at the same parenting techniques, then this may not be the marriage partner for you.

Remember this truth. If you do not have children, there will always be something about which you would think or say: "I would *never* allow my child to do that." But it is only when you have your own child that you may see the other side of things. Pray for discernment.

Neat idea: Perhaps one of you wanted their own child earlier on, but it did not happen or may not. Sponsor a child from say Compassion International. Perhaps chose a child whose birth date is your wedding date or *nine months after the wedding date*. (Get it??) You can still make beauty happen. Be a blessing to that child with letters, photos, cards, gifts and prayer.

22
Got Issues?

There are two levels of devotion. Dating devotion must be limited or you may marry the wrong person. Sometimes you have to leave the cart behind. One may feel so devoted (which could actually be co-dependency) that they fail to see the incompatibility in or unhealthiness of the relationship.

Marital devotion, on the other hand, calls for all-out, Gorilla Glue™ devotion. What a flip switching that must take place after vows have been taken.

Take a good look. Are there any elements of your relationship that are dysfunctional? The root word "dys" means painful, abnormal, difficult, labored. Put that together with "functional"—dysfunctional—painful functioning. Are there lingering, unhealthy, prolonged, negative undertones in the relationship? Bring them up gently from a tree of life perspective (in a way that gives life so that the other can bear fruit from it, not get "torn down"). Try to work elements out before marriage.

When there is trouble in paradise, take into account these things: your birth order, upbringing, nationality, prior hurts, unmet needs or fears from your childhood or past relationships. What experiences or lack did you or they encounter? What causes you or them to be a certain way?

It is amazing just how much we are built by our past– good and bad. We are a derivative of our past experiences until we choose to move beyond the negative ones. They call this "back-story" in novel or film writing. What happened previously before the story that affects the main plot? Don't be critical, just do an honest assessment together.

Our baggage, like our sin, can come from either "the world" (the sins of others that affect us), "the flesh" (mistakes we have made), or "the devil" (situations strategically brought on by the enemy of our souls). We may have to drop and unpack that baggage.

Let's consider the great Old Testament Bible stories. Why did Joseph's brothers throw him into a pit? Why did they sell him into slavery? How did Joseph feel about this? How did he react? What did he have to go through or do to get the victory over all of it? How did he behave and live life out victoriously afterward? We need to study our lives and the lives of others as well. Search with respect instead of inspecting for fault. If you are trying to have a relationship, but there are road blocks, try to really understand where each of you is with regard to how the past has shaped you. How does it cause you to behave and think of each other and treat each other now? We have to unpack what happened to a person—and then leave the baggage behind.

Jesus can heal our hearts. He will give us the strength to work out the practical changes we need to make. We, with the help of the Holy Spirit, need to acknowledge former thoughts, motives and actions, then purposely and intentionally adapt to new healthy ways and habits. Do it on purpose.

Consider some of the *500 Questions* below regarding former events, disappointments, tragedies or losses or even positive things. God can show you all these things.

Unpacking the bags:
- − What happened to you?
- − How did you think of the occurrence then?
- − What sticks in your memory the most about the occurrence?
- − What did you continue to carry with you from the occurrence?
- − How do you feel now?
    - ▪ About the former situation?
    - ▪ About the situations you are in now?
- − Why do you do what you do?
- − What do you hope to get out of doing what you do?
- − What do you actually get out of doing what you do?
- − How many good things/situations/opportunities have you turned down or prevented because of your past experience(s)?
- − What further difficulties have the past issues brought into your life?

Rachel Scott was the first student killed in the tragic Columbine High School shooting of 1999. Rachel has left behind a major legacy to the nation through her interactions with others and her diaries. She was known for her kindness and compassion to classmates and strangers. She befriended bullied, quiet and downtrodden students. She had a way of getting students who sheltered themselves and who were even contemplating suicide to open up to friendship. Rachel's theory was to be a "look-througher" into someone's life and emotions, not a "look-atter," only viewing them from the outside at face value. And that is what we need to do in our relationships too—be a "look-througher," not a "look-atter." *Rachel's Challenge* is a presentation challenging students, corporations and groups to start chain acts of kindness. *Rachel's Challenge* has affected many lives of all ages and walks.

Marriage experts Drs. Les and Leslie Parrott of the Center for Relationship Development present that 90% of all marriage troubles could be solved by each spouse truly having empathy toward the other. Problems in dating/courting relationships can be solved by the same tool of empathy. We should want to be a blessing to the person and improve upon as many aspects as possible before marriage. Both parties should step back and put down their own philosophies, thoughts and feelings, then listen openly without judgment to where the other is coming from. See a situation through the other's eyes, their history, background and point of reference. We need to accurately see things from the other's perspective. Dr. Leslie Parrott said in a Focus on the Family radio interview on 1/31/09, "Awareness is really curative." Their book *Saving Your Marriage Before It Starts* teaches how to operate in empathy by asking:

1) What does this situation, problem, or event look or feel like from my partner's perspective?

2) How is his or her perception different from mine?

~p. 80

Here are some of my *500 Questions* to help more in understanding the other person:
- How do they process events, conversations or information?
- How do they think?
- How do they handle emotions?
- Can there be any other way of perceiving this situation?

Drs. Les and Leslie Parrott further teach:

> [most of us] use either our head or heart, one
> more than the other, it takes a conscious-effort to
> empathize (p 80).

and:

> Loving with our heart alone is only
> sympathizing, while loving with our head alone
> is simply analyzing. Empathy, however, brings
> together both sympathetic and analytic abilities,
> both heart and heard, to fully understand our
> partners (p 80).

and:

> Empathy always involves risk, so be
> forewarned. Accurately understanding your
> partner's hurts and hopes will change you—but
> the benefits of taking that risk far outweigh the
> disadvantages (p 80).

Cindy Lee Webster says in *Effective Counseling: A Client's View* gives the following powerful example of empathy:

> the ability to feel as if you were me…a willingness
> to descend into the depths, to feel my terror, and to share
> the ugliness inside me. Empathy is the courage to be
> open to me, even at the risk of being changed yourself
> through our encounter. Empathic response demands
> courage and fortitude. You could escape the trauma of
> our encounter by imposing advice or cheerfully mindless
> reassurance upon me. But even though there must be
> times when you want to retreat, you hang in there <u>with</u>
> me, and that does more for me than any counseling
> "technique" or inspiring philosophy. If you are willing to
> endure this hell with me, then perhaps there is hope.
> (Personnel and Guidance Journal Vol. 52, No. 5, Jan
> 1974

Bear in mind that single people have set their life up in very specific, sometimes quirky ways that are particular to their individual needs, habits and idiosyncrasies. You may not agree with a particular habit/way they have of doing things. But think of how your two sets of idiosyncrasies might blend for a more effective household. Maybe one of you is a stickler about paying bills…so your bills would be paid on time! Maybe the other one is meticulous about housework…so your house would be cleaner! Two can do a better job than one. Expect to take some time to learn how to dance together.

Also, go to Christian counseling together. When only one person gets counseling, it is just to cope with the other partner, and little improvement usually occurs. It takes both to share their story, discuss and make changes when necessary. It doesn't matter how right each one thinks they are. "IAR" Disorder (I Am Right Disorder) is usually present in both individuals. You need outside eyes to see and give fresh wisdom. It may be necessary to try more than one counselor for best results. Don't use not liking a counselor as an "out" to all counseling. Commit to it.

It's likely in your situation, that neither of you are "completely right" nor "completely wrong" in your beliefs or actions. It is a blend. Do not make a statement with "never" such as "You never say you love me." Do not make a statement with "always" such as "You always arrive late." These are usually untrue statements.

Problems are like an onion. The skin comes off one layer at a time. We usually change in increments, not just in one fell swoop. In this wonderful world of reality, most situations in life take *wayyyyy* longer to resolve than we like. Many fears, mindsets, tendencies and sin have been inbred in us for years. The issues don't come on us overnight and they don't come off overnight either. Seek what else has gone on in the person's life. Some people have had large responsibilities to keep up or substantial hindrances (divorce, death(s), sickness, family issues, career changes, etc.) along the way. They may not have had the physical time available to work out their issues. It's easier to work out problems when we have time for learning, searching, seeking counsel, praying, thinking and fleshing out the changes. Maybe we or they will take the necessary time to figure out issues now though.

Typically psychology says "A string of 'successes' produces healthy development and a satisfying life. Unfavorable outcomes throw us off balance, making it harder to deal with later crises. Life becomes a 'rocky road,' and personal growth is stunted" (Coon, Mitterer, 2009).

This is basically true for believers and unbelievers, but for the believing believer, with Christ in the forefront, it is only a setback. Thank God that as Christians, we have *Him* to take us through the changes. The Bible refers to us as sheep sometimes, because we tend to be foolish (that's a nicer word than dumb) at times. Sheep are not so smart. In this world of sin, speed and chaos, it can be difficult to hear the Lord. Praise God for when we get the full healing through work and purification! How utterly rewarding and beautiful it is! You can participate, with your intended, in this wondrous process.

> They overcame him by the blood of the Lamb and by the word of their testimony.
> ~Revelations 12:11

Apply the blood and power to your situation.

Let us not become weary in doing good, for at the
proper time we will reap a harvest if we do not give up.
~Galatians 6:9

Pray for, look for and expect "A-ha" moments. "A-ha"
moments are when the light bulb will come on and you get
an understanding about something.

If any of you lacks wisdom, he should ask God, who
gives generously to all.
~James 1:5

One of my favorite verses is "'Come now, let us reason
together,' says the LORD" (Isaiah 1:8). Let's hash this out
and work it through. And Jeremiah 29:7 says "*work* for
peace." It won't always be easy and most problems take
longer to work out than we want to take time for. They key
is willingness to make changes.

God gives grace to everyone. "Through the Lord's
mercies we are not consumed, Because His compassions
fail not. They are new every morning" (Lam 3:22, 23
NKJV). He gives us "each day our *daily* bread" (Luke
11:3). This has begun to sound cliché, but He truly is the
God of again and again and again chances. Have you ever
had an issue? Did God ever say you were stuck in that issue
without hope for change? How long was God patient with
you? How long were others patient with you?

The Lord has shown me that patient people seem to be
slower in making changes in themselves also. Because they
are patient with others' shortcomings, it seems they do not
quickly realize a priority need from another to change or
spiff up certain areas of their life. What you are, you also
need given back. For instance, I'm sensitive, caring and a
good listener. But because of that, I also need someone to
treat me with the same softness as I can be easily hurt. So

there you go again, your best trait can also be your weakest trait, unless one purposefully shores up the imbalance with Christ. Also take for instance your own love language; we tend to give out what we ourselves want and need. But your particular love language or other elements are not necessarily what the other person needs to be fulfilled. We need to step outside of ourselves, serve and fill them in their way. Empathy will enable us to understand them and accomplish this.

The key is BALANCE. It you are unhappy, try to work it out under the direction of the Spirit. Don't look for perfection. This is a fallen world. If you leave the relationship too soon, you may miss your blessing.

Do a word study on "grace" and "mercy." You can give grace and mercy to your significant other even as you set the proper *Boundaries*—another good book by Drs. Cloud and Townsend. God loves us perfectly even in our imperfection. He gives us grace, not what we deserve.

The word "grace" in Hebrew is "hen," which means "favor, mercy, kindness, graciousness." It is derived from the word "hanan," which means "to favor, to grant mercy." When I think of the word grace, I think of a warm spring. I think of someone extending grace to me as a spring flows out. I think of a warm running over me. Warm, clear waters flowing, refreshing me when they could have drowned me. A pure form of love or water washing over me, touching my skin instead of consuming me. Drinkable, gentle waters of love strengthening me and my relationship with them.

Don't you want to be a warm spring to someone? Grace. Wouldn't you love a refreshing warm spring to come over your mistakes after you messed up? Grace.

And what does the Lord require of you? To act justly and to love mercy and to walk humbly with your God.

~*Micah 6:8*

I love mercy…getting it…and therefore I have to love giving it in return…mercy. Judgment without mercy will be shown to anyone who has not been merciful. Mercy triumphs over judgment!" (James 2:13) "Blessed are the merciful, for they will be shown mercy" (Matthew 5:7).

How long do you wait for change in someone? The book *Safe People* says:

> Only you and God know. But it is usually longer than we think. It is past the point of pain, past the point of revenge, past the point of despair, as he gives us the supernatural ability to love and to keep seeking an answer. That is what he did for us and that is what he calls us to do (p. 196).

What is the person's overall character? On a whole, are they striving to be more Christ-like? Have you seen them come through in other areas of their life? Choose someone with an 80/20 situation. 80% of them is stable and whole. Those are pretty good numbers. They likely have strong character and will apply themselves to the other 20%.

Try not to take your significant only's requests for change or adaptation for granted. Try your absolute best not to wait too long to make improvements. For Christians as well, it often takes a drastic loss or event before they can see to make changes themselves. You would think this would be different for Christians, and it really should be if we are seeking the Lord like we ought, but…unfortunately…

Most people on the unhappy end of issues have a "give out point." It seems not everyone will persevere to the nth degree in a dating/courting relationship (even in marriages now days). According to Dr. James Dobson, a person may become strong in their desires to leave. They may stay in the relationship for a bit yet, but in a lesser involved way. Eventually, after a period of time and trying, they will make a decision to walk over that good-bye bridge. They will not change their mind or return, otherwise known as "the point of no return." Unresolved conflict can kill a relationship. Time is of the essence. Seek to hear the Lord and respond with more urgency to your intended's requests for change. It is crucial. Seek answers to the problems sooner and initiate consistency with a strong conscious effort in solving them. Obtain help from your counselor, mentor or mentoring couple to encourage you in this and hold your feet to the fire for change. The most regretful thing is to hear "too little, too late." But if this has happened to you, know this…most people don't make a significant change until there has been a great loss, even, sadly, Christians. You are not alone. No one is perfect. "Shall we go on sinning so that grace may increase? By no means!" (Romans 6:1). So do right the first time, or as much as you can.

Grace be unto you. Forgive yourself and go forward with the Lord. He loves you with an everlasting love.

> I will repay you for the years the locusts have eaten—the great locust and the young locust.
>
> ~*Joel 2:25*

Gordon Pennington (2009) says, "Know this; you marry your healer. They will be your forgiver when you falter. Do not marry someone who does not forgive or cannot forget your past." Proverbs 17:9 teaches "Love forgets mistakes; nagging about them parts the best of friends." (TLB) and 1 Peter 4:8 admonishes us to "Above all, love each other deeply, because love covers a multitude of sins."

The best instruction I have ever read regarding change in people is found in *Boundaries in Dating*. My favorites Drs. Cloud and Townsend wrote practical, easy to understand, clear advice on probably an overly common desire of humans…for people to change. Their "Kiss False Hope Good-bye" chapter should inspire many of what to do and look for when measuring change.

What does change in a person look like? How can you tell if real change is in process? I would not do their instruction justice if I was to adapt its size to this book. You simply must obtain *Boundaries in Dating* for your library.

Cloud and Townsend relay the difference between false hope and real hope (which is a virtue). In following their course for change, you will see your hope come to pass or know that you followed a well thought-out process so that you will not doubt decisions afterward. I highly recommend reading the entire in-depth chapter with excellent examples.

Boundaries in Dating "Take Away Tips:"
- Sometimes you need to realize that you are holding on to incompatible wishes. You want something to be true that is not reality, and there is no evidence that it is going to be.
- Good hope is rooted in reality.
- The best predictor of the future, without some intervening variable such as growth, is the past.

- Ask yourself, "What reason has he or she given me to hope that things are going to be different? Is that reason sustainable?"
- Are you seeing evidence of true change and growth? Is there more ownership, a growth path, hunger for change, involvement in some system of change, repentance, or other fruits of a change of direction? Is there self-motivation for change, or is it all coming from you?
- Are you doing something different in the relationship that could bring about change? Or are you continuing to do the same things expecting different results? If you have not tried something different, there may be some hope if you change.
- Have you changed whatever dysfunction you have been bringing to the friendship?
- Have you followed God's path of being the kind of influence that helps people change? Or are you just wishing and nagging?
- Are you hoping for someone to go deeper who is not going to? Or are you hoping for a noncommitter to commit?
- Is there some reality about a relationship that you need to truly face?
- The best hope is to be involved in God's growth process yourself and pursue good character qualities. The more you are a person of the light, the more you will be able to recognize people who are worth hoping for.
- Ground yourself in values and character. Those are things that do not disappoint.

~pp. 201-202

If a situation is going to change at all, "God's kindness leads you toward repentance" (Romans 2:4). Mercy and grace with boundaries will encourage one to change above harshness, nagging, arguing or begging.

Could you be pleased with short-term improvement items and some items moved to a slow- growth pattern list? No? Don't marry if you *must* have certain things changed in order to be happy…or if your intended is unrepentantly unfaithful to the commitment you have made to each other. No shirt? No shoes? No wedding service.

Watch and Pray
Cover your heart when any red flags are noticed or bombs drop while dating. The neglectful continuance of staying in a relationship with awareness of unworked upon red flags (because of bliss or comfort you feel with the person in your life) would be similar to driving all the way to Wally World for 14 hours only to find out the park is CLOSED, or the relationship is CLOSED or should be CLOSED to marriage. This happened all because you ignored the thoughts to call the park and check the hours of operation. You neglected to take into full account exactly what you were doing in the relationship. You ignored the Holy Spirit. What a waste of time, energy, emotions and hopes. What a huge disappointment and frustration even to others beyond yourself. We are to be good stewards of our efforts, resources, finances, time and bodies. Time is gone, and the people involved ended up getting a different kind of roller coaster ride.

But I Want You
There is more to love
Than wanting it.
~*Lois Wyse*

If red flags or bombs go unchecked before marriage, more time, energy and frustration will be spent trying to come into agreement than perhaps enjoying the married life afterward. You will have less time and energy available for the things of God. The right mate can make life more enjoyable or the wrong one, much more challenging. Which do you prefer?

Nutritional experts say regarding food choices we make: There are good, better and best choices available. The same is true in our spiritual, emotional and relational lives. There are good, better and best choices of how we conduct ourselves and carry things out. Some choices will bring increase, others will bring decrease. Which do you want? Increase or decrease?

Your flesh can desire a relationship or a person so strongly, you may think it's God's will. Your flesh can desire sinful actions or things, or even a good Christian who is not for you. It may not mean something is wrong with either of you, but God's plan may just be different and better for you both. "Put no confidence in the flesh" (Philippians 3:3).

"And the peace of God, which transcends all understanding, will guard your hearts and your minds in Christ Jesus" (Philippians 4:7). Pay attention to when God may put a check in your spirit not to go forward with someone. Use God's peace or lack of peace to guide you. It says that it is the *peace* that will be our protecting nudge. The working of God's peace reminds me of the working of God's glory (in a cloud) when Moses and the Israelites were moving the Ark of the Covenant on their journey toward the promise land, Canaan. "In all the travels of the Israelites, whenever the cloud lifted from above the tabernacle, they would set out" (Exodus 40:36). When the peace of the Lord leaves you and you have a check in your spirit that something isn't just quite right, move on—keep on toward the real promise land God has for you."But if the cloud did not lift, they did not set out—until the day it lifted" (Exodus 40:37). When the peace of the Lord is with you, the glory of the Lord is upon the relationship. Continue in that relationship. Maybe this is your Promised Land. We use God's peace and direction to discern. Follow His peace.

I was surprised. As I read this manuscript *again* going over it with a fine-toothed comb, errors and places for improvement jumped off the paper at me. Why did I not see these imperfections before? I had read it *several* times already. And it occurred to me, this is how we don't see answers to our problems. We can look at a problem various times with complaint or feelings of hopelessness. Then one day, "Bam!" You will see a new answer before you. (I am not Emeril.) God can always bring fresh revelation.

There was a woman engaged to a man. She had concerns about what would happen to her financial provision when her future husband would pass one day. Due to unfair events and hurts that took place in the woman's younger years, this was important to her. This was not the only situation going on in the relationship and unfortunately the engaged couple did separate. Sometime after they broke up though, an insurance agent explained that life insurance would have provided her the financial security she also longed for had they stayed together. Most always, I believe there are answers to the nitty-gritty of life. It sometimes takes a while to find them.

23
Ending a Relationship

I pray that you read this chapter with a wide open heart to know that God can and will carry you through anything. If you're life is committed to Him, He will make your endings into beginnings—good beginnings. I am living proof.

<u>Top 10 Reasons Not To Get Married</u>
(Dr. Randy Carlson)
Read this with care, as it could encourage you to either make the right decisions, or positively build on some you have already made! Please do not marry if:

1) You are unwilling to put the needs of another person above your own.
2) You are easily offended, carry grudges and are unwilling to forgive.
3) You are an abusive person (mentally, emotionally and physically).
4) You are unwilling to commit.
5) You have an unresolved addiction problem.
6) Your career is the most important thing in your life.
7) You do not share the same beliefs, values, life priorities or vision.
8) You are unwilling to be an active partner sexually with your spouse.
9) You are unwilling to agree on an approach for handling finances, children and life decisions.
10) You expect your spouse to change after you get married.

Remember, successful marriages are not of perfection, rather of two people willing to grow closer to Christ and each other. Don't be discouraged if you struggle with any of the above reasons, but before you get married, do yourself and your future spouse a favor by first committing to grow stronger in each area.

~Dr. Randy Carlson, © 2009 Family Life
Communications

There is another reason not to marry: it is when someone has an effect on your temperament. Do you go from being relaxed to strained or uneasy when you're around them? Honestly, do you? That's a tough one to admit 'cause you know it means perhaps you shouldn't be in that relationship. Is your creativity stunted or squelched with them? Do you move from joy into being reserved? Perhaps you are not the ones to like, enjoy and continue to bring out the best in each other. My friend says, "It's better to want what I don't have, than to end up with what I can't handle."

Don't be one of the sad stories heard where one or both individuals *knew* it was not right to marry. If you are just plain *not happy*, don't do it! And if you are happy, but are experiencing any of these ten or more reasons here, reconsider!

Different Roads

Hope deferred makes the heart sick

~Prov. 13:12

There's a point when if you don't like things or love someone by now, you've got to let the other go. I believe neither person is happy at that point. One isn't content with the relationship; the other wants to be truly loved and move forward with it. If you don't like or love them in spite of the hindrances, the love probably won't be coming any later either, though I have seen exceptions. Real love approved by God can't help but go forward. Real love given permission to flow by God cannot stand to be without the other person. Real love is ready to be closer to them.

If you think you would love someone *if* their hair was the right color, *if* they weighted less or *if* they made more money...no. The truth is that you wouldn't; you just wouldn't. This has happened to me. I thought I would love someone *if...and* then that thing, that "if" started to happen and they still were not the right one for me. So you are either going to love them in their own right now state or you don't. You're either going to love them or they are not the right one for you. No "if" business.

Sometimes, we argue with our internal selves about parting. We may know the relationship isn't exactly what we want, or good for us, or God for us, but we don't want to feel rejected or lonely without them either. So we hang on to the possibility of the relationship or put the break up off. All the while, this is preventing you from moving on in God's plan for you.

Pastor Christopher W. Brooks of Evangel Ministries asks in his message *Lord Prune Me*, "What is there that I have ordained and what is there that you have ordained? Because there are certain things that God has not ordained."

He goes on to further teach, "And you can't make something that's not God, God. You can't make something that God never ordained, ordained."

He stresses, "But those of you who are single, you have to evaluate: 'Am I trying to take something that's square and fit it into a round hole? If God did not ordain it, why am I trying to paint it up and make it pretty and make it cute and make it fit? Why am I trying to put a suit and tie on it and trying to show it off at church as if it's really God? It's not God and if it's not God, run away!'"

You gotta' go through to get to. By avoiding the pain of final parting, you may actually be prolonging God's real blessing for you. It's hard, but not impossible to do the courageous thing...the tough thing.

> I can do all things through Christ who strengthens me.
> ~Phil. 4:13 KJV

It is not easy, but you must go *through* the mountain or *over* it. There simply and honestly is no other way. It can be excruciating, but not more than Jesus bore for us in order to be the comforter for us in times like these. There was no other way to save us from our sin. He simply HAD to go to the cross for us. He didn't want to:

> Father, if you are willing, take this cup from me; yet not my will, but yours be done.' An angel from heaven appeared to him and strengthened him. And being in anguish, he prayed more earnestly, and his sweat was like drops of blood falling to the ground.
> ~Luke 22:42-44

It is okay to break up with someone and to do it crying as it tears at your insides. Sometimes we have to do things afraid and sometimes we have to do things *while* crying. But just like the angels did for Jesus, He and His angels will come along and strengthen you.

In a time of love and longing, you cannot always bear to see, admit or accept that the relationship is not God's will. That thought may be merely unfathomable at that time. But in time...in time...and it may be a few years time…you will be able to make a better assessment of the relationship. Maybe it never was God's will or neither person would have left, perhaps even more than once. Sometimes when I write on the computer, the sentences and paragraphs get confusing; it doesn't feel like there is a good flow. I scroll up, I scroll down to see where to insert a new piece of info, but it's confusing. Sometimes I just have to print out the whole chapter and look at it on paper from up above. Then I can see better what rearranging or editing is really needed. God has the up-above planning and protection skill.

God will take our catastrophe and create a trophy out of it. He will extract the best from it and use it for His purposes. I love Barbara Johnson who says,

> "The best thing about this very minute is your ability
> to recognize the possibilities in it. Any fool can count
> the seeds in an apple. But only God can count the apples
> in a seed. There is something in every problem that
> holds potential for something better.

> ~Taken from *Boomerang Joy* by Barbara Johnson.
> Copyright © 1998 by Barbara Johnson. Used by
> permission of Zondervan. www.zondervan.com, (p. 71)

He will polish each willing one up to press on in the race. He will bind up, restore and beautify. Receive this today, oh won't you.

By all means end the relationship compassionately and friendly. Apologize for whatever your contributions were to the relationship no matter how little or how much a portion. This is your just assignment. Respect and honor your brother or sister in the Lord. When you apologize, don't make it a general blanket apology. Make it specific. State the exact things you were wrong in and apologize for them.

This is much more meaningful and helps each of you in the healing and growth process.

Apologizing is a two-step process. Step 1: The apology on specific offenses. Step 2: Literally saying "May I have your forgiveness?" If you skip Step 2, your partner may doubt your sincerity and humility. This two-step process says you really care. It is the pill, the medicine, the shot, the massage, the fuller offer to healing. You are the only one who can make forgiveness easier and open the door for God to come in and do the rest.

Give the other person proper, respectful and kind closure to the relationship. Answer questions they may ask of you honestly with compassion. This may help them in their next relationship. You got involved with the person; it is your full responsibility to see it through properly. Clean up the kitchen after you've cooked in it. You want to build a place where friendliness and harmony can exist after healing.

Dr. Jim Talley says, "In five years from now when I look back on what I've done, can I really stand there with three things: A pure heart, a clean conscience and clean hands before God?" (*Divorce Care*, Session 12.)

Gentlemen, generally if it is a tough breakup, women may need more communication and time to get closure from a broken relationship. *Believe me*, they much prefer an instantaneous healing. Generally, God did make us more emotional which may be why generally we take longer to detach or let go when things don't work out. Men make matters worse when they leave wreckage behind without communicating things through. You can be through with the relationship, but there may be some delicate cleanup and sweep-up left to do. Like a death of a loved one, you may have to go through their home and clean it out in order to move on.

Men and women, please do your best to go the extra mile and be sensitive to this for the other person. Please stretch yourself kindly to get through all of it—after all, she or he is a dynamic child of God whether you are to be together or not. Then after a certain time, which is probably longer than one of you may think necessary, you may need to sever ties and communication totally. No contact.

> If it is possible, as far as it depends on you, live at peace with everyone.
>
> ~*Rom. 12:18*

Pastor T. D. Jakes in his YouTube message called *Nurturing Pain* teaches that men can let go much easier than women. They just don't need as much grieving time. Big bullet point here: **"Men cry hard, but they don't cry for long."** Over Jake's ministry years, he's rarely seen a man coming for prayer broken-hearted over a former love he just can't let go of that he knows is still supposed to be with him. It's always the women. Generally, women don't detach as quickly.

Here is why. Women were created to give life and are the nurturers of it. Nurturing is a beautiful trait toward babies and new life, but it is a negative trait when we nurture pain deep within. You can even have a **soul tie to grief itself.** This could be debilitating over years if you continue in it. Don't keep the pain alive.

Men disconnect and release relationships radically. They're just not built the same way. Consider the history of David and Bathsheba (2 Samuel 11 and 12). A son was born out of their adultery. Then David had Uriah,

Bathsheba's husband, killed. David was made aware of his sin. God said their son would die by him. David fasted and lied on the ground at this word in hopes that the Lord would have mercy and change His mind allowing the son to live. David's servants were very worried about him, so much so that they were afraid what he would do learning of the boy's death. When David heard their son died, he got up from the ground, washed his face, anointed himself, changed clothes, went to the house of the Lord to worship, came home and ate. He understood there was nothing more he could do after that point; the son would not come back to life. He realized the finality quickly and moved on. So he grieved hard, but not for long.

Bathsheba on the other hand was still grieving, understandably so. David went to comfort her as she was nurturing her pain. Are you holding onto something that you need to let go? Holding onto the pain does not make the person come back to you and love you. David realized this. Holding on and on and on to pain and what you thought should have happened in your relationship is similar to unforgiveness. It hurts the pain hanger-onner or the unforgiving one far more than the other person who has moved on. Be good to yourself; try to give it up by the power of the Holy Spirit.

When a relationship ends, it's not always possible to remain platonic friends. Depending on how you met or where you know your loved one from, you may continue seeing them in work, social or church settings. This may be thorny or you may be able to deal with it. Everyone is different. If it was a long-term relationship, hard for either of you to get over and it takes its toll on your emotions, you may need to find other settings for yourself. This is not uncommon. There should be a respect of each others' whereabouts or stomping grounds. Defer to each other for the season. Consider their needs above your own. Assist in each other's healing in that way. They are your brother or sister in the Lord.

> ...rather, serve one another in love...Love your neighbor as yourself.
>
> ~*Gal 5:13-14*

If it is a difficult break up for one or both of you to get over, you may need to avoid *any* further contact in any form (phone, email, texting, letter, seeing them one-on-one or in groups). Take this very seriously. One may not heal or move on with continued contact. Contact or friendship may also tempt either or both of you to reunite. My very wise friend who has watched singles for years taught me that first time breakups from serious relationships rarely take. That missing of the person may drain you even though reuniting may not be in the long-term best interest of the couple. You can't live just for today. Carry yourself with dignity.

Psychologist Dr. Henry Cloud (2006) said the same neurological pathways that develop feelings toward someone are the same pathways that experience sadness or grief. Staying in contact with one you still love just simply causes too much confusion of the mind and heart for one or both people. Your mind is attempting a break away, but the pathways are simultaneously experiencing warm, desiring feelings and sadness. Your methods are simply contradictory and are fighting each other, causing chaos and unrest inside of you which one cannot heal or move forward with. It would be like an alcoholic trying to stop drinking even as they keep going to the bar! Why put yourselves through that? Don't go into the bar three months from now either! DO NOT DO THE BACK AND FORTH THING! (That is, break up, get back together, and do it all over again...and again...and again.) This is extremely destructive to people's emotions. A soul won't know up from down the more it is done. "He is a double-minded man, unstable in all he does" (James 1:8). This is all the more reason to follow some good relationship principles to avoid becoming entangled with someone. I was involved in this scenario myself and have seen and heard Christian couples in this pattern for up to twelve years. It is excruciating to be in that kind of relationship and even to watch from the outside. Love me or leave me, but please don't deplete me.

So you say that you're involved in a godly relationship. Is it really? You may both be saved, serving the Lord, attending church, attending fellowships, are not involved in sexual immorality, but if you are hurting each other back and forth, then how is this godly? Something isn't right.

Don't fall back into the same traps and patterns that kept bringing you both back together every time. I know how it goes. You run into each other somewhere, have a little conversation and that wonderful spark and chemistry (relational and physical) surfaces. A few days later or so someone sends an email or extends a phone call. And off we go again onto the circular track. I've done it and have seen others go through it. This is how all that hullabaloo takes place. Are you feeding a wishy washy relationship? Are you still calling them? Do you need to pull back from a dead end situation? You will need to make a deliberate turn.

Henrylito D. Tacio quotes E. Merrill Root:

So far as I am concerned, I would never choose a woman unless I were sure she had also chosen me. I could not love a woman unless I felt in the depths of my being that she also loved me; I would wish her to seek me even as I sought her; were she not made to have me I would be tepid to have her.

~Retrieved 9/13/08 from the website
http://htacio.wordpress.com/2008/12/01/kelvin-lee-
on-your-wedding-day/)

It is the heart that takes us into victory. It is the giving of our heart to Christ that takes us into the victory of salvation. It is a woman capturing the whole heart of a man that leads him into the next level of commitment. It is our heart of devotion that causes one to work so many daunting hours on a labor of love. If a man or woman's heart is not fully invested into the other, the relationship is not a good or fair thing to either of them and should be called off unless God changes someone's heart.

You will never see the commitment you want, need or deserve from the other person unless they have given their whole heart to you. The Bible speaks repeatedly about serving the Lord and loving Him wholeheartedly. How can we do anything properly with less given?

After a brief relationship ended I once felt (okay, various times) displeased that the thing people seem to notice about me is a "sweet spirit."That is great and I am happy about that, but if I was different, maybe so-and-so would love and want to marry me. My heart cried to the Lord, "Lord, why did you make me like this? Why couldn't you have made me with a really high I.Q. or to be a strong, career money-making woman?" I was comparing myself to others. That afternoon after my tears, a friend texted me. It read, "God made you the way He did so that He could enjoy you." I knew that text was really sent from my heavenly Father. At that, I fell back into tears again, but with the comfort and contentment of my loving husband, Jehovah.

> For your Maker is your husband—the Lord Almighty is His name.
>
> ~*Is. 54:5*

Lay it down—the past relationship, the current hurt, the future. Nothing is more rewarding or more peaceful than pure, pure trusting in Jesus. A wise man does at once what the fool does last.

Rejection Junction, What's Your Function?

If you get that chapter title, you're telling your age! Sing it to the old Schoolhouse Rock cartoon jingle. You know the cartoon about the use of conjunctions in the English language. "Conjunction, junction…What's your function? Hookin'up words and phrases and clauses." Still love it! Every Saturday morning! But I *sure* don't like rejection! It's worse than brussels sprouts, getting up early, a root canal without novocaine and debt combined!

So what is the purpose of rejection in your life? Only God really knows, but nothing will come to you before passing through His hands; everything is Father-filtered. That has given me great comfort and allows me to further see how I am to get, give and grow from of an ended relationship.

There were days when I just could not conceive why I wasn't wanted or why the trials or differences couldn't have been resolved. There were days when I argued and was frustrated with myself; why, oh why, wouldn't my devotion or love die out? But I encouraged myself that I had the fortitude and ability to truly love another—through the ups and downs, through the smiles and the frowns, by the sweet rivers and in the storms. I can remain faithful, devoted, determined and see one's good. This is skill, a gift, a healthy ability and in the right relationship will be a blessing and vital glue. It is an ability to be able to say to another before God "I love you still." In the words of the late Adrian Rogers, "If you leave me, I'm going with you." To be able to say to my love, "If I met you today, I'd still be hoping you'd ask me out for a date." "A three chord strand is not easily broken." I'm just in training to learn how to fight like heck for my marriage one day. In this process, I am learning how to build those needed boundaries for a future marriage around my heart and body now.

If you are experiencing rejection, know that it can feel worse than the physical death of your loved one. After all, in death, usually no one had a choice in the matter. In rejection, someone had a choice to stay or leave and they chose to leave. Someone gets to see the other person walk away and carry on with their life without them. Rejection can be a mauling monster.

But rejection is God's protection...God's protection, not rejection...God's ordainment, not rejection.

If you are going and working through rejection now, do not let it take root in you. I would suggest reading specifically on the subject.

These are simple truths about you my brother or sister. Verna Birkey (1977) shares them in her book, *You Are Very Special.* The below represents her Table of Contents. Think on and accept that each one of these statements is true about you from the Lord.

You are someone very special

You are deeply loved
You are fully known, yet fully accepted
You are a person in process
You are God's redeemed child
You are a person of value
You are uniquely designed
You are designed for a purpose
You are given an assignment
You are continually sustained
You are accompanied by God
You are God's responsibility
You are under God's constant care

Brother Pat O'Meara of Worship Word Ministries declared in worship:

You were rejected, but God receives you. Start adoring Christ and realize how much He adores you. Start seeing yourself as the gift God made you. Start seeing yourself as a gift to the people around you, your family, friends, church and community.

God will never leave you.

Sing and declare out loud with worship leader Jason Upton's song *Apple of His Eye*: "I am the apple of my daddy's eye. I am the apple of my Father's eye." Jason describes a guitar that says "'God loves you, but I'm his favorite.' And that's the mystery of heaven, that we're all His favorite. That's the mystery of heaven." Knowing that, beautiful child of God, melts all the inferiority away. You are the apple of your Father's eye.

Forgiveness
God is all about forgiveness. That is everything He stands for. Jesus is His biggest statement of forgiveness. He means for you to receive it, for you to give to others and He

means for you to give to yourself. We must forgive others or it will hinder our own forgiveness. That's how big of a deal forgiveness is. Unforgiveness and not letting the wrong go, is too much for you to bear.

An outstanding issue of unforgiveness can literally bring sickness and destruction upon you. Don't let Satan have that benefit!

Forgiveness of yourself can be more difficult than forgiving others. "I ruined it. How could I have been so stupid? Why couldn't I see it? I blew it. I'll never have another chance to love. I've messed mine and others' lives up. I'm such a fool. I don't deserve anything."

But just like unforgiveness toward another, holding yourself punishable for a crime injects a spiritual and physical poison through your body. Just like forgiving others does not mean you condone what they have done, it does not mean you condone or think less of what you may have faltered in either. God was not condoning the sins Christ took on for us either. Forgiveness whether extended toward another or toward yourself does not make light of or make less of what occurred. It just doesn't, and that is the truth. The absolute truth is, you do deserve to be forgiven. It is a lie from the devil to tell you otherwise. Let yourself out of the penalty box.

"Two wrongs don't make a right." An error plus unforgiveness toward another or yourself will not make "a right." Holding one in a drastic state of penalization will not bring the person wronged back. What *may* bring them back is when you step beyond that stuck state and do something about the problem you may have experienced or caused. This still may not bring them back to you, but you will have grown in two ways then—forgiveness and sanctification.

You can't move on if you have unforgiveness in your heart. Like rejection, you cannot let this take root. Left to fester, it will spoil everything you have going for you including God's intimacy and blessings, which will be hindered and blocked. Bitterness taints everything. You can tell when someone is bitter; they have this putrid aroma about them. Transfer hurt, bitterness, anger and regret onto Jesus. Come out from underneath the heavy boulder; receive your lifting by the gifting provided to you. His love will radiate the hurt away. Say, "I can't handle this Lord; it's about to destroy me. I feel taken over by these feelings." "Cast all your anxiety on him because he cares for you" (1 Peter 5:7) and know that "He who began a good work in you will carry it on to completion until the day of Christ Jesus" (Philippians 1:6). He will help work all those feelings out. Receiving or extending forgiveness is working smart not hard.

Decide to forgive now. If you wait till you feel like it, it may be a long, long overdue time or you may never do it. I realize it can be a tall order. Forgive out of faith and sheer obedience to Christ even when it goes against every strong and determined fiber in your being. You may have to pray, "Lord, make me willing to forgive. There's no way I can do it on my own." You may not feel any different right after you pray, but you will begin a process of your emotions catching up with the decision you made out of your will. Sometimes we do what is right and the feelings catch up later. Ask God to bless the ones hurt and the one(s) who caused the pain.

We are instructed to forgive regardless if we are offered an outward apology in words or actions or not. The injurer may say they are sorry to God in their moments with him or not; you may never know, but it doesn't really matter as far as our responsibility. God will deal with them directly in His own way.

Once you start the process of forgiveness, it will transform you and peel off of you in layers. The spirit of unforgiveness may come back and prick you on the shoulder if a new event transpires or triggers you to recall the original offense. Go into the next deeper layer again; forgive again.

Just like Jesus was the only one who could take the cross for us, only God has the ability to forgive and forget. Forgive and forget is an untruth out of the world. We as humans do not always have literal mental erasers.

Forgiving means you no longer hold guilt and enmity against someone. Forgiveness does not mean you have to leave yourself in the same open place of vulnerability for more hurt from the person. If someone's actions show no sign of change or repentence, you should consider a status change in the relationship. If someone keeps hitting you over the head with a 2 x 4, take the 2 x 4 out of their hands and no longer put yourself in those harmful situations. You change the situations.

Thank goodness for wood up against a head though— the wood that Jesus laid his head up against for our transgressions...forgiveness! Kind and sweet.

After you have forgiven yourself or another, give yourself a humungous hug, because you have just grown. You will then live a more healed life and be more in place for "*the* relationship" when it comes. Life will begin to thrive and you will be able to show yourself or the other person love. "But for you who revere my name, the sun of righteousness will rise with healing in its rays. And you will go out and frolic like well-fed calves" (Malachi 4:2). I never wanted anyone to call me a cow before, but I like what this verse says about you and me! Forgiveness is not about what you will give up; it's about what you will gain.

24

The Grieve, Acceptance and Healing

Let me talk to you about the pink elephant I'm about to let into the room…the gaping hole in the wall I'm about to explain to you. Let me just tell you right up front what I am about to do and why.

Lamentations. I am going to talk a lot about the pain of separation and breakups in this chapter. My editor suggested I whittle it down as it could cause some readers to close the book, you know, "Overdone; don't you think?" But I have chosen to leave it all in because it's *real*. It's how much pain some of us feel after some breakups. If I was to have streamlined this chapter--cut it down, watered it down—you who are dying on the inside may still think you are unusual and hopeless. If I don't share the depths of my former despair, how would you understand the full healing power of God and my praise?

So if this does not apply to you and you need to, bypass this chapter, skip it, or rip it out. Complete permission to do so. I'll catch up with you ahead. But just know that God may have you reading it to help someone else at another time. Now, read on.

Take the past Lord
Take the past Lord and every pondering
Take the past Lord and every pain
Take the past Lord
Faint the memories
Take the past Lord, seal the pain

Take my present Lord
All be for you
Take my present Lord and all my longings
My hopes and desires
Take my present Lord
Each new hour
Holy Spirit, calm me this day
Holy Spirit power show me the way

Nehemiah was cupbearer to King Artaxerxes of Persia. It is written: "I took the wine and gave it to the king. I had not been sad in his presence before; so the king asked me, "Why does your face look so sad when you are not ill? This can be nothing but sadness of heart" (Nehemiah 2:2).

The TLB version reads, "as I was serving the king his wine he asked me, 'Why so sad? You aren't sick are you? You look like a man with deep troubles.' (For until then I had always been cheerful when I was with him.)" (Nehemiah 2:2 TLB).

Lovely single Laura (2006) shares, "You miss them so bad your heart pains. When you are together, the pain goes away, but the issues get louder. When you separate, the issues get forgotten, but the pain is magnified." Reuniting without former issues resolved will avail happiness for a bit, but then the issues arise and spoil it. Limbo land will resurface and contemplation to separate comes all over again.

The hardest thing to do is to let someone go from your inner heart spot…to relinquish the efforts of trying…to give it up. It's like two people whose arm is extended out from their bodies toward each other while being pulled in opposite directions. Only the curls of their fingertips are still holding on to one another. The fear of letting the loved one's fingertips go is terrifying. The person could very well be gone forever if you do, and the loss is unthinkable and unspeakable. To let the last bits of those fingertips loose will create the separation and feared permanent loss so very dreaded. Oh, no one wants to open themselves up for that kind of pain when allowing those fingertips to be released, but do it my friend. Trust God.

Do you want to know why breaking up is so hard? It is because we attach with our hearts, minds and souls. It is the heart which contains our will that takes us into the levels we want to go to in a relationship. We think about the person in special ways with our mind. The soul is what holds the seat of our affections—our emotions. So you see, every facet of your being has the chance to become attached and involved with another. This is why it is so important to act wisely. This is why it can be so painful to separate from one we love.

These same three areas are what God requires us to give to Him fully—"Love the Lord your God with all your heart and with all your soul and with all your mind" (Matt. 22:37). This is what the Lord is telling us will provide a full bond with Him. Thank goodness we don't have to detach from the Lord! But these same parts of our insides and bodies can attach to people too. The full bond can be wrenching to separate.

Consider this; you had a "first love" before you were saved (B.C. first love). You may likely have another "first love" after your salvation (A.D. first love). Two believers falling in love for the first time as a new creation is more serious. You've that spiritual connection in common. It is a very special relationship. Don't be surprised that it may be more difficult to let go.

A strong, strange and surreal oddity: If and when you do see your missed one at an event, you will be leaving separately. While once you were both so involved in each other's lives, now you don't talk at a gathering. While once you came in the same car together, now their GPS has different directions on it than your GPS. While once you left a gathering together with a good-night kiss at the end, now there is a simple, courteous "Bye" said to each other and one leaves out the door alone. One is left feeling like a stranger. Hmm…Lord help someone hurting to keep accepting, adjusting and prospering through these times by your great love for them.

For a woman, a most gut-wrenching experience is when you see your former guy and he no longer has anything in his eyes for you. That sparkle and adoration are gone. That is one of the ways love shows itself outward. I caught a quote in the story *Westland by Charles Baxter (p. 249):* "the lenses enlarged those eyes, so that the love was large and naked and obvious." I love that quote, when it's happening, but when it's died out…OUCH. When times change, your former love could be kind and courteous to you, but that spark is completely extinguished. Just know you are not alone. Others have been your way and you remain the princess of the King of Kings. He is in love with you. And men, you are a prince of the King of Kings. Walk tall in his love and promises for you.

If you need to avoid seeing your past love, change and looking for new surroundings can be challenging. But look on the bright side. Think of other times when you were forced, unwillingly to do something. You would not have met some particular new and wonderful people in your life or seen more opportunity without that force to move. See what else God has for you. Ask Him for strength to make any changes necessary for your own healing (new people, new directions, etc.).

Men may not be able to relate to this, but in my healing, I even had to get rid of some of my articles of clothing to purge remembrances of my former relationship. As a feminine female, I endeavored to look pleasing to him. He was attentive to my doing so, always complimentary of how I looked. Unless I had eaten a cheesecake the night before, he could always make me feel beautiful and a woman really misses feeling that from her man. So afterward, even as I would roam through my closet, a dress or blouse would remind me of being with him. I gave 98% of those articles away. I didn't need any reminders at any point further in my life. This may sound drastic, but drastic needs call for drastic measures. I knew that others could be blessed by what I gave away. I gave up a pretty ivory jacket he had given me. I loved it. It looked really sharp on and made me feel like a million bucks whenever I wore it. I hated to part with it, but God replaced that jacket with a white one for only $20 on sale. I love you Kohl's! Let go.

I share those types of events, feelings and outlooks in hopes that you will be able to bring out what you are possibly feeling too. I hope it will help you to process things. You can acknowledge the feeling, recognize it and label it for what it is. When you label it, or put your finger on it, you can then work through and release the feeling. Though you may have to do this various times, it is freeing. You can continue to move forward in your healing process. Claim your healing. Speak it out loud. Declare it. This is YOUR healing *process*. You will not stay here. Evangelist Tim Story says, "When you're going through hell, don't stop." God is big. Big enough to heal whatever we have gone and are coming through. Notice I say "*coming through*." You will.

Purge as many items, mementos and communications as you can from the relationship. They are like little or large strongholds. The ridding of these things brings another level of release. At bare minimum, bury them in the most remote spot of your basement or at a friend's house. Then the next step is el burno or whatever.

Don't go on and on praying for the person. Prayer also keeps them close to you. You pray because it's all you have left to do and you feel the intense need to do something to reunite the relationship. But cease praying for them. It keeps the hope alive for you and keeps an attachment going to them. If they are a Christian, they have others praying for them. If not, if they are sincerely hungry enough for healing and growth, they will find their own way to grow in Christ.

A college instructor was about 35 minutes late for the very first day of class due to the heavy snowfall in Michigan. A student came in late, a few minutes after the instructor and took her seat. I can imagine the student must have been feeling a bit worried or guilty for being so late to his class. But the student had absolutely no idea what had just gone on—that the instructor himself arrived only minutes before she did!

I saw all this happen right before my very eyes and thank God for that revelation. This is like Jesus. Only He can see all. Only He knows all. We know nothing—so very limited. "Now I know in part; then I shall know fully" (1 Cor. 13:12). "As the heavens are higher than the earth, so are my ways higher than your ways and my thoughts than your thoughts" (Isaiah 55:8, 9). When he steers us away from something or someone, we must trust He knows what and who is good for us. I wonder if any classmates sitting near the late student ever broke the relieving news to her. We may not find out God's reasons or plans until we see the Lord face to face. We see life in a 1 x 1 picture frame, while God sees, knows and plans the panoramic, aerial view.

> All this also comes from the Lord Almighty,
> wonderful in counsel and magnificent in wisdom.
> ~*Is. 28:29*

Learn to Q.U.I.T.:

Q   Quiet, humble surrender to allow God to work out
      His will
U   Understand your fighting alone cannot make it
      work. Some people are not the best for
      each other
I   I really do understand what you are going through.
      I've been there, and in time you will be well.
T   Tomorrow you <u>will</u> feel better

> To let go doesn't mean to stop caring; it
>   means I can't do it for someone else.
> To let go is not to cut myself off; it's the
>   realization that I can't control another.
> To let go is not to enable; but to allow
>   learning from natural consequences.
> To let go is to admit powerlessness, which
>   means the outcome is not in my hands.
> To let go is not to try to change or blame
>   another; I can only change myself.
> To let go is not to care for, but to care about.
> To let go is not to fix, but to be supportive.
> To let go is not to judge, but to allow
>   another to be a human being.
> To let go is not to be in the middle arranging
>   all the outcomes, but to allow others
>   to effect their own outcomes.

To let go is not to be protective; it is to
    permit another to face reality.
To let go is not to deny, but to accept.
To let go is not to nag, scold or argue, but to
    search out my own shortcomings and
    to correct them.
To let go is not to adjust everything to my
    desires, but to take each day as it
    comes and cherish the moment.
To let go is not to criticize and regulate
    anyone, but to try to become what I
    dream I can be.
To let go is not to regret the past, but to
    grow and live for the future.
To let go is to fear less and love more.
                ~*Author unknown*

You can see their face in your mind. You know how they walk, their little actions, things they say. You know what makes them happy. You know how they think. You may know where they are and what they are doing right now. You go out to enjoy fellowship and actually laugh, but "Even in laughter the heart may ache, and joy may end in grief" (Proverbs 14:13).

For the life of me, I could not get the man's phone number my heart ached over out of my mind! All the gas price signs would read "$2.59" a gallon. It never failed, so many times I would glance at the clock and it would read "2:59!" Each time that happened it was like a javelin through my heart. It felt like a bad trick was being played on me repetitively. Like the movie *Groundhog Day*. When haunting thoughts or moments come upon you, know you are not alone. This too shall pass. The thoughts *will* diminish. Come back at the thought with scripture. Pull out that sword—the Word.

When we go through grief and anguish, sometimes we feel like we are going to lose our mind. You may contemplate that you are crazy and that if anyone knew what goes on in your mind, they would surely run. This is normal. Emotions are swirling around in our head and heart as ferocious as a hurricane. We no sooner take one thought captive and the next one bombards us. Our mind flickers back and forth from questioning how we can change to make them happy so they'll come back, to our personal shortcomings and failings blowing up inside of us like a nuclear bomb. You are normal, not insane. It's a time of critical pain. You're on the gurney but Jesus is your great physician.

You may think, how can there be another so perfect for me, who I'll be that crazy about and love that much? God made at least four wonderful fruits on the earth: Pineapple, cantaloupe, berries, mango and more. God made more than one beautiful person. His ability to grow us and bless goes beyond our near-sightedness and our thought limits.

This may be a critical time of loneliness. Press into God's love and your faith. Pull on God's anointing like the woman pulled on His robe. "Bring joy to your servant, for to you, O Lord, I lift up my soul" (Psalm 86:4).

Many have heard the saying "take it day by day." This has become cliché and rather meaningless. Buy a bag of M&M's. Besides letting them remind you of *Marry Me!*, let the "m" & "m" remind you to take this time "moment by moment." When one is flooded with pain, thinking of a whole day is too large of a picture—overwhelming. You have to take your feelings moment by moment. All you may be able to do is write one or two scripture verses down, keep them in several places, and cling to them moment by moment. Ask people to pray for you. Spend time in worship. You may not want to, but offer it up to the Lord and He will lift you up.

Suicide. Not many people openly admit their thoughts of it when going through a very emotional loss. They may not be able to put it into words or may not want to be looked at as faithless or unstable. But I can tell you that even strong Christians can have thoughts about it at a time like this. Satan won't miss an opportunity. I felt those feelings. A freeway bridge took on a different look from time to time. For a few days, I thought of who would receive and clean out my belongings. I knew my son had his father to live with.

DO NOT TAKE YOUR LIFE!! YOUR PAIN WILL GO AWAY!! I just want you to know that you are not strange. Tell your closest, safest family, friend or pastor. If thoughts continue for more than two days, you should seek professional help from a counselor or psychologist (preferably Christian). Call 911 if you feel tempted to take your life. *Suicide is a permanent answer to a temporary problem.* You will have an abundant life again.

Psalm 23:4 says "Yea, though I walk through the valley of the shadow of death, I will fear no evil: for thou art with me; thy rod and thy staff they comfort me." Take further comfort in that, in order for there to be a shadow that you have, there must be light. He is the light, so He is with you just as the Word says in those times.

A gentleman shared his suffering and turn-around experience with me. It was late summer and he stood at the river's edge with a grievous heart. The water was deep, carried itself with a 7mph current and the man thought it would carry his misery away. He was beside himself from the loss of his cherished spouse. In agony, he intended to end his life right there. "I was so beside myself I couldn't see straight," he recalled and expressed in a somber voice. As he stood there weak, contemplating his pain, a big, heavyset gentleman came up and said, "That's not the way to go." Those were the only words this visiting angel said and all of a sudden he vanished. The saint who shared this story testifies, "Thank God I didn't do it because it would have been a stupid move on my part. But even the closest to the Lord deal with things like this because we're not infallible. I am glad I am able to admit it and share it."

I am your angel here sent to tell you today, "That is not the way."

> For I know the plans I have for you," declares the LORD, "plans to prosper you and not to harm you, plans to give you hope and a future
>
> ~*Jer 29:11*

God will heal you and you will truly live and smile once again. You will experience wondrous, hopeful thoughts again having nothing to do with the other person. But for now you are in pain, perhaps agony. Jesus felt the same as He was about to be taken by the soldiers for his destiny. He said, "My soul is overwhelmed with sorrow to the point of death" (Matthew 26:38). He understands your sorrow. Adonai Yuree—the Lord sees. He sees what you are going through; He knows and intercedes on your behalf to the Father when you can't pray for yourself.

Wear purple. I am not kidding. Purple is the color of royalty. You are royalty because you are the son or daughter of Almighty God through Jesus Christ. Get this into your head and heart. Digest it fully because it is fully truth. Envision yourself wearing purple and sitting with Jesus as He treats you lovingly. You are the beloved. Buy and wrap yourself in a shiny, deep purple cloth. You are the son or daughter of the Most High God. You are incredibly made and loved by Him. Seek a greater understanding and experiences of your heavenly Father's love for you. This is how you will come up from the pit after a heart shattering break up or out of a bout of loneliness. Know that He delights in you.

> He will take great delight in you, he will quiet you
> with his love, he will rejoice over you with singing.

> *~Zeph. 3:17*

He has your hand in marriage. You are the bride of Christ. Arise.

Listen to the words of this Christian psychologist: "When there is a severing of a limb, there is always new growth. New life will come. You have the choice and ability to move ahead in this."

I was driving home one day and a grounds crew was in action outside a church. They were strategically moving fresh top soil and mulch around the shrubbery of the landscape. My attention was drawn to the lush green bushes with their soft needles. Even from the street I could easily see a few inches of new, lighter green fresh growth at the tips of each branch. How vibrant and pretty it looked! When I lived on acreage, we planted additional spruce trees for interest and to create a border from the road. Each spring and throughout the summer I'd walk the grounds checking to see how much fresh growth had come and how tall and fat the trees had become. I'd touch and feel the soft, light green tips and know the trees were maturing into something even more desirable. They provided visual pleasure and blockage from the road. The trees were grew sturdier every year. How's *your* new, green growth? Look back and see the progress you have made in your healing and what you have come through thus far. See? Healing is happening and will continue to, if you praise God and do the work that goes with it. How far is it from here to there? Where am I in the "there"? I am clearly not where I was!

The Gate of the Year
And I said to the man who stood at the gate of the year:
"Give me a light, that I may tread safely into the unknown!"
And he replied:

"Go out into the darkness and put your hand into the Hand of God.

That shall be to you better than light and safer than a known way."

So, I went forth, and finding the Hand of God, trod gladly into the night

And He led me toward the hills and the breaking of day in the lone East.

So, heart, be still!

~Marie Louise Haskins

Still Grieving and Remaining Apart

Be careful not to leave the back door open! When you get in your car, you lock all the doors for safety. Don't leave *one* door of your mind unlocked for Satan's negative thoughts to take seat and grow!

You cannot afford any negative thinking or "stinkin' thinkin!" Thoughts will enter your mind about the past relationship, the memories, their looks, the things you are missing about them and thoughts of going back. Stop it! "Take captive every thought to make it obedient to Christ" (2 Corinthians 10:5). Refocus your attention elsewhere, onto Jesus. Call out for prayer. You cannot afford not to. If you fail to do these things, you are only leaving yourself open for continued depression and remaining stagnant from the loss. I know you may not feel like it, but this is fightin' time and no one else can do it for you.

Are you thinking your missed one is pining for you? Maybe they are. Maybe they are not. But what is reality? What are your longing emotions fabricating? What is wishful thinking and what is not? Sorely so, as much as *we* long for someone, it does not encourage their feelings toward us. The mind can play tricks on us. Distinguish between these things to help you remain on course for your new beginning.

Jealousy alone is not a healthy reason to reunite. If it is real love, why would it take jealousy to show someone? Jealousy is one of the strongest emotions. I would be extremely cautious of reuniting as a result of hearing or seeing that your "ex" is with another person. You either love or you don't; it should not depend upon of another person's interest. We are looking for genuine love, not induced, jealousy-fueled love. In a reunion stemming from jealousy, those eyes better be open and the accountability friends better be asking lots of questions.

When you are quitting a bad habit, the habit spot needs to be filled with a good replacement (not another relationship with the opposite gender). The same goes with the loss of a relationship. Fill that void with a healthy filler: more of Jesus, serving others, meeting other healthy people, new hobby/interest/goal, renovating your home. Do something you've always wanted to do. Join a new group, a new ministry. Each time I did this I always grew.

This is an opportunity to examine yourself and make improvements in your life. This is the time to develop you! In doing so, you'll be happier individually, more useful, more interesting and an even greater catch for the right relationship. It can take much to come to this degree of acceptance, but you will. A great relationship is an obvious win. A lost or failed relationship is a lesser obvious win, but it is. It is a promotion to a better you and love. It's kind of like the initial growth of the body of the Christian church. Because of intense persecution, believers were driven out of Jerusalem. Their dispersing ironically caused the gospel to be shared with Samaritans and Gentiles. Out of a bad situation, good growth will come. God will turn it for the good. In or after your situation, it's your time to disperse and reach out for greater venues. "And we know"—do you know?—"that in *all* things God works for the good of those who love him" (Romans 8:28).

You go back or contemplate going back into the relationship because you think there is nothing better for you ahead. You go back to get out of the pain; you think there is no other way to rid yourself of the black looming cloud over your heart, but God can and will heal you. You

won't have any idea how, but He will:

> bestow on you a crown of beauty instead of ashes, the oil of joy instead of mourning, and a garment of praise instead of a spirit of despair. You will be called oaks of righteousness, a planting of the LORD for the display of his splendor.
> *~Isaiah 61:2-4*

Say, "God, I need peace and joy today."

It's going to take at least one of you to be strong about staying apart. It will need to be. You may have to take a tough approach; in order to get through it, this means NO CONTACT. You may feel cold or heartless (depending on how sweet you are) not returning calls or emails, but you are really protecting each other's hearts instead. This is more loving and the higher, but harder road. You must draw the line. If you decide to block or filter the other's communications, you should delicately make them aware of those plans before you set that block up. Otherwise, it will be like the movies where the soldier goes off to war and writes his girl every day. The mother blocks the daughter from receiving his letters, and the whole relationship is misperceived. The soldier thought his girl had been reading the letters all that time and ideas, thoughts and actions were totally misunderstood. Unless you're trying to get a big movie deal out of what you're doing, better not to go about it that way. Better to say to the other, "I care for you, but this relationship is not the best for both of us. For that reason, I will not continue to keep communication between us in any way. We have to be strong."

If your lifestyles overlap, see them ever so sparingly in larger groups. Do not converse with them one-on-one. Do not linger in smaller, intimate groups. Keep your eyes focused ahead. Don't trust your emotions; they have the tendency to surprise you. While at one time you used to plot to see them, now you must plot NOT to see them for the sake of healing and new beginnings.

In any breakup, to the degree that you loved, is to the degree that you will hurt. Be not surprised of the depth of hurt you may feel. How beautiful you can love like you did. One day, another will appreciate your ability and gift to love. To get to that place though, there are several stages of grief that are normal. If you feel them, be encouraged, because you are IN the process of healing. The roller coaster of these emotions is called "the slippery slope." The emotions wax and wane, switch from one to another and back again to the third or fourth at any given time. This is unpleasant but normal. You will move through this. The common emotions are shock, denial, bargaining, anger and depression.

Some friends were having landscape put in around an already established, mature tree. The workers dug near the roots of the established tree, bothering its roots, and the tree's leaves withered. Special root stick fertilizers had to be placed next to the tree roots for restoration of the tree's vitality. If your love for your former man or woman went down deep into your roots, your roots have been dug at. Your leaves are temporarily withered, but given deep roots in the Lord, you can be re-fertilized, watered and stand strong and beautiful again. "We are hard pressed on every side, but not crushed; perplexed, but not in despair; persecuted, but not abandoned; struck down, but not destroyed" (2 Corinthians 4:8-9).

It would be soooo easy and nice to turn around in the middle of processing your loss and get back together again, but if that is not the right relationship for you...don't do it!!! Don't go back to Egypt! Have an accountability friend(s) whom you call when you get those aching voids and desires to contact your missed one. Ask friends to call you at times when you normally would have received a phone call or visit from your missed one. Ask them to fill in the gaps through this adjustment for a while. They are going to be part of your healing balm. They are your Jesus with skin on. They are part of your scaffolding to hold you up. Charles Spurgeon said, "Friendship is one of the sweetest joys of life. Many might have failed beneath the bitterness of their trial had they not found a friend." You can make it through. This is survivable. Others have gone on to heal before you.

Jesus is not a placebo! He is real! He is working on your behalf even as you read! Our faith should be of such belief. We can pray something, but if you are truly wavering in receiving any kind of answer, it is void. Believe that God really is involved and working in your prayer life. No placebo results—the real thing—the real power. We need to have "the peace of God that just don't make sense" as Sister Angela Rankins would say.

Bishop T. D. Jakes on a YouTube message called *Let It Go* emphatically reminds us that God knows everything you have been through. "Nothing just happens!" "When people can walk away from you, let them walk!" He instructs, "Don't try to talk another person into staying with you, lovin' you, calling you, caring about you, coming to see you, staying in touch with you."

Jakes pleads with people,

> I don't care how wonderful they are. I don't care how attracted you are to them. I don't care what they did for you twenty years ago. I don't care what the situation is. When people can walk away from you, let them walk because your destiny is not tied to the person who left.

Hear this from Jakes; *"Your destiny is never tied to anybody that left."*

The fact that the other person just was not for you is proven out by 1 John 2:19 which says "They went out from us, but they did not really belong to us. For if they had belonged to us, they would have remained with us; but their going showed that none of them belonged to us."

Jakes begs listeners, "People leave you because they are not joined to you. And if they are not joined to you, you can get super glue and you can't make em' stay. Let em' go!"

It doesn't mean they are a bad person. It just means their part in the story is over. Jakes continues, "And you got to know when people's part in your story is over so that you don't keep trying to raise the dead." David realized his and Bathsheba's son was dead. He washed his face and went to Bathsheba and she bore another child.

Accept what Jakes says to you. "You got to know when it's over!" Sometimes life only comes after death. Need proof? Consider Jesus's resurrection.

Jakes continues,

Nothing just happens. If they walked away it's no accident. If they left you it's no accident. If you tried to make it work and it wouldn't work it's no accident. Accept it as the will of God. Clap your hands, wash your face, do your dance and keep going!...I got the gift of goodbye. It's the tenth spiritual gift. I believe in goodbye. It's not that I'm hateful. It's that I'm faithful. I know whatever God means for me to have he'll give it to me. And if it takes too much sweat, I don't need it. Stop begging people to stay. Let 'em go!

Nothing just happens! Look deeply at the story of Naomi and her two daughter-in-laws Orpah and Ruth. The history begins when Naomi, her husband and two sons, who were Ephrathites, came from Bethlehem where there was famine to live in the country of Moab. Naomi's husband died. Her two sons who were married to Moabites Orpah and Ruth, died ten years after her husband. Naomi surely required care and finances. Widows were taken advantage of and left uncared for in those times. Naomi was in the dark night of her soul.

Naomi heard that God had brought provision to their home land. She and the girls began traveling back to Judah. Since she had no other sons left for Orpah and Ruth to remarry, she encouraged them to go back and stay in their homeland Moab, while she returned to hers. Orpah and Ruth both had the right to separate ways and make their own life now. Perhaps they could remarry there and find rest.

Both girls cried out and said no, but Naomi insisted again. Orpah "kissed her mother-in-law good-bye" (Ruth 1:14) and retreated. Ruth on the other strong hand chose to cling to Naomi (Ruth 1:14). Again Naomi urged her to go back to Moab, to which Ruth replied "'Don't urge me to leave you or to turn back from you. Where you go I will go, and where you stay I will stay. Your people will be my people and your God my God. Where you die I will die, and there I will be buried.'" There was such an attachment between them. Ruth could not hear of parting. Ruth was joined in the spirit to Naomi; there was a soul tie. Ruth's destiny was intertwined with Naomi.

And as the story God wrote unfolded, Naomi instructed Ruth, a godly woman, how to connect with Boaz, a godly man. Ruth became his wife and everyone was blessed. Their story went down in history. Do you see how devotion looks? Do you see that God created that devotion within Ruth and that it led to their destiny? Orpah's destiny was not the same.

Let's also look at Ruth 2:8. Boaz did not want Ruth to leave right from the get-go. He had a destiny tie to her right from the beginning. He said, "My daughter, listen to me. Don't go and glean in another field and don't go away from here. Stay here with my servant girls."

Look at Ruth 4:9-10! Boaz is proud to boast of his bride! Boaz proudly and boldly and confidently announces their engagement! "Then Boaz announced to the elders and all the people, 'Today you are witnesses that I have bought from Naomi all the property of Elimelek, Kilion and Mahlon. I have also acquired Ruth the Moabite, Mahlon's widow, as my wife, in order to maintain the name of the dead with his property, so that his name will not disappear from among his family or from his hometown. Today you are witnesses!" If your man isn't beaming about your streaming together…you deserve finer, Sister, and I am with you.

Then Ruth 4:11 tells "Then the elders and all those at the *gate* said, "We are witnesses. May the Lord make the woman who is coming into your home like Rachel and Leah, who together built up the house of Israel. May you have standing in Ephrathah and be famous in Betheleh." Wow! The gate? Isn't this the Proverbs 31 woman who makes her man respected at the gate of the city? "May you have standing…and be famous in Betheleh"? Ruth is Proverbs 31 all over the place! Go Ruth! Go ladies! This verse is totally blessing Boaz; it's saying "may you do great things for God together!" This sounds like "Destiny and Calling" to me.

In the Old Testament there were kings who would not serve the Lord. Some of them would not tear down the high places where sacrifices were still being made to other Gods.

They would not put their idols away. They would not go the full measure and get rid of all sin.

Do you have any high places? Any "exes" lingering in the background that you know are not "the one?" Tear them down! Put your idols away, and get the full measure of what God has for you. If this is not the person God has for you, then you are in disobedience. Partial or passive obedience is sin; delayed obedience is sin. Obedience needs to come first, understanding later. What things tangible or otherwise keep you in a spot that keeps you going back to them? What sightings of them or interactions with them keep you bound up in emotions and thoughts preventing you from being free?

You must get rid of everything, change anything or any habit that keeps you going back to that person. You need to be completely free. Burn the ships so you cannot go back.

> If your right eye causes you to sin, gouge it out and throw it away." "And if your right hand causes you to sin, cut it off and throw it away.
> ~Matt. 5:29-30

If you find that seeing that person causes you days of emotionally sitting on the bench afterward, segregate from one another further. Does seeing them cause reminiscing? Yearning to be with them? Does Satan poke you with rejection or inadequacy? Does seeing them steal your joy? If these things make you unable to function alive in Christ because you are out of commission from sadness, then it is time to take another route. Attend alternate events. Do whatever it takes not to go back even in your mind. Tear down the high places. Press on fully and focused in Christ. Spend time alone with Him.

There is a time for everything, and a season for
every activity under heaven.

~Eccl. 3:1

In 2 Kings 21, the kings kept doing the same dumb
things over and over again. In 2 Kings 21:3 King Manasseh
of Judah rebuilt the high places his father Hezekiah had
destroyed. Then King Josiah took down the high places in
2 Kings Chapters 22 and 23. Leave no chance for re-
entrance into that former relationship that was not going
anywhere or God did not want you in the first place. Do not
get back together again. If…If…If…you do…*it better be*
with Christian counseling and with a plan for
accountability, change and improvement.

In college, I had an Intermediate Algebra teacher (the
thought of that subject makes my face scrunch up). He was
nice, very friendly, fair and caring. However, Mr. Dougal
(name changed) was at heart a Trigonometry and Calculus
teacher. That is where he really thrived and sat in his
specialty. He of course, could teach Intermediate Algebra,
but most of the students found him to teach over our heads,
too quick and too intense. Consequently, Mr. Dougal was
not an effective teacher for a good number of students. He
was out of his true calling. He did not provide the best
teaching and we did not put out the best results.

We do not want to be out of our calling. What will be
thwarted and left unaccomplished for the kingdom of God
if we allow ourselves to settle for anything less than His
plan? How many lives will not receive what God desires
because you are out of place? Where do you really believe
God wants you concerning that old relationship? In or out
of it? Go with God. Follow Him wholeheartedly.

You may have times of sobbing—a cry so painful your friends will not recognize it's you—like that of a wounded animal as my friend describes it—an emptiness great as the Grand Canyon. A longing and hurt so intense that only your heavenly Father can know.

> In the same way, the Spirit helps us in our weakness. We do not know what we ought to pray for, but the Spirit himself intercedes for us with groans that words cannot express. And he who searches our hearts knows the mind of the Spirit, because the spirit intercedes for the saints in accordance with God's will"
>
> ~*Rom. 8:26-27*

Really, truly, honestly, I promise…you WILL rise again! It may come sooner than you think. I have experienced this and have witnessed others in new life. Jesus was resurrected and He will resurrect you, if you press into Him.

Brokenness can be painful, but can also bring a stunning, deep beauty like nothing else. You will learn a tenderness and compassion for others not learnable any other way.

When I struggled a bit to get over another short-term relationship, I made a sign for my wall next to my bed. It read: "No. Not it. No peace. Keep moving. Don't misjudge. Boundaries." This helped me keep myself accountable to not pondering or wishing the relationship would work out or still try to get it to work out myself. Many times His spirit would say to me "Greater things have I for you."

Sometimes we fall back into disappointment that no former relationship turned into marriage. But God has just one for you, so be glad and grateful you didn't marry the wrong one. There's a saying in the sales world, "Every 'no' just brings you closer to the 'yes' (the sale)." With every 'no' you've just been saved from marrying the wrong one! So you're closer to the right one! Go on a fast as talked about earlier. Break the emotional tie between you both. Gain greater insight for your own life. It's kind of about God, you and others right now—anyone other than your former significant other.

While we press on, some days are harder than others. I would have a good streak for a few days and be so disappointed when the feelings of grief, sadness and longing only returned. There was so much to fight off. There were days I thought my heart was hemorrhaging and bleeding out. There was no one-time "deliverance" from the loss, but each time I went to the altar for prayer…each prayer that was said over me, was lifting. I had to ask the Lord for new grace every day, which is normal. And some days more than others I leaned more heavily on friends.

Get your vitamins and nutrients! You need healthy dosages of A, B, C, D & E!

A = *Always*. You are always in first place with Him!
B = *Because*. Just *because* you're His kid, you've got it made!
C = *Constantly*. You are *constantly* on His mind!
D = God is fully *devoted* to you, wanting you always!
E = *Everything*! Jesus is your multi-vitamin. He is your *everything*!

You can't possibly overdose on these thoughts! God has an insatiable desire for you! Are you getting this deep into your spirit? God is crazy with a capital "C" about you! My brothers and sisters, if you were any richer, you'd be in heaven!

Shane Willard's partial remedy for depression is this: make your eyes smile—open them big, bright and happy! Your mouth will automatically smile too! Yeah, you look good! You've got to make yourself do this sometimes. You'll be strengthening your character by pressing into something you really don't want to do, and you'll feel better! "This is the day which the Lord hath made; we *will* rejoice and be glad in it" (Psalm 118:24 KJV). Sometimes you have to *will* yourself to victory with Jesus. You look so much better when you smile!

There may be a particular time or day of the week that is particularly lonely for you. Some singles say Sunday is that day for them. I challenge you to shake things up a bit on that day. Don't grocery shop or do laundry if you can help it. Go out to lunch, fellowship, go out for a favorite activity. Plan it ahead of time.

Don't try to rush through your healing, though you may very well want to. Trust me I did this unintentionally and intentionally. God did bring good out of that too, but it may have caused others hurt. Do your healing right; you owe it to yourself and others. It's like weight loss. There are weight loss fads that will take your weight off quickly by means of pills, very low caloric intake or other methods. They will not keep your weight off though. If you do not heal through, somewhere, somehow, that untended to root of hurt is going to pop its head up and surface.

Immerse yourself in the Lord. Go deeper in Him. Go deeper in your involvement with strong, praying believers. Perhaps one love affair has ended for you, but you have the opportunity to have an on-fire love affair with Jesus. There is no fluff in this. There is no embellishment in this. He will make you feel the highest degree of love available.

As you are in community with strong, solid believers, God will put it on someone's heart to pray and intercede for you. God woke up my prayer warrior at 2am telling him what I was up against and that he was to pray for me for two hours each day for three days. I prospered again. God loves me enough to talk to direct someone else on my behalf. My value is great to God. Your value is great to God. He will do this for you too as you build your relationship with Him and others.

My girlfriend attended a concert and bought me the song below, *If You Let Me*. The words and the melody are very healing. The song carries an anointing. God used this song to minister to me. I sobbed on my bed (or healed on my bed I should say) many times listening to it. God lets those healing tears come.

If You Let Me by Sarah Dalton
Stand still, let go
I love you more
More than you know
I see the things
That you can't see
I'll make a way if you let me
If you let me,
I'll hold you like a lover
If you let me
I'll listen like a friend
If you let me
My love is like no other
If you let me your broken heart I'll mend
Stand still, let go
I'll wait for you my love to show
I see the wounds that you can't feel
If you let me I'll come and heal
If you let me
I'll hold you like a lover
If you let me

I'll listen like a friend
If you let me
My love is like no other
If you let me
Your broken heart I'll mend
Stand still, let go
I'll wait for you, my love to show
I see the wounds that you can't feel
If you let me, I'll come and heal
And I will make a way
If you let me

You can hear *If You Let Me* at www.SarahDalton.com..
You'll want to purchase *If You Let Me* at
www.Redletterrecords.com or *www.Cdbaby.com.*

Let Him.

Gold

Move toward the gold in your circumstance. Ask yourself, amongst the hurt, what did I gain from the relationship? For me, it was definitely coming into a spiritual revival and romance with my Lord. Along with my deeper relationship with Christ, it was the gift and the world of music he brought back and stronger into my life. I took things before the Lord and did what I needed to do according to God, not man. I'm not even the same girl. My insides and outsides have been through a metamorphosis. We can keep becoming a "new creation." I am "butterflying" as I call it! I am at a new level in the Lord, experiencing many new places, things, people and blessings. I am changing and evolving in the beauty of the Lord. I am convinced age 46 is the new 26 with Him! "With God all things are possible" (Matthew 19:26).

Ask yourself, what did I help someone else learn from the relationship? What did it bring out in me or teach me that I could do? For me, I pressed into the Lord more than ever and found new levels of His love and steadfastness. "We also rejoice in our sufferings, because we know that suffering produces perseverance; perseverance, character; and character, hope" (Romans 5:4).

When you go through a particular trial, only then are you really able to "get it." Only then are you able to truly relate, feel accurate compassion for, and understand what another person is going through in that trial. Until you experience that particular trial, one can only say to another, "I don't truly know what or how you feel or to the depths that you hurt. I can only imagine that it is so great a hurt. I am truly sorry." I heard a girl once say to someone upon an explanation to her, "I overstand you." I love that! It's like "I *really, really* get you!" Now you can overstand someone and help them.

But this pain you have gone through, while I'm sure you would not wish it upon anyone, it makes you more valuable to the kingdom. It makes you sensitive to those issues. It develops a deep love and compassion only brought about by the silversmith's hand. It is the refiner's fire. It causes you to be able to weep over the things God weeps over.

"But he knows the way that I take; when he has tested me,
I will come forth as gold"

~Job 23:10

25
THE SWORD...Power Verses for Victory

Speak these scriptures out loud throughout the day and night. Insert your name into each verse.

He tends his flock like a shepherd; He gathers the lambs in his arms and carries them close to his heart. *~Is. 40:11*

But one thing I do: Forgetting what is behind and straining toward what is ahead, I press on toward the goal to win the prize for which God has called me heavenward in Christ Jesus. *~Phil. 3:13*

Let us throw off everything that hinders and the sin that so easily entangles, and let us run with perseverance the race marked out for us. Let us fix our eyes on Jesus, the author and perfecter of our faith, who for the joy set before him endured the cross, scorning its shame, and sat down at the right hand of the throne of God. Consider him who endured such opposition from sinful men, so that you will not grow weary and lose heart. *~Heb. 12:1-2*

The Sovereign Lord will wipe away the tears from all faces. *~Is. 25:8*

You keep track of all my sorrows. You have collected all my tears in your bottle. You have recorded each one in your book. *~Ps. 56:8 NLT*

He will wipe every tear from their eyes. *~Rev. 21:4*

So I will be with you; I will never leave you nor forsake you. ~*Josh. 1:5*

We take captive every thought to make it obedient to Christ. ~*2 Cor. 10:5*

Thou wilt keep him in perfect peace, whose mind is stayed on thee: because he trusteth in thee. ~*Is. 26:3 KJV*

Finally, brothers, whatever is true, whatever is noble, whatever is right, whatever is pure, whatever is lovely, whatever is admirable—if anything is excellent or praiseworthy—think about such things. Whatever you have learned or received or heard from me, or seen in me—put it into practice. And the God of peace will be with you. ~*Phil. 4:8, 9*

Weeping may remain for a night, but rejoicing comes in the morning. ~*Ps. 30:5*

So if the Son sets you free, you will be free indeed. ~*John 8:36*   (Pray this to break the emotional bond you feel toward your missed one.)

Now the Lord is the Spirit, and where the Spirit of the Lord is, there is freedom. ~ *2 Cor. 3:17*

The LORD is close to the brokenhearted and saves those who are crushed in spirit. ~*Ps. 34:18*

Oh Lord, truly I am your servant; I am your servant, the son of your maidservant; you have freed me from my chains. ~*Ps. 116:16*

I run in the path of your commands, for you have set my heart free. ~*Psalm 119:32*

He upholds the cause of the oppressed and gives food to the hungry. The Lords sets prisoners free. *~Psalm 146:7*

For the joy of the Lord is your strength. *~Nehemiah 8:10 KJV*

He healeth the broken in heart, and bindeth up their wounds. *~Psalm 147:3 KJV*

And we know that in all things God works for the good of those who love him... *~Rom. 8:28*

My grace is sufficient for you, for my power is made perfect in weakness. *~2 Cor. 12:10*

Forget the former things; do not dwell on the past. See, I am doing a new thing! Now it springs up; do you not perceive it? I am making a way in the desert and streams in the wasteland. *~Is. 43:18-19*

My flesh and my heart may fail, but God is the strength of my heart and my portion forever. *~Ps. 73:26*

Come, all you who are thirsty, come to the waters. *~Is. 55:1*

My "Never Again" List
by Pastor Jerry Weinzierl

Never again will I:

Say "I CAN'T"...for I CAN do all things through Christ who gives me strength. (Phil. 4:13)

Confess LACK...for God shall supply all my needs according to his riches in glory by Christ Jesus. (Phil. 4:19)

Confess FEAR...for God has not given me a spirit of fear but of power and love and a sound mind. (II Tim. 1:7)

Confess WEAKNESS... for the LORD is the strength of my life. (Ps. 27:1)

Confess UNWORTHINESS...He has made Him to be sin for us who knew no sin; that we might be made the righteousness of God in Him. (2 Cor. 5:21)

Confess CONFUSION... for God is not the author of confusion, but of peace. (I Cor. 14:33)

Confess DEFEAT...for God always causes us to Triumph in Christ Jesus. (1 Cor. 2:14)

Confess fear of PERSECUTUON...for if God is for us, who can be against us. (Rom. 8:31)

Confess SICKNESS for He took my infirmities and bore my sickness and with his stripes I am healed. (Is. 53:5 & Matt. 8:17)

Confess WORRY...for I am casting all my cares upon the Lord because He cares for me. (1 Peter 5:7)

Confess BONDAGE...for where the Spirit of the Lord is there is freedom. (2 Cor. 3:17)

Confess Dominion of SIN in my life...for the law of the Spirit of Life in Christ Jesus has made me free from the law of sin and death. Sin shall not have dominion over me. (Rom. 8:2)

Confess FRUSTRATION...for Thou will keep Him in perfect peace whose mind is stayed on thee, because he trusts in thee. (Is. 26:3)

Confess FAILURE...because in all of these things we are more than conquerors through Him
that loved us. (Rom. 8:37)

You have to be like the old hymn. You have to get to the point where we say "I shall not be moved. Like a tree that's planted by the water's edge—I shall not be moved."

26
Experiencing Love

The king is enthralled by your beauty; honor him, for he is your lord.

~*Ps. 45:11*

Wow. This of course is written for men and women and it is not speaking of physical beauty. God is captivated and pleased greatly by you. His love for you causes Him to whirl all about you. He is fascinated by you. That is the truest form of love from the truest one—and it is all for you.

I used to cringe when I would see fanciful items encouraging little girls that they are princesses. It seemed like instilling arrogance or self-centeredness into young girls—worldly confidence if you will. But I have a new take on the princess concept now.

I went to a yard sale and the Lord prompted me to buy two very unique items, which I purchased at an extravagant price of $6 for both! It was wall art for a little girl's room done in the pink princess theme which I used to have such an aversion to. However, with some changes to the pieces and an adapted view of them, I mounted them on my bedroom wall straight onward from by bed. They would be the first and last images I saw in my day.

The first item was a large canvas design of four representations. The first image was a pink ballerina dress, which I painted over transforming it into a long flowing, white bridal gown, reminding me that I am the bride of Christ. I am loved. I am not incomplete. He is my husband

and loves me more than could ever be understood. The second image was a flower, which is to remind me that I am a beautiful flower and to think on things that are pure true, noble, right, pure, lovely, admirable, excellent or praiseworthy (Phil 4:8). The third was a large heart, again reminding me how much God really, really loves me. The forth was a wand with a star on the end and bright streaks. I covered the handle by painting two other stars. This was to remind me that I am a star to God and that he named all of the stars by name. How all powerful is He!

The second piece of wall art was an oval plaque that said "Princess" with an image of a crown. This was to instill in me that I am a princess in His eyes. I am the apple of His eye. He adores me and always follows me with His loving eye. And because of Him I will receive a crown of salvation when I reach Him in heaven. It will be adorned with jewels based on my efforts in this life. Then I will cast that crown at his feet in deserving worship unto Him.

This is all about receiving and knowing the Father's love and adoration for us. How securing, comforting and surrounding this concept of truth became to me. Take to it indelibly as your state of belonging to someone strong and loving.

I bought a large dry erase board for that wall in my room too. I would write on it certain scriptures I needed to meditate on. I wrote messages like "Jesus loves me this I KNOW just the beautiful way I am." When you write out scriptures in large print, write them like they are a declaration and you are professing this as your belief. Another time I drew a large heart shape and wrote my name inside of it. And I know that's what God is thinking of me and you with your name in it.

Hephzibah. Say that five times over! Hephzibah! Hephzibah! Hephzibah! Hephzibah! Hephzibah! Yes…speak it over yourself constantly. It is God's thoughts and devotion to you. Isaiah 62:4 calls you Hephzibah, which in Hebrew means "my delight is in her." This section of scripture was referring to Isaiah's hopes that Israel would be saved. But as God's word is the living word, Hephzibah and the verses below are what God calls you and how He deeply cherishes you today. If you have ever felt forsaken or deserted by a person or by life, read what God calls you here.

For Zion's sake I will not hold My peace,
And for Jerusalem's sake I will not rest,
Until her righteousness goes forth as brightness,
And her salvation as a lamp that burns.
² The Gentiles shall see your righteousness,
And all kings your glory.
You shall be called by a new name,
Which the mouth of the LORD will name.
³ You shall also be a crown of glory
In the hand of the LORD,
And a royal diadem
In the hand of your God.
⁴ You shall no longer be termed Forsaken,
Nor shall your land any more be termed Desolate;
But you shall be called Hephzibah, and your land
    Beulah;
For the LORD delights in you,
And your land shall be married.
⁵ For *as* a young man marries a virgin,
So shall your sons marry you;
And *as* the bridegroom rejoices over the bride,
So shall your God rejoice over you.

~*Isaiah 62:1-5 NKJV*

<u>Verse 2:</u> God divinely appoints a new name—"The church shall be more renowned than ever, both in respect of her condition, and so called Hephzi-bah" (John Wesley).

<u>Verse 3:</u> *Crown of glory*—An expression to set forth the dignity of her state.

> *In the hand*—"Preserved and defended by God's hand." (John Wesley)

> *Diadem*—an ornamental, jeweled crown signifying sovereignty. You are sovereignly safe with God.

<u>Verse 4:</u> (per John Wesley):

> *Forsaken*—As a woman forsaken by her husband.

> *Thy land*—The inhabitants of the land.

> *Hephzi-bah*—My delight is in her; a new name agreeing with her new condition.

> *Beulah*—Married; agreeing to her new relation.

> *Married*—Thou shalt see the increase of thy children again in the land, as the
> fruit of thy married condition, which by reason of thy being forsaken of thy husband, were in a manner wasted and decayed: and this refers to the great enlargement of the church in the gospel days.

Female and male, if you are saved, you are married to Christ and look at all that gets you! You receive a loving relationship and

God's protection over you. And as we continue to sanctify ourselves, we are in a new condition…Hephzibah.

Hephzibah!

Hephzibah!

Hephzibah!

Hephzibah!

Hephzibah!

27
My Testimony

Born in 1965, I was raised in a good Polish, Italian Catholic family as the youngest surprise baby eleven years later than my youngest of three brothers. Our parents raised us as children of integrity, yet I had my lies and times. It was a stable, loving home. We went to church each Sunday, attended Sunday school, catechism and made the sacraments.

As the "surprise" only girl of the family, I was treated very well, loved and protected. My mother did special things with and for me. She helped me earn my Brownie badges and we went on shopping and field trips. My father escorted me to the debutant ball in 10th grade. I still have the earrings and bracelet we received that night as well as the shiny, silver cummerbund belt he gave to me another year. There was never any sibling rivalry between my brothers and me. Because they were so much older and busy with college and starting their careers, it was kind of like growing up as an only child. The only arguments we ever had were whether one of them could watch Star Trek instead of my show. I'm still not a "Trekkie" to this day. Lord, please don't bring me a "Trekkie" husband! Although the tickle fights were brutal. Our home was very much like the Cleaver family.

I played "house" as a little girl and had a sizable collection of Barbie doll campers, houses, jeeps and salons. I thought I would become an architect; I used to design floor plans (top view sketches) of new Barbie doll houses. (Wonder where that came from, seeing my father was a draftsman.) And of course, I felt how lucky Barbie was to have Ken in her life.

As that young girl turned high school age, I was active. I had popularity, pretty looks and a pleasant, engaging personality. Sometimes too engaging...I fought with Mr. Kildegard when he wouldn't let me do my Shorthand homework in his Social Studies class. Anywho...my dream was to graduate, have a family and be a stay-at-home mom because I was boy crazy. I didn't think about going to college. I don't recall being inspired to either. My parents perhaps saw my lack of desire to study and the draw towards boys consistent. Their generation's belief was that women married and raised families as a career. In the depths of my heart, I yearned for a man to love and adore me to the heights of the heavens—someone who would never leave me because they were so crazy about me.

After graduation, I went to work at the Big Three as a secretary of a large engineering department. Two ministers showed me what Jesus looks like in their lives and at the age of 19, I accepted Christ's love for me. I never in a million years dreamt that the man I longed for in my soul would be Jesus Christ! I was not that kind of girl desiring anything more of religion. Ahhh...but show me Jesus and relationship and my empty soul accepted Him by surprise. He is that forever lover, Savior and husband of my soul. He is my dream come true and far more than I ever could have thought of.

I experienced a radical transformation upon meeting Jesus. My friends changed and so did my activities and the relationship with my parents. It was hard for me to find new Christian friends though; I experienced social loneliness for the first time in my life. Though I had a few new friends and attended a large singles group, I just didn't find fun connections. And I really wanted to find my man. The two ministers that led me to Jesus told me I could be content being single for then, but I was head strong. I was young, pretty and wanted marriage and a family. I just could not understand and accept that "His grace was enough for me." Actually, I guess you could say I refused to believe it. I refused God into that hole and dream of my heart. I refused him that niche. I wouldn't surrender that top spot of my heart.

My anger with God caused me to become rebellious and I wandered away from Him. I got into messes. At the age of 25 (1990), I married someone who did not share my spiritual perspective after more than a year of dating and a nine-month or so engagement. I was advised by two believers not to, but I was too co-dependent to break up. It was a difficult marriage lasting twelve years of for the most part oil and water. We didn't have our largest passions in common. In the later years of the marriage I drew back to the Lord once again. You see, sin only tastes good for a short season.

Entry: August 2002
My former spouse divorced me against my desire. I was a good and faithful wife, yet could have used more spiritual and emotional maturity and wisdom. Well, that's what you don't get when you fail to walk close with the Lord. I was devastated and *soooo* angry at various people through the divorce. I went through rages of anger. I was dumped by an attorney for an outburst of anger in a mediation meeting. I then had to undergo a court mandated interview to assess my emotional stability and fitness as a custodial parent. I was beside myself. You would not have recognized me. My good brother had to shake me and wake me to senses. The Lord had to teach me about "be angry and do not sin." I was just so hurt and devastated.

Divorce was the last thing I ever wanted; it wasn't anywhere on my wish list. The thought of my family breaking up and losing time with my son...there's just not enough I could say to convey the sorrow of that to you. All I can say is that when my mother called me with the news of "9/11" that morning in September, I was totally numb to it. I was in my own "9/11." My own buildings were burning and crashing. I was in a tower, but I was no longer the princess.

I attended not one, but two rounds of divorce recovery classes and personal counseling. That's how much it was going to take to even take the edge off this thing.

I had to watch my former spouse date and become engaged. I fasted and prayed for reconciliation until after his remarriage ceremony. She eventually became expectant with a child of their own...everything I yet wanted. But God held so me so tightly through this all and I had the strong support of a godly circle of loving friends.

I came to the willing place of selling and giving away all the baby items I had kept from my son, in hopes of having more children. I accepted at that time, that if I was to ever have another child with another man, it would be a better experience to recollect all those exciting items with him.

I believe that I hate divorce as much as God does, but I have overcome through it. It's not what I chose, but I was clearly chosen to overcome its destruction.

Entry: 2003
As instructed, I waited 1.5 years to date anyone after my divorce. I then met and dated the man spoken of

previously in this book and below. From the moment I noticed him, I was smitten.

Entry: Final Break up, November 29, 2008 (Thanksgiving weekend)

The final break up from my boyfriend was Thanksgiving weekend. Happy Thanksgiving to me. Pain, pain, lots of pain.

Entry: Break up to February 2010

Literally, right after the break up until February 2010, I kept some company with a man and briefly dated two other godly men, but none of them worked out. I brought disappointment to another from a Christian Internet site whom I never met in person. All but one of the situations I went into prematurely and unhealed and unintentionally inflicted disappointment and pain. You're probably thinking, "Golly, this girl needed her own book!" I thought I was ready to move forward with the right man. **But how can one even move forward with the right man when they are still crying over the wrong man?**

Really, I should have hung up my skates for awhile. Should've gone on a relationship medical leave. Some athletes miss participating in the Olympics for sake of injury, which is tragic, but it happens and they have to deal with it. Sometimes it is degenerative to play with an injury—it just worsens it. Trying to date again while your heart is not over another is unsteady ground; it's just not a good or fair foundation for either person.

The good that did come out of those relationships was that those men did bring some, joy, healing and affirmation to me and I blessed them as well.

<u>Entry: April, 2009</u> (Reflection)

He was a talented praise and folk musician. His golden-toned guitar and soothing voice was alluring, and kept me loving him. Afterward, when I heard the achingly sweet sound of guitarist's fingers sliding up and down the strings, it piercingly reminded me… For a long, long time I missed my musician—his melody; his softness; his wild, gentle creativity; his euphonic lyrics. I missed my musician and I wanted him back again.

I don't think anyone knew what I would go through when I heard a worship song in church that he used to frequently play. There was such irony in it. I had to struggle to dedicate the song unto the Lord instead of allowing my emotions to sink me as I was reminded of him. Yet when I stood and sang the song, God truly knew it was a sacrifice of praise unto Him.

<u>Entry: 10/15/09</u>

I waited with baited breath. (Where did that saying come from anyway? Pop an Altoid.) I thought, "Isn't anyone going to call and tell me he wants to get back together again?" Mutual friends would call me and I would hang up the phone shocked when they didn't say to me, "He's sorry. He knows he was wrong. (Isn't that what women usually think about the man?) He misses you." I finally realized my naïve thoughts and foolishness. But I think they were just natural thoughts while grieving. I think that's how a broken heart thinks. I'm a smart and wise woman thanks to the Lord.

I recall getting my mail and deep inside hoping there would be an apologetic "let's reunite and try counseling" letter. A little over a year after our final break up, a mutual friend encouraged him to reunite and I did receive a letter. He declared "our relationship is truly over." It wasn't quite how I imagined it going. I was devastated. My smallest of hopes were even dashed—sliced with a Ginsu knife. My yearning and desire for him felt like phantom pains from an amputation—so real, but of no chance of happening. The door slammed shut.

Tight social circles are good if you're looking for close community, but bad if you're going through a tough break up and you see and hear of your "ex" often. I couldn't get away from seeing him or hearing about his music. I am sure he thought that people would feel bad for me if he dated anyone in our social circles. A woman may have felt guilty and sorry for me in doing so. I wanted to go underground and leave no Reese's Pieces trails so no social circles could follow and invade my new territory. Siberia couldn't have been far enough away for me.

Entry: 10/22/09 (Reflection)
We were either "my plan" or God's initial "Plan A" that he didn't want. We met at a Christian home gathering where he was leading worship. His leadership, personality, guitar and looks made me say, "Wow." We dated in four intervals—five years spread out with friendships and no contact in between. I couldn't have loved him or adored him more from the heart, from the start. I couldn't have been more attracted to his handsome face and stature. If I were to allow myself, I would still recall the romantic dance and the dazzle my eyes felt each time I saw him. He was altogether lovely to me.

There was always some email, some reason or some fellowship encounter that found us back together again in earlier times. A season before our fourth reuniting, he was not interested in doing so. The fourth reuniting (like the other two) never should have happened, but it did. There was another difficult tribulation going on, which I believe caused vulnerability, clouded thinking and emotions. Out of respect, I'll let that remain private. There were also some positive changes in both our lives that had taken place that would have seemed to benefit us this time. I was so happy; I attributed being back together as the answer to prayer. It seemed like a long awaited dream.

I wished we had both been willing to work out the issues together; tough stuff doesn't change quickly. Frustrated, it was our seemingly unworkable situations and differences that prevented him from proposing, or so I thought. But, after and even during our relationship, I realized that we were not compatible. Our upbringings, temperaments, needs and expectations were different. Our communication styles were different. I *was* willing to work on the areas together.

The last parting felt like another divorce. The fact that he was my first Christian boyfriend and first awaited Christian love, only deepened the experience for me making it really hard to say goodbye.

There were days so dark I went into the restroom at work to release tears, dry them, cling to the Lord and go back to my desk to happily call another customer. Talk about needing to flip the switch—only by the grace of God went I. There were times I thought of not waking up the next day and who would sort and take my belongings—I'm just being honest with you. Yes, there are others who have been deeply wounded.

There were a few times we both attended a church separately with a visiting speaker. I had so hoped for the speaker to prophesy to him amidst the crowd, "That is your wife over there." That pain and longing was so deep. Those were points of such desperation.

We traveled in the same singles groups. The groups of singles overlapped greatly, more so than ever because each group was trying to establish fellowship with the others. Just when I thought I was getting comfortable hanging out with new people, we'd each show up in the same spot. This made things much more difficult for me. Upon seeing him almost a year later at an event, we ended up sitting one person apart from each other. Everyone went out to eat afterward and I could not even look across the table at him or at his groomed hands which played out the gifting I loved so much. Emotions bombarded me. I spent several weeks in emotional recovery after that encounter, so I had to revert back and avoid places where he would be.

But "Praise be to the God and Father of our Lord Jesus Christ! In His great mercy He has given us new birth into a living hope through the resurrection of Jesus Christ from the dead" (1 Peter 1:3). He will resurrect you! Hang in! Get close--as close as you can to Him. And that's real close, 'cause He'll let you. That's exactly what He wants. I had to let the Lord love on me like never before. I had to realize again how much I mean to Him. Only His thoughts about me matter. I learned to pour my love on Him.

Entry: 12/2009 – 1/2010

I went on the Daniel fast. I was desperate enough to do it even over the Christmas and New Year's holidays. In that time I received two confirmations (one of them a dream) that we were not to be together.

Through drawing close to Jesus, worship, convalescing, prayer, support, counsel and a ferociousness to move my life forward in His strength, the pain eventually dulled to that of a red, stubbed toe. I turned a corner, though an unexpected paper cut of a memory could still make me wince. The loss gradually became not the hanging broken bone or laceration it once was, but a scratch from a kitty claw.

Entry: 2/11/10

Kiss the Son

Kiss the Son

Don't cause me to plead for your affections

Lavish me with your pouring, giving heart

Bless me

Pour onto me

I want that so much from you

Tell me that you love me

Sing unto me your sweetness, for you are

Put your praises forward to me. I receive them like a gift you've sought hard for and spent much on. They mean everything to me

So many areas in life to hold back on, but not on me. You can give all to me

And in return …I am like a devout lover who does not hold back

I make promises that will be kept

I can hold you like a tight envelope and seal myself around you

And in our time of sweetness, an exchange will come

Your thoughts, emotions for my peace, hope

Your emptiness and longing for my filling and love

Stay and linger in my aroma

Have my presence

Let me see your smile when you finally have my love for
you on your mind

Let me put my adoration for you on your face

Carry yourself like you have my power, because I am
accessible to you

A love relationship

Kiss the Son

Entry: May, 2010

At one-and-a-half years post-breakup I attended a folk music concert *by myself*, listened to a sappy, break-up love song by another mellow guitarist and suddenly realized…I was fine! No tears, no needing to run from the song. No sadness, no memories--just magnificent feelings of relief and thankfulness for no pain. The hurt spot was no longer there. The languishing was gone! Halleluiah!

God had brought healing just as He said He would. There were plenty of times when I struggled with the miracle of ever getting here. I victoriously made it through seeing him at a home Bible study of fellowship, dinner, study, personal sharing and prayer. Amazing. I couldn't honestly say at that point that I was ready to see him with someone else, but I believed that would be okay one day too. YOUR healing WILL come too.

I did keep a tight band around my heart when our paths crossed. I was cautious. I did not look at him much, converse one-on-one or linger in any close group discussion if it could have been helped. We are off-limits to each other. Not only his, but now my life has moved on, and great blessings have been bestowed with more great things to come. I vowed to continue to move on, but I was also wise. I knew how history had gone in the past with my feelings toward him.

My healing came in increments. One-and-a-half years post-breakup I still had one last increment of healing to go. Usually it is said "the last straw broke the camel's back." In my case it was the last increment of healing that broke the way through to the flow of full freedom. The last increment that needed healing for me was of the mind. There was a groove of thinking that needed to be filled in for me—one last crack in my heart that needed healing and that was that. I was very fearful that my old feelings would re-erupt. The further healing and changes started coming and happening so fast it was hard to document them all and too many to list here.

Whether the relationship was good or difficult, I hated to be forgotten and left out of his life and heart. That is pride, ego and self-love—wanting to think that my own good qualities are powerful enough not to be forgotten. But either way, forgotten or not, it does not change my true value. My Maker assigns that to me and it is high, high, high!

I let you know these circumstances to assure you that through all of this, even the frequent group contact, the Lord still healed. I still pray for him from time to time— blessings over him.

I see him differently now, only once in a blue moon with minimal effects. I am able to see him, say hello, make short small talk, move on, and go on my merry way the next day without former thoughts or yearnings of the past. I have no other special man in my life at this time filling that spot. It's all the Lord's doing, healing and satisfying. It's not like I never think of him or Satan doesn't still try to get me feeling rejected over it, but I just don't go there anymore or allow Satan to twist things. Where once I had to struggle to look forward, I now forget to look back! I know my purpose. I am held, healed and whole.

A good man from church told me, "It's hard to keep a good woman down." John Hughes, I thank you for that blessing. In times of doubt and in times of pursuit that was encouragement to me. You see we never, ever know how the kindness, affirmation and declaration we speak to and over someone will live on to bless them and carry them through.

I do believe my "someday" with a new beau will come. What a caressing summer breeze he will bring upon my heart. I don't like Michigan's frigid winters, but it is no longer winter within my soul. What I once desired so badly, I am better off for not having. Lord bless us both. I am convinced I should always rather have God's "Plan B," which is no less, but greater than "my plan" or God's "Plan A." He and I are buried in the Lord. "You *(the enemy)* intended to harm me, but God intended it for good" (Genesis 50:20).

Entry: August 26-29, 2010
It isn't good to hang around liquor stores, magazine racks or those former loves. And since I'm not real good at focusing on someone else's "bad," I will easily see your good I once loved. Really, I think we all need to get better at not seeing someone else's "bad".

I had a relapse. I surprisingly saw him at a singles' weekend retreat for three days. We all participated in many beautiful summer activities in the sunshine and water (Mackinac Island) in front of orange sunsets and under the brilliant stars. He played his guitar and sang worship at the intimate bonfire with the lake and the sunset behind him. I saw his tent, Bible and special mug that I knew. I heard him pray. It all sent my thoughts, desires and emotions flying in reverse. I once again saw and was confronted by those things I loved in the present and wished for a different future. I saw the qualities I loved about him in full swing. Yep, they're still there.

He did not seem bothered by my presence, bothered as in "Gosh, I miss her." He acted like he had totally moved on and over it. So I went through another round of rejection. He *still* was not choosing me. It didn't matter how godly, pretty, vivacious, talented or otherwise I was, he was not choosing me, so therefore he was still rejecting me. It was a permanent ongoing status. He still was continuing on without me. I frequently have felt over this course of grieving probably the exact way Jesus must feel about the ones He died for but have not given their lives to Him: If you're still not with me, then you are rejecting me. That's honestly tough, but it's the truth.

Entry: 9/4/10
He was with our fellowship, activity group the following Saturday as well.

Entry: 9/10/10
I shed tears again. I needed prayer. I had to re-elevate myself in the Lord again. He said to me, "Hold on through the hurt." I felt worse than a fool, like a fooled fool for relapsing. But I was ministered to again by my Lord and the icing on the cake (my friends).

Entry: 9/11/10
The Saturday after that we both had community events going on and everyone was talking about his event at my event. Someone willingly babbled something that affected

me as well. It was like large snowballs rolling down the mountain at me at top speeds.

The next day, Sunday, I drove 50 minutes to visit another church just so I wouldn't know a soul there and no one would mention his name around me and create more common fellowship ties. I wanted to go into the Witness Protection Program, move to Lemon Grove, California and get a whole new life.

It's not that I wanted the same relationship back again; I did not. I wanted a transformed relationship—redesigned with the guy who had some traits I loved. And bottom line, I just didn't want to feel booted by a man I loved so much. Do I make no difference to you? And that's probably how the Lord feels as well. And I think that because I saw him in that way again and had no one else romantically special in my life, my emotions just had the understandable tendency to revert to the familiar.

I'm not this, I'm not that, I'm this, I am that, I don't own that, got too much of that. I felt like chopped liver, yet I *knew* I wasn't. It was Satan's ploy of condemnation. I was convicted that if I continued to put more value on what Satan was telling me my former love does or does not think of me, then I am allowing Satan's lies to supersede what God's thoughts and truths are of me. Continuing in that thinking is sin.

I thought, "How many times do I have to do this, this "get over" thing?" I don't want to do anything. I am tired and frustrated. Satan had used my failed relationship to press me down for a long time. It took so much to come back from that—fighting and many trips to the altar for prayer and healing. But my friend brought 1 Kings 18:43 to me: "And seven times he said, 'Go again'" (vs. 43). "Get up and go again" was the theme of the devotional. Elijah told King Ahab that rains were coming to bless the drought. Elijah told his servant to go look toward the sea. Finally, on the seventh time the servant was told to look, there was a "cloud, as small as a man's hand, rising out of the sea!" (1 Kings 18:44 NKJV) If we don't acknowledge the small miracles, we will not see God's big destiny or plan for us. Persist God's dear one, persist. Reach out and fight for your inheritance. Don't let the devil take it from you. Do not relinquish what God wants to do in your life.

For me, it was get up and move through or perish. Satan would not be liberal or gentle with me. Inside I felt I had great things put upon my life and Satan would do all to prevent that coming forth. Satan loves nothing more than "to cripple you and then put you down for limping" (Adriane Rogers).

Sometimes it feels so tough—so many hurts and stresses I have gone through, so many burdening scenarios. Then I get to the place where I say, "For you Lord...okay, but only for you Lord...okay...and the others who need what I'm going through." Deep, deep inside, I felt that the more I was allowed to go through, the more I could share with you, relate to you and help you. Now I am meeting with you by way of paper, sharing with you. "When God is going to use you greatly, He will hurt you deeply" (Jentezen Franklin).

Entry: 9/25/2010
He was at another bonfire bash, presumably with a date. Hearing that, I decided to go to a Saturday night church service instead. When the pastor prayed for me, he broke off strongholds and soul ties. I thought soul ties only occurred between individuals that were fornicating. I learned that a soul tie can develop between any two

individuals in relationship; and the genesis can come from a deep love, a genuine liking, or a giver-taker relationship.

The next morning Satan began to bombard me with thoughts of "Nothing's different. You're still the same. You'll never get over him." But I declared "No! I am different! Things have changed!" I envisioned the cutting of ropes and the cutting away of ties. I envisioned freedom. I began to experience a detachment from him again—for good.

I had asked the Lord earlier on, "Lord, why is he so hard to forget?" And the Lord answered me, "Because I made him beautiful too."

I had some things working against me. I loved his music. I still missed his gifting terribly. I had the inner fight all the time with that, yet I could never fully understand why. Finally, I sat in persistence and wrestled with the Lord like Jacob for an answer. "You said you would give me wisdom liberally Lord. What is it that had kept me in bondage to his musical gifting? Why was that always so painful for me? Why was there such a draw to him through music?" This is what the Lord showed me:

- I used to be Karen Carpenter and Marie Osmond as a young singer girl in my bedroom. My hairbrush microphone and mirror sure made for a great performance and when Mom walked in, I died of embarrassment. So I have always had a passion for music. I sang in several performances. This drew my heart to his gifting.
- When I was young, my brother Ralph used to sit me on his lap and let me strum the strings of his guitar. Did these seeds blossom into a deep passion for music? Music ran deeply through me, but I had

forgotten that during my marriage and I had never had the opportunity to be around the guitar. The strings serenaded me in.

- Yes, there is just something about a guy with a guitar to many women. Admittedly, that too must have been part of it for me. Maybe I was partly infatuated with his gift of music and voice as with Keith Partridge and Donny Osmond as a girl. A guy with a guitar *and* a crystal clear, soft, melodic voice. I tell my son he should take up guitar.
- Because he was a worship leader and a folk musician, I often heard of the praise nights and concerts he would be leading or performing at. I always heard about what he was doing, and I couldn't be a part of it. It would have killed me to sit in the audience like any other person—not the girlfriend any longer. And when I could not participate, I felt left out.
- He wrote a song for me in earlier days when he was hoping for love with me—spoiling.
- I love worship music and to be emerged in worship deeply. The fact that he wrote and played Christian music was a blessing.
- I wanted the gift of music and worship in my home as much as possible. I still do.
- My thoughts were that there would always be a musician for gatherings and to have our own personal worship together.
- Another reason I believe I loved him so much was because we connected in our primary "love language."

Entry: 9/26/10

The next day I was moved to visit another church known for greatness. The message was about affirmation, the very week I was writing about it in this book. Love how you do that Lord! At the end of the message, Pastor Loren Covarrubias (2010) gave a prophetic word. "There is someone here today that wants to run away. You feel that the discomfort and anxiety of the situation is too much for you. But the Lord would say to you, if you stay in that situation, watch and see what I will do."

That evening I attended the intercessors class, as I was pressing into the Lord. The lead intercessor guided by the Holy Spirit prayed, "Wholeness over Denise." She said it was no mistake that I was there.

I picked up my heart and moved on again. I evaluate my relapse to be a blip on the radar screen.

Entry: 10/9/2010

So tonight I go to a bonfire where he likely will be and possibly with a date. This is big. You see, in all the seven years of knowing him, I never saw him with another. This is the thought that people dread in breakups. It might not have been such a big deal earlier, but I was informed that he was dating while I was in relapse. But I will trust the Lord. He said, "Watch and see what I will do." I anticipate goodness. I have determined that I will meet her and bless her with a smile and a compliment. It is finished. He is not mine. It is His will that perfect healing and restoration come from this. This will show His power and deliverance out of any sour situation.

I did have butterflies in my stomach during the night as I knew he would probably be coming with someone. It wasn't that it was no big deal driving up the ramp to the situation. But God brought the strength for the situation right on the spot. The opportunity did not come to give her a compliment, but I did pleasantly go to greet them, welcome her and converse a little.

Entry: 11/6/2010
Another month later I attended a conference at another local church on singleness and met a few new wonderful, fun…ok—*crazy* people.

Entry: November 19-21, 2010
A month later I went on a retreat and met more new friends. While in previous times I desperately wanted to break out of my social circle and the connected people, this time I actually was able to meet brand new people. But this time it was a "reaching out," not a "running away from."

Only God knows the plans He has for me (Jeremiah 29:11). I don't know all the future, but I *believe* His ways are better. I can now see His partial plan unfolding and why He did not bring my mate and me together sooner. I needed to heal and become whole. If I had not gone through my heartbreak, I may not have searched so desperately for my true beauty in Him. I may not have discovered so deeply how much God loves me and how much I love His presence. **If I had first been contented in someone else's love, I may not have had the ache to know my Father's so deeply.** Perhaps the Lord knows I would have made a spouse an idol if he had arrived earlier. Perhaps God had to see that I would truly want His deep relationship and not take this earthly marital matter into my own hands again. Perhaps he wanted me and others to see that I am complete in Him alone first and foremost.

Had God not allowed that man to grow apart from me and we had remained together, I would not have reached this calling. Both of our lives would have been different. God gave me the blessing of making the steps into my destiny without having to get permission from another. It was open playing field with just me and the Lord.

I *believe* God foresaw all of my life. I *believe* God had a project set out for me before His world even began because He knew the choices (good and bad) I would make. I *believe* it is more about Destiny and Kingdom living than my own desires.

By going through the hurtles (yes, *hurt*les) and hurdles of life without a boyfriend or mate, no one could ever say "A man made her happy. A man rescued her." No, it was God. He is my deliverer. He is my strong tower and provider. Truly, he put food on my table and made ways for me. His ways were for me and not against me. "What I want from you is your true thanks; I want your promises fulfilled. I want you to trust in me in your times of trouble, so *I* can rescue you, and *you* can give *me* glory" (Psalm 50: 14,15 TLB).

The great part is that now…it's not about a man. It's all about Him…and me. Me and what the Lord will do with me for His kingdom purposes first. I enjoy the unfolding of the gifting and of life. It is as when you fling open a pure white sheet. The air puffs in your face. It bellows, unfolds and brings freshness and a covering of white purity. "Let all that I am wait quietly before God, for my hope is in him" (Psalm 62:5 NLT).

After all the pain has been said and done, I can truly say I know my value in Christ. I am precious as a ruby, unique and valuable enough to secure with nails. And so are YOU!

Entry: October 10, 2011
        Singing and Waiting…

28
Singing and Waiting

*"...may all who love you be like the sun
when it rises in its strength."*

~Judges 5:31

A singer is active in doing something. They are moving their mouth, taking in deep breaths of oxygen, letting fullness of sound out, working with a tool (a microphone) to reach many and perhaps even making gestures with their bodies. Something is going on within their insides and their outsides. When you sing out, often there is passion that is stirred up inside of you—that is, if you are *"sanging."*

If you saw three people on a street, two talking to one another and the third alone but singing out loud, which one would get your attention? The singer would draw your ears, eyes, interest and wonderings. You'd think "What is going on inside that person's head and heart to be singing?" Isn't that what we as believers want for the unsaved to wonder about us? Who and why are we singing about? How are we able to sing?

I want to not just be waiting for a mate, but I want to be found by God and for my own personal fulfillment that I am *singing* and waiting! I'm not talking singing depressing country music. I'm talking singing out music of the gospel of Jesus Christ! We as believers have a lot to sing out about because His love is better than life (Psalm 63:3). Sing out with joy and ambition.

Because you are my help, I *sing* in the shadow of your wings. My soul clings to you; your right hand upholds me.

~Psalm 63:7-8

Let God first establish *you* as the melody of a song to sing! *Then* he can add the harmony, the mate, to your life. Let me say boldly, that because you are reading this book, I am proclaiming over YOU that YOU ARE a prospering, strong Single! In Jesus's name!

Aren't there sometimes in life when your stomach is just hungrier than other times? I just can't feed myself enough sometimes. The growl roars up and I just ate not long ago. That tells me I've either plum stretched out my stomach out from misbehavior, I'm using more energy through ambitions, I'm not getting proper nutrition because I'm too busy to eat well, or I'm not drinking enough water. Water is filling and we need it to be properly hydrated and moving excess out of our systems. When I am craving a serious relationship—like yesterday—I know I need more of Jesus. I need a big, slurpy gallon of Him. I need the drink—the Holy Spirit. He is that living water than can quench our thirst, shortage and desire. I also up my time with the beautiful people He has placed in my life.

Prayer of Wholeness
Supernaturally Lord, fill in the voids. Fill in the gaps where there is longing. Make whole the places where there is emptiness and incompletion. Make solid the hollering places of desire and yearning. Steady the shaking. Plant the shifting heart in footings of your love, your strong love, your undying love. Touch the places that are crying out for acceptance. Satisfy the neediness with your intimate affections. Be my visible strength.

There have been times I have not always been content in my singleness. The status waxes and wanes. I think this is normal, according to what I see in other strong believers. The goal, though, is that the times we do become anxious are lesser in degree and farther apart from each other. The goal is to always come back to the place of joy and contentment like David, even stronger than you were before. And I attest: this is possible.

People say there are freedoms and benefits to being single. Truthfully, in past times I've had to reach far for that understanding. So at one point I counted the number of books on my nightstand—32. I counted the number of books on top of the unused portion of my queen bed—22. C'mon now, that's freedom! My bed and bedside library consisted of everything from Bibles, dictionaries, college books, books on career, healing, prayer, parenting, relationships, singleness, devotionals, personal growth, publishing and fasting. And also there was a CD player atop the bed for my listening comfort and learning! It came down to appreciating *something* about being a single woman. Some things are "only in America!"…other things are "only as a single!" You should count my shoes! Single men speak German, single women speak shoes!

Regardless of your situation in life, GET YOUR JOY ON! JOY-APPEAL is appealing! It will draw the unsaved to Christ, friend to friend, man to a woman and most of all you to your Savior—the one who loves you the most. Nurture in yourself a refreshing spirit. Live out the light that is within you.

Consider the letter below by Shellie R. Warren. Some are not ready to trust like this. I wasn't always either. I just got to a place of such hurt and frustration that I was willing to step back, be with Him, be in His rest, enjoy my relationship with Him and grow.

A Love Letter To My Single Daughter
My Daughter,

You are right where you are supposed to be. So many people have theories and insights on how couples are to come together and the truth is that many miss it by interpreting what they want rather than what I choose. A man pursuing…a girl refusing, these are not necessarily the optimal conditions for mate selection. Adam did not "pursue" the women, nor did she spend her time creating ways to make it challenging for him to do so. Just like one's purpose or date of birth and death, it is *I* who determines the "who, when, and where" of authentic and spirit-led matrimony and intimacy. It is the responsibility of both parties to follow as I, and I only lead.

You are not waiting on some man to "get his act together" or "see you for who you really are," and no matter how it may appear to you in the physical realm, in the spiritual sense, 'he' is right on schedule; my schedule. You are not to be listening to what man says, no matter what form the voice may reveal itself (media, tradition, statistics, naysayers, etc.). Remember, I decided when it was time for Adam to receive the miracle of female assistance and so if you have an issue with physical time, don't take that up with anyone other than me; even then, know that I have your best interest at heart. Far too many of my daughters are consuming themselves with fear and anxiety about things that are really none of their concern. My ways are not your ways and until I unite you with the one you are purposed to benefit, his whereabouts and activities are not to be a priority to you. If you have not been joined to him yet, it's simply because it's not the right moment. He is not ready and neither are you. There are finishing touches that must be placed on you both and no matter how you may feel or what you might think, I am a God of order. I will not be pressured to move outside of my plan. I know it must be hard. Flesh never likes to submit to my will. But please let me continue to mold you. Before you ever existed, you were hand-selected for someone and that has not changed. As the creator, I am excited about my handiwork. Don't go looking for answers to questions you are not able to conceptualize or present in a way that will intimidate me to react or respond. As I did with your parents, let me have the pleasure of presenting you as a gift to your mate. Ask your mother and father if they will ever forget the first time they saw your face. I want "him" to experience a similar thrill. If you want to channel out your energies get excited about how excited I am about you; about how blessed I know he will be to have you!

Again, don't concern yourself about the time. I am timeless. Concern yourself instead with remaining in my hands so that I can perfect you to be all that he needs---so that when it's the right moment, there will be no fear, no hesitation, no question that you are indeed the one that he is meant to live out the rest of his days on the earth with. Far too many women are not praised on their wedding day by their husbands in the way I would've liked because they did not allow me the opportunity to complete them to be what was required, and the man was not discerning enough to know the true purpose that his companion was meant to serve in his life.

I want more for you. Love me enough to let me give it to you. Just as you are to be a blessing to him, he is to be provider and protector for you; he is to bless you as well in ways even your prayers have yet to articulate, but in my infinite wisdom, I know you deserve.

Remember, above all else that, like faith, marriage is a spiritual union. This is the time to remove yourself from your senses, from what the physical is telling you and tap into your spirit. This is when you can please me most by standing and believing that I am true to my word...even when you don't see, feel or hear evidence of its manifestation. The spirit always moves at what you all call 'light years" ahead of the flesh. It takes it some time to catch up. (Hebrews 11:6) Be patient. (1 Corinthians 13:4)

Stay in my will and I will show you the way---a way that leads to love, bliss and happiness. A place where you will feel naked and not ashamed... until death parts you. A place where your future husband will restfully await you.

I love you. Be still and know. *Really know.* I do.

Your Heavenly Father

©2008 Shellie R. Warren

A Love Letter To My Single Son
My Son,
    The day I formed you I was so excited for you to be discovered by the world and then to discover me. The day you were reborn, my angels celebrated your life. Now every day I celebrate you, the apple of my eye.

Ruler of the earth, get settled within me. Hold me as your foundation of life. When you are rooted in me firmly, your character will shine. Allow me to establish you.

My son, I desire for my glory to be shown through you. I desire courage to be seen in you representing the courage I displayed in my walk to the cross for you. No other way can that full courage come than when you are walking closely with me. Deny the lies of the enemy. My Word is what stands and I will stand in you. When you are in my Word, I will poor my ways into you.

When you commune with me, I will supernaturally strengthen you. When you worship, I will do things to work on your behalf. I long for you to settle into me and my presence.

Let me Father you. Let me shore up what you natural father did. Let me fill where your natural father was not. Let me heal, treat and wash what life may have done to you. I will heal you. I will make you whole. I will touch and bind up those places that need tenderness and forgiveness. Seek me for wholeness and I will give you wisdom and love.

Make me the leader of your life and I will show you what real living is. Make me the leader of your days and I will show you how to lead the world. I made you with strength--strength in your physical body and strength in your spirit. Use that strength for my good. I made YOU for greatness. We can do so much together.

My son, I want to see you smile. Even when times are hard, I can still love you to a smile if you will acknowledge me in that way. I want to hear you laugh. I love that sound in my ears; it's almost like worship to me. Let me flow through you continuing to bring out the unique and desirable personality I placed within you. I placed fabulous skills and talents within you. I never make a bad design. I am excited about you. Let's run together.

I love you Son. Maybe you don't hear it enough in the world. But my Word and love for you never changes. It never weakens or runs dry. I love you. Get used to hearing it from me. Oh, and tell someone else too. When you truly know how much I love you, then you can truly love yourself. And only then can you truly love another. I want you to show my love to the world.

My love for you is unconditional. But my holiness must also shine forth. You take me with you wherever you go and into whatever you do. I'd really appreciate for you to keep my commands. My death was excruciating, but I would do it all again for you. Die daily to your flesh and lusts and I promise to bless you through your obedience.

Keep the company of other men whose hearts beat for me. Support each other, and most of all open up and deeply talk to each other—about life, your ideas, your sins, your fears and your dreams. I don't want you waiting around for a woman to share deeply with. She will love that ability and comfort about you when I place you together in my timing. This depth may be a new thing for some of my sons, but again, be my leader and ignite this in the Brotherhood. Set an example of what it means to have a heart that burns for me.

I have Sisters-In-Christ for you to know in fellowship. Learn how to treat them like jewels. Encourage them. Nurture them. Protect them. Help them feel safe. Show brotherly love.

I know you want your Eve. I know you want to experience her love and all the things I have created. Please be patient, even though I know it is hard sometimes, but I will help you with my grace when you accept it. When we have become a solid Father and Son doing life together, then and only then can I see in my infinite wisdom to bring my gift to you.

Keep watch for your bride. Look for the virtuous woman who wants to serve me first and you. When I show you the woman I have provided for you, pursue her. Remember the sport or the game you loved as a child? How you couldn't wait to run in it or play it? Remember that excitement and how much you wanted to do it and purposely set out to do it? Run after her like that, with that passion. Pursue her. I made my daughter to want to be adored, cherished and sought after strongly. Pursue her the way I pursued you. I wanted an intimate relationship with you. I knew it was you I adored all the time. I wooed you to my heart and love. Do the same, Godly man, toward my daughter. I made marriage to resemble my marriage covenant with you, where the bridegroom desires the bride first and goes after her.

Then honor this great woman highly, the way I would. You will never regret this. You will obtain my honor first and hers in return. And I want her to respect you for the great man I have made you. I want her to follow after your decisions and that should come easier when she has watched your walk with me through time. Let her teach you too. I have designed you both very well.

You're going to have to go all out for her. Just like I did for you—gave you everything I had in me. And you are to love her like I love you. I'll consistently show you how to do this when you seek me.

I want this special woman of God to bless you, help you and tell you how wonderful you are. I want her to continue to build you up. I will also love you through her. I want blessings for you that you yourself don't even know you want or need yet from her.

I have great things planned for you Mighty Man of God. Now, for this time together, let me give you richness and fullness of heart. As we move forward together, don't just show the world what a Godly man looks like. Show the world what a Godly man *lives* like.

My beautiful Son, you and I are a match made in heaven.

I love you,

Your Heavenly Father

~Denise Flynn

La La La La La...Keep Singing...

Though I desire marriage and look forward to it, I am not anxious about it. There is a difference. I am content with peace and joy in singleness. I know that if I never marry, I can make it well and be truly blessed. I believe that! I know that God's strong love will be more than enough to be by my side. That doesn't mean I do not wish to marry, because "I Do!"—just practicing. No, that was not a hint or call for attention. It's just a writer not being able to miss the chance to use a great line! I am joyous and thankful about Jesus and others in my life and what is going on in my life. Though I do not know all the answers, I am excited about the fact that I know God does and He has good things in store for me!

Maybe you re-wonder about a special former man/woman in your life or the last fine man/woman of God that just wasn't quite right.

> Of the two evils, choose neither–
> *~Charles H. Spurgeon*

Keep waiting on God.

It's like when you're looking to buy an outfit, a car or a home, and you can't find the right thing...what you have in your heart...what will work for you...what will meet your needs...what you like. Save your money then! Save your heart and someone else's.

I draw encouragement from a Gary Chapman song. Let there be great happenings and wonders in the waiting. God's timing is never out of sync.

"I Will Wait On You"
(by Gary Chapman)

30 seconds in the microwave and my
    burrito's done
Grab a cup of instant coffee anytime I'm on
    the run
Get my news down from the satellite any
    time day or night
Things don't always work that way with you

So I will wait
Let the whole world be in such a hurry
I will choose to trust and not to worry
Though it's so hard to do
I will wait on you

It's so hard to stand in silence while the days
    go screaming past
It's so hard to just be still
In a world that spins so fast
You are good
You are kind
If I'm patient I will find
When the time is right you'll lead me on

So I will wait
Let the whole world be in such a hurry
I will choose to trust and not to worry
Though it's so hard to do
I will wait on you

You do all things right and in your perfect
    time
I know I have a place in your design
Don't want to run ahead or fall behind

So I will wait

I will wait
Let the whole world be in such a hurry
I will choose to trust and not to worry
Though it's so hard to do
I will wait on you
I will wait
I will wait on you
I will wait

The word "wait" has probably more negative connotations associated with it than any other. We think "I'd rather do anything else but wait!" But when we can live life fully functioning in Christ, we will also be enjoying the ride and the experience along the wait. It is not that we won't have times of doubt, imbalance, anxiety over the desire for marriage, loneliness or frustration, but we can get back into the strong stride with Christ again. It won't quite seem like waiting then. There will be an appreciation for the time.

I believe that when I am done being made and fashioned to God's design, God will wake my Adam up and bring me to him. God will enliven my man's eyes to me. Until then, I am coming into more greatness in the image of Christ and my man is naming all the animals in his region and dominating in the supernatural blessings of our Father!

As we sing, God will reward those who place Him first in their life. Watch God's rewarding here. Ezekiel 29:18-20 says, "Son of man, Nebuchadnezzar king of Babylon drove his army in a hard campaign against Tyre; every head was rubbed bare and every shoulder made raw. Yet he and his army got no reward from the campaign he led against Tyre.

Therefore this is what the Sovereign LORD says: I am going to give Egypt to Nebuchadnezzar king of Babylon, and he will carry off its wealth. He will loot and plunder the land as pay for his army. I have given him Egypt as a *reward* for his efforts because he and his army did it for me, declares the Sovereign LORD."

God's character is that of Hebrews 11:6, "And without faith it is impossible to please God, because anyone who comes to him must believe that he exists and that he *rewards* those who earnestly seek him."

Let's take one last look at the book of Ruth. Upon their meeting, Boaz had already heard of Ruth's good reputation. He said in Ruth 2:11 "May you be *richly rewarded* by the Lord, the God of Israel, under whose wings you have come to take refuge." Boaz was part of her reward. God rewards.

While I am singing and waiting for my desire, where do I need to be and what do I need to be doing to meet my mate? I'm telling you, when I get a dog, I may name her Ruth, because there is so much good stuff packed into this book! In Ruth we see God's sovereignty all over their lives. Ruth 2:3 says "So she went out, entered a field and began to glean behind the harvesters. *As it turned out*, she was working in a field belonging to Boaz."

God is in control, aligning things, people, circumstances and places. God knew from His meddling up above that Ruth would end up right in this place with Boaz. For all Ruth's diligence and living righteously for God, He placed her right where she needed to be to receive her and Naomi's blessing. While she was honoring God through Naomi and focusing on taking care of herself and her family, she was brought to the place of her destiny and David and the Messiah were born through their lineage.

Follow Christ and you may follow Him right to your blessing and part of your destiny.

May we be found singing and waiting.

29

The Unveiling

It's who you know and your connections; more and more I see this in the spiritual. The Father and I know each other very well. He knows how I love Him and that I try my best to honor Him and ask for forgiveness and repent when I don't. My Father also knows my future mate. Hopefully my future mate is asking for me too. Our father knows what each of us needs now and in the future and when to bless us with each other. At His right time, He will introduce us. Ecclesiastes 3:11 tells you and I, "He has made everything beautiful in its time." He will blend our needs and purposes together. It's who you know. We have connections. "Therefore my heart is glad" (Psalm 16:9).

As I was writing this book, I was so excited to share it, but only at the right time. If I shared it before it was complete, it would not come across as well and all anticipation and plans for it could go down the tubes. That must be how God feels as He designs us, molds us, changes us and recreates us before bringing us together with our mate at just the right time. This book has been my handiwork from God. Individually we are His handiwork and a marriage will be His handiwork too. If His name is going on it, all the components must be ready to show His good creation and glory!

So many different considerations to dating, relationships and courting. We are still human, flawed ingredients (individuals) hoping to come together to create an envisioned utopia, chiffon-like experience. But when we taste a nibble or a bite of a relationship, we get "clues" about how well it will work. There are emotions indicating pleasure or unfulfillment. They love me, they love me not. Do they or don't they? Do I or don't I? Without listening closely to the Holy Spirit and using the basics and in-depth basics and biblical precepts, there can be quite the array of questions, even confusion.

Sometimes it is hard not to be anxious about the turn-out of a date or a relationship. It's like the urge to turn to the last page of the novel first. However, don't focus on the end. One has to maintain making good plays offensively and defensively. We must consider what good things would move the relationship forward while also observing any yellow flags being through onto the game field that should hold the relationship back. The referees toss yellow penalty flags onto the field "to identify and sometimes mark the location of penalties or infractions that occur during regular play" (Wikipedia.org, 2011).

Sports have rules. If a team plays by the rules, studies their game, practices and stays focused, they usually win. However, even with that, there are surprising upsets. You are blessed if you can play without injury. You'll have a better "single career" (so to speak). Injury could cause people to sit out of games wounded for some time.

Use the basics and in-depth basics of relationships as wisdom so you do not repeat some of the same mistakes others have made. God has His best for you. You have the Holy Spirit plus wisdom. Wisdom is Godly knowledge *applied*. Wait upon the Lord to bring you that spouse that will leave you satisfied and tickled too. You are hand-cut special for someone, and someone special is cut for you. "A longing fulfilled is sweet to the soul" (Proverbs 13:19).

"Marry Me!" God says "Marry Me" to *us*. He says "Marry me again every day. Fall deeper in love with me."

Study the Song of Songs, also known as the biblical chapter "Song of Solomon"—the inspired writing of the sweet marriage between a man and a woman. The inspired writing symbolizes the beautiful marriage between the bride, you and I, and our bridegroom, Jesus.

The unveiling. When the groom lifts the veil to the bride's face and they create covenant and intimacy. The unveiling. When Jesus tore the curtain in His redeeming death letting us see His face in covenant and intimacy without barrier. And you will be able to say on that day to your wife or hear from your husband, "Arise, my darling, my beautiful one, and come with me. See! The winter is past; the rains are over and gone. Flowers appear on the earth; the season of singing has come, the cooing of doves is here in our land. The fig tree forms its early fruit; the blossoming vines spread their fragrance. Arise, come, my darling; my beautiful one, come with me" (Song of Songs 2:10-13).

And until then, and on every day "This is the day the Lord has made; let us rejoice and be glad in it" (Psalm 118:24). And you have made me for this day, Lord. I submit to being all you would have me to be to bring you much glory to fulfill your Kingdom's purposes. I will marry you again. Amen.

> "Now may the God of peace who brought up our Lord Jesus from the dead, that great Shepherd of the sheep, through the blood of the everlasting covenant, make you complete in every good work to do His will, working in you what is well pleasing in His sight, through Jesus Christ, to whom *be* glory forever and ever. Amen."
>
> ~*Hebrews 13:20-21*

Be Salt, Be Light, Be Love, Be Jesus!

30
How's Your Love Life?

So, we've talked about one love life. Now let's talk about another even more important.

I don't know how you have come across this book. But I have prayed that it would be placed into the hands of many (as any author dreams). In order to get the most out of this book (and life), it would be highly suggested that you would have a relationship with Jesus Christ. Let me share with you why you need one and how you can have it.

Here is the problem requiring corrective action. The original sin (of Adam and Eve) is not so original any more. Man continues to be born into and live in it. It makes no difference if it is an attitudinal sigh or a cold lie, an unkind comment or a bloody murder, a slight mistreatment or unlawful stealing. There is no difference between a profane word when coffee spills or a brutal rape, "I wish I could have his job" or destructive gossip, a snippy response or misused organizational funds. There is no difference in drunkenness or using heroin, cheating on taxes or child pornography, unmarried passion with the opposite gender or homosexuality. There is no difference between speeding or sexual pleasures with another's spouse, unforgiveness or deceit, a harsh demand or the denial of God. It is all under the heavy mantle of sin. From the seemingly smallest offenses to the most horrific, it is just one short word—sin, but with abysmal, infinite consequences—punishable by eternal separation from God in damnation.

I was born with brown eyes, red lips, brown hair...and sin. She was born with 120 I.Q., vivacious personality, musical talents...and sin. He was born with curly hair, good attitude, cerebral palsy...and sin. She was born with common sense, no arm, blue eyes...and sin. He was born with humor, handsome looks, athletic ability...and sin. As surely as we were born, we were born into this state of sin. Everyone came with it—this birth defect that carries a high penalty.

It does not matter how nice you are nor how good and loving you treat people. It does not matter how well you are liked by others. It does not matter that you go to church since those things alone are not the healing, corrective remedies for the nature of sin.

I wish I had something else to say or not say to keep you comfortable. I know this may be an inconvenient decision to have to deal with along with life's other demands or temporary pleasures. There is this unavoidable truth. It is our ultimatum. My friend, if there were any other way you could obtain heaven and continue living as is, and no harm was caused to me, I would not tell you this. But it will be too late once you are face to face with God, if I say nothing. You dear one, you are alive still today, this minute, with one more chance to change your awaited ending.

Let Him have you today. Choose His love for you. Give yourself without hesitation away to Him. Give to live.

There is a love more beautiful than anything or anyone to surround you. It is a deeper love than any thought or hurt you could ever feel. God made a way for you to have this kind of love. He sent His only Son, Jesus, from Heaven to be born into this world. Jesus willingly went through an agonizing death for you. The entire purpose was that Jesus was sent to die in your place—instead of you yourself paying the penalty for your own sin. He stood in your place. God posted bail for you, Jesus, so that you could walk out of the cell alive. Jesus came to get you out of big trouble if you'll let him rescue you.

Jesus endured bludgeoning for every person's sin, but not everyone will acknowledge their need for their sins needing to be forgiven. Not everyone will admit they cannot fix their sinful status themselves. Not everyone, even the nicest, will accept the gift of Jesus, who God provided for them. But you...will you? Will you say yes to grace washing your sins away and have them no longer remembered? Will you say yes to God's mercy and unending love for you? His love will be amazingly good to you.

God loves you. He always has, every minute of every day of your life regardless of what you have done. He just cannot agree with or permit the sinful state that every person was born into and those small and big things we all do. Well, rather than fight this invitation, go with it, accept it. God is calling you now to enter into a right relationship with Him. God wants you to know Him to complete the connection, not just know about Him or that He exists.

You may feel a pressing now, an urge, a draw and you feel uneasy about the way your life is right now. You may be thinking...do I really have to do this? Do not contemplate. The feeling is the Holy Spirit urging you to come to Him.

Are you thinking, "I already believe in God"? You still need to go one step further for effectiveness and ask His Son to come into your heart.

Whoever believes in the Son has eternal life, but
whoever rejects the Son will not see life, for God's
wrath remains on him

~John 3:36

For my Father's will is that everyone who looks to the
Son and believes in him shall have eternal life, and I will
raise him up at the last day,

~John 6:40

No one who denies the Son has the Father; whoever
acknowledges the Son has the Father also.

~1 John 2:23

And this is the testimony: God has given us eternal life,
and this life is in His Son. Whoever has the Son has life;
whoever does not have the Son of God does not have
life.
~1 John 5:11, 12

There is a new life awaiting you here, which begins
with one prayer said in one moment of time--your time
today. Do not hesitate. Pray this:

Jesus, I see that I have been wrong. I was born with
something wrong. It is the state of sin in my heart.
Please forgive the offenses I have committed, knowingly
and unknowingly. Come live within my heart so that I
may be pleasing to you and your Kingdom. I ask you to
change me and make me a brand new person. I believe
that you came, died and rose again from the grave so that
I could have this very moment, the rest of my days and
eternity with you and all that that means. Today is the
first day I fully receive your love and love you back. I
pray this in Jesus's name. Amen.

If you have prayed that prayer and mean it from your heart, you are what the Bible calls "saved" or "born again." The Bible says "you are a new creation; the old has gone, the new has come!" (2 Corinthians 5:17). The condition of your heart has been changed from being at enmity with God to being pure of heart and forgiven. If you were to die, you would be guaranteed life in Heaven. You have accepted the gift of Jesus Christ in your heart, giving you eternal life. So smile! Breathe in relief!

Now, Satan is real and he will try to make you believe that nothing has changed for you from the prayer you just prayed. He is lying to you. Counteract that by telling a friend of the decision you have made to invite Jesus into your heart. Send me an email too! I want to rejoice with you! Email me at Denise@TheMarryMeBook.com.

Next, find and attend a church that teaches what the Bible says. Let the pastor or an usher know that you are a new Christian and would like to meet with the pastor. He will help you get started on the new walk you have wisely begun. Begin to read the Bible beginning in the book of John. Before you read, ask the Lord to reveal Himself to you as you read. Ask Him to help you understand His word and to help you do what it says.

Smile heavenly big! You are blessed! The angels are having a party over you now!

You are redeemed!

References

Chapter 2 ~ First Things First

Cerminara, Gina. (n.d.)

Hawkins, Dr. D. "Are You Really Ready for Love." Harvest House Publishers. (2007).

Osteen, J. *Making Plans to Succeed.* Lakewood Church. Houston, TX. Retrieved 2011, Jan. from http://www.youtube.com/watch?v=cd4AiZJ8GpY&feature=autoplay&list=PL455A597D732B5C76&index=1&playnext=4.

Chapter 3 ~ Getting Together

Gibbs, N. and Duffy, M. (2007, June 14). "Ruth Graham, Soulmate to Billy, Dies." *TIME U.S.* http://www.time.com/time/nation/article/0,8599,1633197,00.html. Retrieved November 2011.

Graham, B. *Just As I Am.* HarperCollins Publishers Ltd. Toronto, Canada. (1977).

Kendrick, A. and S. *Courageous.* Sherwood Pictures, Provident Films, Sony/Affirm, and TRISTAR Pictures. (2011).

RBC Ministries. Retrieved January, 2011 from http://www.inplainsite.org/html/choosing_a_marriage_partner.html. Section 13B.

Chapter 4 ~ The Choice Is Yours?

Franklin, J. *Fasting.* Charisma House. Lake Mary, FL. (2008).

Franklin, J. *Fasting Journal.* Charisma House. Lake Mary, FL. (2008).

Hammond, M. M. *101 Ways to Get and Keep His Attention.* Harvest House Publishers. Eugene, Oregon. (2003).

Oakley, P. *Jesus, Lover Of My Soul (It's All About You).* On I Give You My All by Singing Out His Love. (May 2006). Lavender Sky Records.

Storey, T. *Miracle Mentality What's on your mind?* Storey Dreams.

Chapter 5 ~ The Real Deal

Answers.com. *What is the deepest layer of skin on the human body?* Retrieved January 2011 from the website http://wiki.answers.com/Q/What_is_the_deepest_layer_of_ skin_on_the_human_body

Crenshaw, R. *A Ten Cow Woman.* Retrieved 12/8/10 from the website http://ezinearticles.com/?A-Ten-Cow-Woman&id=3750053.

McVeigh, K. *Single and Loving It.* Harrison House. Tulsa, OK. (2003).

Chapter 6 ~ Gender Similarities

Beck, A. *What is a Girl?*

Beck, A. *What is a Boy?*

McGee, Dr. J. V. "The Greatest Sin in All the World." Thru the Bible Radio Network (1995).

Chapter 10 ~ Relationship Status

Mitchell, M. Produced by Zelznick, D. *Gone With the Wind.* Selznick International in association with Metro-Goldwyn Mayer. *(1939).*

Witty Profiles. Retrieved March 15, 2011 from http://www.wittyprofiles.com/q/2548336.

Chapter 11 ~ Heart in Pocket

Buri, J. R. Ph.D. *Psychology Today.* Blog: Love Bytes Insights on Our Deepest Desire. '"Tis Better To Have Loved And Lost..." Not Really.' Retrieved March 17, 2011 from   http://www.psychologytoday.com/blog/love-bytes/201101/tis-better-have-loved-and-lost-not-really.

Tennyson, Alfred Lord. *Works* (London: Macmillan, 1891).

Tennyson, A. L. *Poems* (Boston: W. D. Ticknor, 1842).

Chapter 12 ~ Keeping Hope Alive

Hagee, J. *Faith Under Fire.* John Hagee Ministries. San Antonio, TX. 8/12/11.

Chap. 12 (cont.)

LeLacheur, S. *Circle Your Wagon.* Zion Christian Church. Troy, MI. April 3, 2011.

Shirer, P. *Going Beyond Life Interrupted Simulcast.* Lifeway Christian Resources (2011).

Chapter 15 ~ *Frankly Speaking*

Harris, J. *boy meets girl.* Multnomah Publishers, Inc. Sisters, OR (2000).

Linkletter, A. *Art Linkletter: My Life and Times 1.* Recorded at Chick-fil-A. San Diego, CA. Aired on Focus On The Family Daily 6/3/10. Also retrieved 3/10/11 from http://www.focusonthefamily.com/popups/media_player.aspx?MediaId=%7BD289B220-463C-4BE9-95CA-A7D466C4D9D1%7D

Meyer, J. *The Wisdom of Making Right Choices - Pt 1.* Joyce Meyer Ministries. Fenton, MO. Airdate: February 7, 2011.

Satir, V. Retrieved September 6, 2010 from http://www.brainyquote.com/quotes/authors/v/virginia_satir.html

Chapter 16 ~ *Living Fruit*

Evans Sr., L.H. Prayer for a Bride and Groom. Love, Marriage and God [Recording]. Word Records. (1960).

Chapter 16 (cont.)

Kendrick, S. and A. *The Love Dare.* B & H Publishing Group. Nashville, TN. (2008). Reprinted and used by permission.

Pruden, C. P. *Building A Beautiful Wife.* Arc Press. Southfield, MI (2010).

Stewart, K. Dr. "Choosing a Mate." Harrison House. (1984).

Chapter 17 ~ *Mirror This Radiant Marriage*

Dobson, Dr. J. C. "Straight Talk." Word Publishing (1991).

Kim Betty Show. 103.5 FM. Detroit, MI. *Single and the City* series. February 2010.

Chapter 22 ~ *Got Issues?*

Cloud, Dr. H. and Townsend, Dr. J. "Boundaries in Dating." Zondervan Publishing House (2000).

Cloud, Dr. H and Townsend, Dr. J. "Safe People." Zondervan Publishing House (1995).

Coon, D., Mitterer, J. O. "Psychology Modules for Active Learning," 11th edition, Wadsworth Cengage Learning (2009).

Chapter 22 (cont.)

Parrott, Dr. L. III and Dr. L. *Saving Your Marriage Before It Starts.* Zondervan Publishing House. Grand Rapids, MI (1995).

Parrott, Dr. L. III and Dr. L. *Shattering Marital Myths & Expectations.* Focus on the Family radio broadcast, 1/31/2011.

Pennington, G. Rochester First Assembly of God. Rochester, MI. (November 21, 2009 sermon).

Webster, C. L. *Effective Counseling: A Client's View.* Personnel and Guidance Journal, Vol. 52, No. 5, January, 1974.

Wyse, L. "How Come Holding Hands Feels So Good?" American Greeting Corporation. Cleveland, OH. (1971).

Chapter 23 ~ Ending A Relationship

Brooks, Pastor C. W. *Lord Prune Me.* Series: *Spiritual Spring Cleaning.* Evangel Ministries. Detroit, MI. www.evangelministries.org.

Carlson, Dr. R. *Top 10 Reasons Not To Get Married.* Family Life Communications. Tucson, AZ.

Jakes, T. D. *Nuturing Pain.* The Potter's House. Dallas, TX. Retrieved Jan. 2011. http://www.youtube.com/watch?v=LrJ2rsKvJU0&feature=related

Chapter 23 (cont.)

Johnson, B. *Boomerang Joy.* Zondervan Publishing House. U.S.A (1998).

Talley, Dr. J. *Divorce Care.* Session 12. MMIV The Church Initiative, Inc. Wake Forest, NC. (n.d.).

Chapter 24 ~ The Grieve, Acceptance and Healing

Baxter, C. "Westland." Short Fiction by 33 Writers. Thomson Wadsworth. (2005).

Birkey, V. *You are very special.* Fleming H. Revell Company. U.S.A. (1977).

Dalton, S. *If You Let Me.* Like A Child. Red Letter Records. Waterford, MI (2008).

Haskins, M. *The Gate of the Year.* The Desert Collection. (1908).

Jakes, T. D. *Let It Go.* The Potter's House. Dallas, TX. Retrieved Jan. 2011 from the website http://www.youtube.com/watch?v=pCTUZWIo00Y&feature=related

Schoolhouse Rock. *Conjunction Junction.* Bob Dorough, Music & Lyrics. USA (1973).

Rankins, A. Zion Christian Church. Troy, MI. (April 24, 2010).

Upton, J. *Apple of His Eye.* Open Up the Earth *CD/DVD. (2006).*

Chap. 24 (cont.)

Weinzierl, J. *My "Never Again" List.* Grace Christian Church. Sterling Heights., MI. (no date).

Chapter 26 ~ Experiencing Love

Wesley, J. *John Wesley's Explanatory Notes.* Retrieved Jan 2011 from http://www.christnotes.org/commentary.php?b=23&c=62&com=wes

Chapter 27 ~ My Testimony

Covarrubias, Pastor L. Mt. Zion Church. Clarkston, MI. (Sept. 26, 2010).

Franklin, J. *Praise The Lord.* Trinity Broadcasting Network. Santa Ana, CA. May 17, 2011.

Chapter 28 ~ Singing & Waiting

Chapman, G. "I Will Wait." Outside. Provident Label Group, LLC. (1999).

Warren, S. R. "A Letter To My (Single) Daughter (From God)." (©2008). http://en.wikipedia.org/wiki/Penalty_flag. Retrieved 10/31/11.

Bible Copyright Information